OECD PROCEEDINGS
CENTRE FOR EDUCATIONAL RESEARCH AND INNOVATION

CHILDREN AND FAMILIES AT RISK

New Issues in Integrating Services

ORGANISATION FOR ECONOMIC CO-OPERATION AND DEVELOPMENT

ORGANISATION FOR ECONOMIC CO-OPERATION AND DEVELOPMENT

Pursuant to Article 1 of the Convention signed in Paris on 14th December 1960, and which came into force on 30th September 1961, the Organisation for Economic Co-operation and Development (OECD) shall promote policies designed:

- to achieve the highest sustainable economic growth and employment and a rising standard of living in Member countries, while maintaining financial stability, and thus to contribute to the development of the world economy;
- to contribute to sound economic expansion in Member as well as non-member countries in the process of economic development; and
- to contribute to the expansion of world trade on a multilateral, non-discriminatory basis in accordance with international obligations.

The original Member countries of the OECD are Austria, Belgium, Canada, Denmark, France, Germany, Greece, Iceland, Ireland, Italy, Luxembourg, the Netherlands, Norway, Portugal, Spain, Sweden, Switzerland, Turkey, the United Kingdom and the United States. The following countries became Members subsequently through accession at the dates indicated hereafter: Japan (28th April 1964), Finland (28th January 1969), Australia (7th June 1971), New Zealand (29th May 1973), Mexico (18th May 1994), the Czech Republic (21st December 1995), Hungary (7th May 1996), Poland (22nd November 1996) and Korea (12th December 1996). The Commission of the European Communities takes part in the work of the OECD (Article 13 of the OECD Convention).

The Centre for Educational Research and Innovation was created in June 1968 by the Council of the Organisation for Economic Co-operation and Development and all Member countries of the OECD are participants.

The main objectives of the Centre are as follows:

- *analyse and develop research, innovation and key indicators in current and emerging education and learning issues, and their links to other sectors of policy;*
- *explore forward-looking coherent approaches to education and learning in the context of national and international cultural, social and economic change; and*
- *facilitate practical co-operation among Member countries and, where relevant, with non-member countries, in order to seek solutions and exchange views of educational problems of common interest.*

The Centre functions within the Organisation for Economic Co-operation and Development in accordance with the decisions of the Council of the Organisation, under the authority of the Secretary-General. It is supervised by a Governing Board composed of one national expert in its field of competence from each of the countries participating in its programme of work.

© OECD 1998
Permission to reproduce a portion of this work for non-commercial purposes or classroom use should be obtained through the Centre français d'exploitation du droit de copie (CFC), 20, rue des Grands-Augustins, 75006 Paris, France, Tel. (33-1) 44 07 47 70, Fax (33-1) 46 34 67 19, for every country except the United States. In the United States permission should be obtained through the Copyright Clearance Center, Customer Service, (508)750-8400, 222 Rosewood Drive, Danvers, MA 01923 USA, or CCC Online: http://www.copyright.com/. All other applications for permission to reproduce or translate all or part of this book should be made to OECD Publications, 2, rue André-Pascal, 75775 Paris Cedex 16, France.

FOREWORD

This collection of papers was presented at a conference held in 1996 in Toronto, Canada, to disseminate work completed by the Centre for Educational Research and Innovation (CERI) of the OECD concerned with integrating services to meet the needs of children and youth at risk and their families.

Integrating services was identified in earlier CERI work on children at risk as being the most useful way forward for improving educational outcomes and social integration for the most disadvantaged members of our societies. This approach then became the focus of further study with detailed work being carried out in collaboration with the governments of Australia, Belgium (Flemish Community), Canada, Finland, France, Germany, Italy, the Netherlands, Portugal, Slovenia, Sweden, Turkey, the United Kingdom and the United States. The publication *Successful Services for Our Children and Families at Risk* (OECD, 1996) brought together the completed case studies and formed the basic text for the dissemination conference.

This book is the fourth and final publication arising from the work on integrating services for children and youth at risk. It provides an up-to-date account of progress made in the development of integrated services and discusses some of the challenges still to be met. It has been prepared by Peter Evans of the OECD secretariat and is published on the responsibility of the Secretary-General of the OECD.

TABLE OF CONTENTS

Introduction
  by Peter Evans and Philippa Hurrell 7

Welcoming Address
  by Paul Cappon 11

Opening Address
  by Donald Johnston 13

Setting the Scene: Some Personal Experiences
  by Lisa Dore and Mei Chen 17

Part One: Transitions

Making Services Work for Children and Youth at Risk and their Families:
Two Ways of Integration
  by Guido Walraven 21

Transition to Pre-school: Britain and Finland
  by Jennifer Little 35

After School Child Care
  by Marjorie McColm 41

Trends in Youth Employment and School-work Transitions in Canada
  by Doug Giddings 47

Part Two: Community Involvement

Missouri's Caring Communities
  by Marilyn Knipp 63

Redesign of Services for Children and Families
  by John Lackey 73

Parental Involvement in Pre-school Education in France
by Josette Combes 83

Professional Social Work: Education and Service Integration Roles
by Mary R. Lewis 89

Part Three: Implementing System Change

Implementing System Change for Effective Client Services
by Alex Dingwall 107

From Programmatic to Integrated Services in New Brunswick, Canada
by Alex Dingwall 111

Issues in Managing and Sharing Information for Implementing System Change
by Hermann Rademacker 113

Preparing Professionals to Work in a Co-ordinated System of Services
for Children and Youth at Risk
by Phyllis R. Magrab 119

Innovative Strategies to Provide Integrated Children's Services: Going to Scale
in Ontario, Canada
by John H. Lewko, Michael Shea, Richard Volpe and Cynthia Lees 127

Part Four: Research and Evaluation of Outcomes

Knowledge from Evaluation Research
by Richard Volpe 149

Evaluating Policy Initiatives
by Alejandro Tiana Ferrer 167

The Building Blocks of a Cost Effectiveness Analysis of Integrated Services
for at Risk Children and Youth
by H.M. Levin 173

Models of Community Development
by Jennifer Evans 181

Issues in the Evaluation of Intersectoral Initiatives: A Background Paper
by Craig Shields 193

Issues in the Evaluation of Intersectoral Initiatives: Survey Findings
by Coletta McGrath 199

INTRODUCTION

by

Peter Evans and Philippa Hurrell

Background

OECD countries are generous in their provision of education, health and social services for their citizens. However, the different demands that are being made by the knowledge economy, heterogeneous school populations and changing family structures (allied to the changing demographics of decreasing birth rate and increasing survival rate) are stimulating change in their structure and function. This problem is further exacerbated by growing social and employment difficulties.

Public services currently have a strong supply side element. They provide programmatic services which are agency driven, and focused on individuals. For all their good intentions, public services all too often do not work effectively together to take account of the real needs of individuals and their particular circumstances. For example, hospitals may set appointments to meet their own schedules, not taking account of what best suits the family. Schools may be unaware of family crises and thus be insensitive to their impact on a child's school performance. Social services may be unaware of the demands schools are making on students' time. Indeed the way in which services have to account for their funding may of itself stimulate the creation of additional services dedicated to tackling problems out of context and may well lead to the provision of irrelevant, overlapping or duplicated services; worse excessive form filling or professional rivalry can even inhibit the provision of support that is actively required.

Over the past decade it has become increasingly clear that this kind of programmatic structure is ill-adapted to satisfying the demands of the individuals and families it is intended to serve. Furthermore, the services required are often difficult to find or are unavailable. They can lack continuity, respond to crises instead of being preventive and steadily supportive, and they are generally unaccountable to the people they are intended to help. Many countries, reacting to escalating costs and a trend towards decentralisation, are therefore moving towards a rationalisation of the way services work and in particular are examining their co-ordination in the context of community development.

The CERI work on children at risk

Over the past years OECD/CERI has been studying the ways in which education, health and social services are increasingly being co-ordinated in order to meet the needs of at risk client groups. This approach was first signalled in 1995 in the publication *Our Children at Risk* and taken up as a central theme in the publications, *Integrating Services for Children at Risk* (1996), *Successful Services for our Children and Families at Risk* (1996), *Co-ordinating Services for Children and Youth at Risk-- A world view* (1998). A videotape, readied for public broadcast, entitled "Children of promise" which shows examples of co-ordinated services in Australia, Canada, Finland, the Netherlands, and the US has also been produced and was "premiered" at the Toronto conference.

A central aim of the CERI research was to collect information on examples of best practice in integrated services for students at risk in three distinct phases, namely, pre-school children, school age students and youth in the transition to work. The decision to study them separately was based on the different spectrum of services they require. Families with pre-school children are important consumers of health care; school aged students of educational services; and youth in the transition to work are more likely to take advantage of vocational and employment services. Hence the character of "integrated services" for each of these groups will differ in a significant way.

While the term "integrated services" often seems to imply collaboration between professionals at the front-line, the ability to work together is just as dependent on initiatives to support integration at the administrative, management and policy levels. Therefore, for the case studies carried out by CERI had two components. In the first, countries were asked to complete a report covering laws and policies relating to integrating services. In the second, OECD experts interviewed actors from the strategic (senior management) and operational (middle managers) as well as field level workers and the consumers themselves, students and parents.

In order to collect a comprehensive body of information which would allow us to analyse how and why integrated services work, we addressed four conceptual areas: context, input, process and product, which have been widely used to study human services. Context refers to the history and background to integrated services, providing a setting in which to contextualise them. Input refers to the different resources which have been invested in integrated services by both public and private bodies. Process alludes to ways in which services are planned, organised and delivered by administrators, managers and professionals. Finally product refers to the outcomes of service delivery, such as the level of client satisfaction and the success of treatment programmes.

A team of seven, comprising two members of the CERI secretariat and five experts from Canada, France, the US and the UK carried out the research by visiting the countries and sites where the integrated services approach was being used and developed. The countries visited were: Australia (New South Wales, South Australia and Victoria), Canada (Alberta, New Brunswick, Ontario and Saskatchewan), Finland, Germany, Portugal, and the USA (California, Missouri and New York City). Further studies were also carried out by agencies representing the Dutch and Finnish governments. This work has been reported in the volumes noted above.

The Toronto conference

The proceedings reported in this book, the last in this series of work on integrated services, formed the basis for discussions at the final dissemination conference held in Toronto, Canada, in October 1996. This was predicated on the CERI research on integrated services just described. The individual papers have been thoroughly brought up to date for this publication. They are brought together under the four themes around which the conference was organised: transitions (*e.g.* pre-school to school and school to work); community involvement; implementing system change; and research and evaluation of outcomes.

The conference was opened by Mr. Donald Johnston, Secretary General of the OECD; Dr. Paul Cappon, Director General of the Council of Ministers of Education, Canada (CMEC); Pr. Alejandro Tiana Ferrer, Chair of the CERI Governing Board; Ms. Mary Johnston of Health Canada, and Ms. Ila Bossons, Counsellor in Metropolitan Toronto.

Mr. Johnston noted the importance for OECD Member countries of capitalising on the opportunities offered by free trade and of bringing public budgets back into balance, while at the same time maintaining social cohesion. Children at risk were perhaps "the most important problem" that needed to be addressed and he emphasised the role of services integration in achieving stability in government expenditure in this sector, and not necessarily at the expense of service quality. He also pointed out that the work will be used in informing a forthcoming OECD conference on social policy in the next millennium.

Ms. Mary Johnston noted the importance of developing comprehensive systems to prevent health problems which require shared data for better decision-making and the need for inter-ministerial teams to analyse the impact of policies on each other's departments.

Professor Tiana Ferrer emphasised that social justice should be a starting point to be nurtured in schools. A culture of commitment and not intolerance must be fostered to stimulate and help to create social cohesion. He noted that reactive services were unfortunately more common than preventive ones and that public responsibility needs to be developed which will inevitably require investment of resources if children are to be adequately valued. He then pointed to the importance of the work carried out. It had brought the idea of integrated services back on to the agenda as a way of tackling social exclusion. But Professor Tiana Ferrer noted that the work had gone further and stressed the important role that should be played by education in a holistic approach to dealing with problems faced by children and families at risk. The study had also developed new concepts for the field. It stressed the importance of co-ordination in the delivery of services, of prevention, of the chain of responsibilities and of community involvement.

The challenge of integrating services

The problems presented by children and youth at risk and their families cannot be effectively tackled, let alone solved, without a co-ordinated and lifelong approach which emphasises people to people relationships, working "with" rather than "for" students, as described by the personal reflections of Lisa Dore and Mei Chen in this volume. The delegates at the conference agreed that pre-school children should be prepared for the school curriculum; that schools should be important community centres providing a range of services; and that school-employer links, such as those embodied in apprenticeships, have an important role to play. Community involvement is central to achieving the necessary continuity and flexibility, and policies of decentralisation are very helpful in stimulating the development of the civil society. The process of decentralisation should give communities the necessary power and resources to undertake local programmes and develop the training necessary for working in an integrated way.

But integrating services requires implementing system change. And for this to be successful it is vital that staff are fully supportive and do not feel threatened by the prospect of job losses. Indeed, integrating services should not be seen as a means for down-sizing and short term cost-cutting expedients. This may be a long term outcome, but in the short term extra resourcing may be required.

The implementation of system change and evaluation were identified as areas that still need to be tackled. Evaluation, in particular is weak with relevant models still to be developed. Other difficult areas such as the reluctance of agencies to co-operate and resistance on the ground among professionals and their training and the difficulties in managing and sharing information again need a great deal of further work.

Finally, and picking up on the introductory comments made by the Secretary General, it was noted that change towards integrated, customer driven services cannot come soon enough. The impact of globalisation and free market economies on social exclusion in the developed world as seen in the growing gap between elite and disadvantaged groups (especially in educational, health, social and employment outcomes) must be addressed.

Concluding comment

The failure of services to meet customers needs, and the realisation that many problems need to be treated holistically, have resulted in the need for integrated services. Many countries are now moving in this direction since it represents perhaps the only way forward compatible with the broad commonalities of our social democracies and the perceived social needs of the next millennium. The chapters of this book provide up to date examples of what these new services may look like, the contexts in which they may function and how they may operate. It also identifies some of the challenges still to be met.

WELCOMING ADDRESS

by

Dr. Paul Cappon
Director General, Council of Ministers of Education, Canada

On Behalf of the Council of Ministers of Education, Canada (CMEC) and its chair, the honourable Gordon MacIniss, I am very pleased to welcome you to this final dissemination conference on Integrated Services for Children and Youth at Risk and their Families.

Mr. MacInnis would have liked to be here to welcome you personally this morning but previous commitments have kept him at home in Prince Edward Island. He has asked me to extend to you his warmest welcome and best wishes for a successful conference.

I would like to say a special word of welcome to our international visitors. We are very pleased to have you join us here in Canada for this important conference. I hope you will find time to visit some of the sights during your stay.

For those of you to whom CMEC is not a household word, I will take just a few moments to explain what the organisation is and what its role is in Canadian education. As many of you know, education in Canada is the constitutional responsibility of the provinces and territories. There is no Federal Ministry of Education.

The CMEC was set up in 1967 by the provincial governments to give the Ministers of Education a forum where they could exchange information and carry out projects collectively. The necessity of having such an organisation in a decentralised country like Canada is obvious. Over the years, the council has been the collective voice of Canadian education authorities, both nationally and internationally.

It does not proceed from the automatic assumption that Canada needs national goals to produce quantifiable results. It is not constructed along the production-line model of education. What it does do, is recognise, first and foremost, that Canada is a federation in which the constitution has placed responsibility for education with the provincial governments.

It recognises that this decentralisation is the only way to deal with the great diversity of this country, which requires education systems that are responsive to the social and economic context of different regions. It is convinced that this system is a source of richness and not of weakness.

It recognises, however, that provinces and territories have an interest in working together to share scarce resources, to learn of best practices, to give each other common services, to develop common instruments and, increasingly, to join together to address issues that are of national concern.

Twenty-nine years ago, when the council was founded, the pressure to work at the national level was much weaker than it is today, for the simple reason that, while much was to be gained by sharing information and working together on projects that might have been difficult for any one province to accomplish, the essential thrust of main-line educational problems remained within provincial or regional boundaries.

The last decade has seen a major change in this regard. As we know, the most pressing questions in the education field now know no boundaries. The OECD is working on many of the same questions that are of immediate concern, not only to Member countries, but also to school administrations everywhere in Canada.

Indeed, this conference, which represents the conclusion of one phase of OECD's work, is indicative of the partnerships required between several policy levels if we are to address effectively major policy questions that concern us all.

CMEC has a long standing relationship with OECD. As the national voice for education in Canada, CMEC has been and continues to be a player -- and we would like to think a valuable player -- in the activities of the organisation through the education committee and the CERI Governing Board. We have learned much from the education-related activities of OECD and we hope we have, in turn, made a useful contribution to the organisation.

This conference marks the culmination of several years of activity for OECD and its Member countries. I am sure that, like me, you are all looking forward with keen interest and anticipation to learning of the results of this work.

Again, on behalf of CMEC, I welcome you all and wish you good luck in the few days you will spend together here in Toronto.

OPENING ADDRESS

by

Donald Johnston
Secretary-General of the OECD

Welcome -- Madame Deputy Minister, Mr. Chairman of the conference and of the CERI Governing Board,, Ladies and Gentlemen.

It is a great honour and pleasure for me to able to open this joint OECD/CERI Canada dissemination conference concerning children and youth at risk and their families.

While I would very much like to be here with you in person, the pressures which we are all under require that we maximise the use of modern technologies and it is good to see CERI continuing its history of innovation in this area. I certainly hope that more use will be made of multi-media methods in the future.

Your conference addresses one of the most serious problems to face OECD countries today. So let me start by putting the work of the conference into the context of the broader economic and social pressures that confront us.

Each OECD country must meet a triple challenge. First, each country must be in a position to respond positively to the opportunities that are provided by the opening of the world's economies to free trade, to avoid protectionism and to benefit from the economic growth that will certainly accrue in the medium to long term.

Second, there is little disagreement about the need to bring government expenditure under control and to get public sector budgets back towards balance. This can often mean a reduction in the size of public services although not necessarily in their quality.

However, both of these moves towards increasing the health of our economies lead to the third challenge. And that is, how they can be achieved without at the same time threatening social cohesion, with the risk of increased exclusion and the attendant political uncertainty.

Today there are signs of such a fragmentation as witnessed by increasing unemployment and the emergence of the "new poor"; In your own area, the statistics reveal, all too clearly, the scale of the problem and the potential damage that could be done to our societies if they are not heeded.

As the most recent CERI publication, *Successful Services for our Children and Families at Risk*, reminds us, 15-30 per cent of school aged children are identified in many OECD countries as at risk of failing in school with the likelihood that they will not attain the standards necessary for active labour market participation. In other words, on average, one in four of our children are at risk. For instance, in the USA 20.4 per cent, or one in five, children live in poverty. In Ontario 30 per cent of adolescents drop out of high school. These are frightening figures which are reinforced by the large numbers of unemployed young people which can be counted in many of our countries.

The latest "Employment Outlook" cites the horrifying unemployment statistics for young people. For example, in the age group of 20-24 year olds for males in France 24.6 per cent are unemployed. In Finland the equivalent figure is 32.1; in Ireland 24.7; in Italy 27.8 and in Spain it is 36.4 per cent. The equivalent figures for females are just as bad -- sometimes a little better, sometimes a little worse than for the males.

From both humanitarian and economic perspectives, we literally cannot afford to waste the lives of these your people -- for they are our future -- and live with the guilt of not having fully explored and analysed every possible avenue to ensure their full integration into society. Furthermore, we cannot accept that our systems, whether they are concerned with education, health or welfare, could be held responsible for aggravating the problems through lack of coherence and co-ordination.

Most OECD countries have introduced policies and measures to try to cope with these challenges and this conference focuses on a number of cornerstone issues in attempting to identify, elaborate and disseminate possible solutions that may prove effective in meeting them. For instance, your work looks particularly at innovative approaches that stress multi-disciplinary partnerships between education, health and social services in planning to meet the needs of families and their children across a wide age range. In doing so, a better balance between prevention and redemption has been achieved.

These innovations at the local level have flourished in the context of decentralisation, and are avoiding waste and duplication and are encouraging greater involvement of the community. This includes, for instance, the police, local businesses, senior citizens, parents, charities and foundations in developing realistic and relevant strategies for targeting interventions more effectively.

But most importantly of all, where a co-ordinated approach has been adopted, there is growing evidence of improved standards in education, and health with less drop-out from school and increased chances of integration into the world of work. In addition there is evidence of financial savings and increased satisfaction for all of the stakeholders concerned. However, the evaluations that have been carried out, although encouraging, are still incomplete and need to be greatly strengthened in order to learn more from successful innovations.

Because your work on successful services for our children at risk and their families also relates strongly to other areas of OECD work, the outcomes of this conference are eagerly awaited as part of the input into a conference in November at OECD which will be looking at the role of the welfare state in the millennium and the reforms that will surely need to be made in order to achieve the twin goals of equity and efficiency.

Being Canadian myself I am pleased that Canada has agreed to host this meeting and helped to bring together such a wide range of representatives from different government departments who share the same concern to develop families. Canada is a particularly appropriate venue, since the country has a great deal of experience in implementing and experimenting with reforms in this area, some of which you have been able to witness first hand from your field work in Toronto.

I will conclude by thanking the many individuals and organisations who have contributed to the organising and funding of the conference as well as the research work itself. I would particularly like to thank the Council of Ministers of Education Canada, for the work that they have done in organising this conference with CERI. I am looking forward to the results because it is my conviction that we all have a very important role to play in sharing our experiences about what works in social innovation leading to greater social cohesion. I wish you every success with your work.

SETTING THE SCENE: SOME PERSONAL EXPERIENCES

by

Lisa Dore and Mei Chen[1]

"This is the real challenge for governments: how to help chosen families happen, and how to support them when they do. Because, integrated services or not, when you come down to it, it's not systems working with people so much as people working with people."

When I was 17 years old, I was asked to be part of a Children's Aid education working group, because the agency saw me as an example of a "successful" youth in care. And I was succeeding: I had been with the same foster parents for five years, I was doing well in school, I was a member of my school's volleyball team, and I had been working in the same part-time job for almost two years.

At this working group, I met a man named Irwin. As the end of the school year approached, Irwin learned that I was looking for a summer job. Before I knew it, he was offering me a job, working at a day camp with small children. Ever since I had met him, Irwin had been talking about PARC (Pape Adolescent Resource Centre), the place he worked at, and particularly about the Network group. I had never gone, because the idea of spending time with youth in care did not appeal to me in any way, shape, or form why would I want to go to a place full of messed up people?

However, after Irwin got me that job, I went to a Network meeting, out of guilt or as some sort of repayment, maybe; but I was going to go that one time and never return. I found out much later that Irwin expected this to be the case; I was one of two new people at that week's meeting, and when he was asked, Irwin predicted that it would be the other young woman who would come back to the group, not me. But it turns out both of us were wrong, for in the more than four years that have passed since that meeting, I have attended Network meetings almost every week; I regularly take part in PARC social and recreational activities; I have lived in PARC housing with other PARC youth; I have volunteered as a tutor; and I have worked at PARC not only on a part-time basis, but also full-time for more than a year. I was dragged to PARC practically kicking and screaming, and now I'm a PARC geek.

The question asked of me by others, and myself, is "Why?" Why -- when I didn't want to go in the first place, when I was doing so well, when I needed none of PARC's resources, when I already had a strong circle of friends whom I could count on for anything -- did I become so attached to PARC? It took me a long time, but I finally came up with an answer, and this is what I think I have to offer you today.

---

1.   Although this paper is written in the first person singular the authors prepared the paper jointly.

This conference is on integrated services for children and youth at risk; you have come from all over the world to share knowledge, ideas, and practice models on this, so you can better serve the youth of your countries, and I agree wholeheartedly that it is a good direction to take. However, I did not keep going to PARC because it was the product of two agencies or ministries; because it could help me with housing, employment, education, or advocacy; because its policies and procedures complemented, not contradicted, each other. To this day, I don't think I know which ministries are responsible for funding PARC, or even what many of PARC's policies are, per se. And when I found I did need help with a place to have, or a job, or filling out student loan applications, it was simply a bonus that I could get that at PARC, instead of going elsewhere. I stayed at a PARC for a more basic, non-systemic reason; I stayed because there, I felt accepted.

As a youth in care, I live with labels, with stigma, with a feeling of shame. I was "an abused kid", "a foster kid", "I did not have a family". Some of these notions came from myself, while others came from outside; the origins do not matter. What does matter is that I saw myself as "different". I had always felt a need to explain and justify myself and my past. But at PARC, I didn't have to explain, because everybody already understood; I did not have to justify, because being in care wasn't automatically a bad thing. All of a sudden, it was okay: okay to talk about my foster parents and not worry about uncomprehending, strange looks; okay to not have a "family" to go home to for holidays; okay to have to be on my own at 18.

Acceptance, support, encouragement, trust, faith -- these are some of the ideas that people think of when they think of "family". As a youth in care, when I thought of "family", I had lots of negative ideas and feelings attached to it. Later, it became simply a word, because it was not relevant to my life; I didn't have a family. Now, I often think I'm luckier than many normal kids, because I don't have a family" -- in fact, I have several families. Over the years, I have made my families; instead of having no choice about the people whom I can turn to and count on, I have been able to decide who those people are. I have had the opportunity to surround myself with people who care about me, who nurture me, who believe in me, people who help me to do and be whatever I want. Everybody should have the same opportunity.

This is the real challenge for governments: how to help chosen families happen, and how to support them when they do. Because, integrated services or not, when you come down to it, it's not systems working with people so much as people working with people. I have seen people do things they never thought they could, seen them push themselves forward personally and emotionally, seen myself do both, all because of a connection that was made with a person or a group of people. I am able to try new things, take chances, chase my dreams because I know I have people who will catch me if I happen to fall, and help me get back on my feet again. This is what most needs to be integrated by agencies, systems and governments in order to make the greatest difference; the feeling of acceptance, support, nurturance, belonging -- of being part of a family.

PART ONE

TRANSITIONS

MAKING SERVICES WORK FOR CHILDREN AND YOUTH AT RISK AND THEIR FAMILIES: TWO WAYS OF INTEGRATION

by

Guido Walraven[1]
Sardes Educational Services, The Netherlands

Introduction

The CERI project on Integrated Services has led to several important and interesting reports (OECD, 1995, 1996*a*, 1996*b* and 1998). The time has come for each Member country to disseminate those research results and to adapt solutions derived from the research of best practice in other countries to the national situation. In the process of dissemination three parties are involved: research, policy and practice. Those three form a triangle, and I am convinced the three of them need to join forces to tackle the huge problems concerning youngsters at risk that are facing us. In other words it is the linkage between those three parties that facilitates the improvements we are all aiming at: to help the children and youth at risk and their families in better ways, concentrating on their needs and enhancing their own possibilities to cope with their situation.

What is their situation like? As an Englishman said in the 18th century, when asked about the situation in his country: *The situation is hopeless but not serious.* Is the present situation of children and youth at risk and their families in OECD countries "hopeless but not serious"?

The bad news, that I am afraid is the experience of all of us, as people working with and working for youngsters at risk is that their situation is serious in many respects. And there are an overwhelming number of reports from different backgrounds that document the experiences of the groups at risk as well as our experiences in dealing with that serious situation.

The good news is, however is that all over the world there are examples of good practice in which committed people are trying to help youngsters at risk, by delivering services in a more effective and more client-oriented way than usual. That is to say, in a more co-operative, co-ordinated and integrated way. The international study of the OECD brings together such examples and it analyses the factors that determine their success. In that way people in other places can systematically learn from the experiences pioneers have had.

---

1. This is a revised and enlarged version of a paper presented both at the OECD/Canada Final Dissemination Conference on Integrated Services in Toronto, Canada, October 1996 and at what might be called the National Dissemination Conference in London, September 1997.

Our hope is grounded in those examples of best practice and in the commitment of the people making that practice work. During the project we visited schools, pre-school facilities and other institutions, and I know that many of us were impressed by the dedicated ways in which principals, teachers, staff, paraprofessionals and volunteers are working together for their pupils and students, and also at involving other relevant professions and agencies. The people we met were proud of their institutions and the results their teamwork is bringing about; they mentioned how rewarding it can be to work with their students and children. As the principal of the Westview Centennial Secondary School, Toronto, put it: "Working here reminds us of the reasons why we choose education as our profession". In the same manner visiting the sites reminded us why we are involved in projects like the one on Integrated Services for youngsters at risk. In the end what we are doing in this project ought to have consequences for those youngsters.

Improvement starts with a vision of where you want to go, and the more specific the common vision in the local or regional situation, the more energy generated during the implementation process. Against that background I have been asked to give you some more specific information on the concept of integrated services, especially about two dimensions of it: horizontal and vertical integration.

Apart from a common clear vision you will also need a strategy of how to achieve it. Therefore I will also mention some of the conditions that need to be fulfilled or at least considered before the goals are reached.

I will restrict myself here to vision and strategy, the two elements that determine the direction of the process of improvement and implementation. Other elements of the complex game of implementation are discussed in other contributions to this book.

This contribution starts with looking into the question *"Of what are youngsters at risk?"*. Against this background we can make even more clear that integration of services is one of the best answers to those risks. Consequently we need to address the question *"How can we integrate services?"*. Research shows that the main type of integration is organised per age group (horizontal integration). Co-ordinating all services for one age group is of course an enormous step forward compared to the usual ways of service delivery. But we will argue that this is not enough. Integration for age groups should be combined with a longitudinal approach: integration of services for all youngsters from birth till adulthood (vertical integration). Horizontal integration (per age group) and vertical integration (from 0 to 18 or 20 years of age) are complementary. With vertical integration the transition from one developmental phase to another needs special attention, for instance the transition from school to work. There is a need for "interlinked responsibilities" of professionals and their institutions, to smooth the transition between these phases. Some strategic issues regarding the implementation of integrated services of both types are dealt with further on. In the conclusion we show that the two types of integration are necessary to tackle problems of youngsters at risk, but that there are no "magic bullets".

At risk -- of what?

In the operational definition of the term "at risk" the OECD-CERI has given (1995), three elements are mentioned: *1)* school failure, *2)* increased difficulty in making the transition to work and adult life, *3)* social failure or reduced likelihood of making a full contribution to active society.

One might see the three elements as steps in the development of a person to adult life and a full contribution to active society. Consequently the term 'at risk' might be interpreted as a way of stating a long term goal for the development of children and youth. In that sense it is an optimistic term; the film about the OECD Project is therefore titled "Children of Promise".

What we need in working for youngsters and with youngsters at risk, is therefore a longitudinal approach: to do our utmost to help to let them develop into adults with all their personality and capabilities blossoming (cognitive, socio-emotional, motor, creative and other capabilities), and at the same time to try and combat the at risk factors as much as possible (see Figure 1).

The emphasis on capability development mirrors the recent shift from looking to children and youth at risk from a deficit model, towards working with them departing from a resilience model.

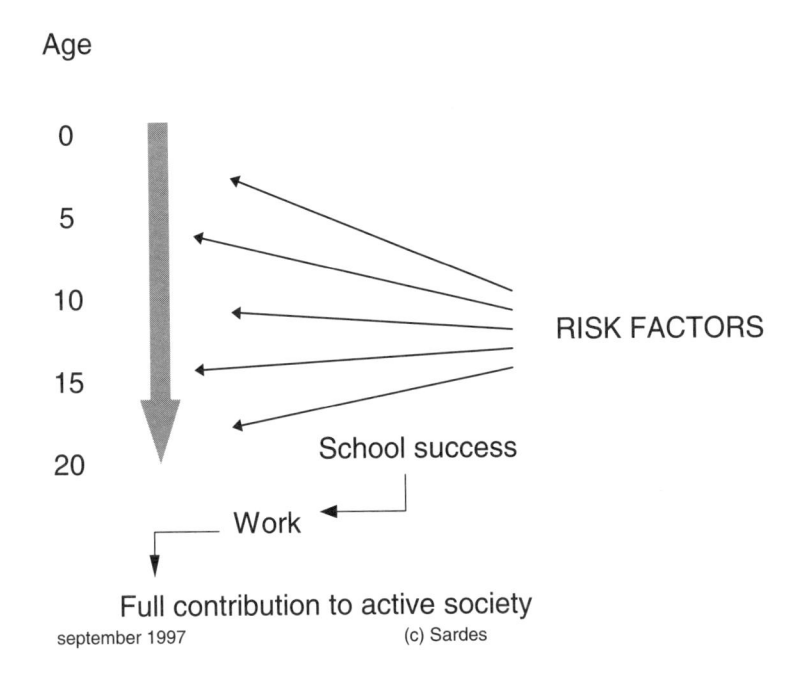

Figure 1. **Aims of integrated services**

Development to adult life is the emancipation of young people from their parents, earning their own place in the family and society at large. This process used to be more a matter of course than it is nowadays. Rituals denoting transition were culturally established (in French or in bilingual Canada this is called "*rites de passage*"). Today's society offers young people much less opportunity to win a clear place. Compared to the old days, society no longer seems to need its young people. That has great effects on the emancipation process or the transition to adult life. For instance in some ways the period of adolescence is becoming longer, because becoming independent and having your own job and family tend to happen at a later age, while in other ways some children, especially children at risk, grow up at an early age, that means that by force of circumstances they have to stick up for themselves and to fight as adults.

When addressing the problems of youngsters at risk the different dimensions of identity formation need attention: the psychic, the social and the cultural dimensions. It is only by a balanced consideration of these crucial dimensions of successful identity, that the signals transmitted by young people will enable the reduction of problems.

Education plays a crucial role with all three dimensions as far as youngsters at risk are concerned, but there is a growing awareness that schools cannot do it alone, that they need other agencies to co-operate with. That has everything to do with the complexity of the problems, the multiple causality of at risk and the cumulative character of risk factors.

Even if you want to avoid the direct causation, there are a number of so-called predictive factors strongly related to the failure elements from the 'at risk' definition; you can divide them into two groups: on the one hand poverty, family issues, community factors and geography, and on the other hand poor knowledge of the majority language as well as school, and classroom factors.

Many of these factors are beyond the reach of schools and have to do with social economic status or social inequality (especially the first group of factors). It was Bernstein (1970), who stated in the 1960s that "school cannot compensate for society". What schools can do, however, is concentrate on factors they can influence (especially the second group of factors). And that is exactly what innovative schools did in the 1970s and 1980s when they gave priority to the concept of the effective school, with effective instruction and effective learning time.

The environment of schools was part of the idea of an effective school from the beginning, *e.g.* the neighbourhood of the buildings and the role of parent involvement. But with the growth of the problems in society for vulnerable groups, because of economic developments and austerity policies among other things, it was a professional response for teachers in the 1990s to say that they could not work at these problems without support. Effective schools tried to be SMART (set their goals in Specific, Measurable, Acceptable, Realistic and Time based terms). Adequate schools in the 1990s had to be even SMARTER in order to tackle the growing impact of the problems. Within schools they tried to be both effective and affective: to relate to the children and youth in order to awaken their intrinsic motivation among other things, to create an affective school climate and to respond to the basic (educational) needs of youngsters: feeling competent, autonomous and in relation with others. In short, schools adopted an adaptive educational attitude: they tried to adapt to the differences between students within the same classroom.

Adequate schools in the 1990s tried also to be smarter in their external relations by inviting other professionals into their buildings for help with problems and/or by networking with other institutions in order to discuss similar experiences, exchange information and facilitate referring schoolchildren to them. In short, they worked towards more integrated services.

Integrated services -- the age group approach

Co-ordinated or integrated services is one of the solutions to the problems of youngsters at risk which have the most promising perspective. In order to answer the key question "How to develop co-ordinated or integrated services", we need to look at the usual form of service delivery first (see Figure 2). For a certain age group many services are available. In the case study I did on a pre school example, the MOVE project in The Netherlands (see OECD, 1998), there were more than ten services available. Even for professionals it was difficult to keep track of all the possible services, not to mention for families, and for families at risk in particular.

In many cases of usual service delivery the emphasis is on the supply side: professionals develop their services and more or less "wait" until clients come along or get referred to them. This might seem to be overstating the situation, but at least in The Netherlands this was true five or ten years ago, and it certainly has not been overcome everywhere in that country. Unfortunately the OECD study showed that the same goes for many other Member countries.

Figure 2

Usual service delivery

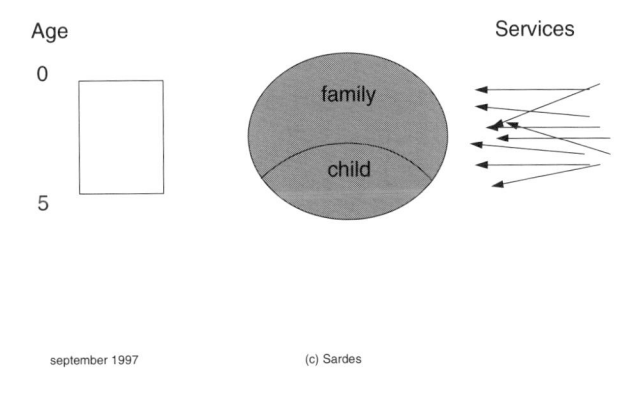

What is needed, however, is a client centred approach and putting the emphasis on the demand side. The exact problems, needs and questions that youngsters at risk and their families have must be investigated with a professional responsible for any subsequent action. Clients should no longer have to go to different institutions and different counters within those institutions, to talk about their problems time and again before those are addressed adequately. Instead, a responsible professional can act as a case manager or client advocate and invite all necessary services and institutions to co-operate. She or he has to take the initiative to make an inventory of all the relevant services, and has to try to make the service provision more co-ordinated or even somewhat integrated.

The process of getting professionals to co-operate is a long one, however. Co-operation has once been described as an unnatural act of non-consenting adults. It might take years before the following situation exists (see Figure 3).

Figure 3

Co-ordinated / integrated services

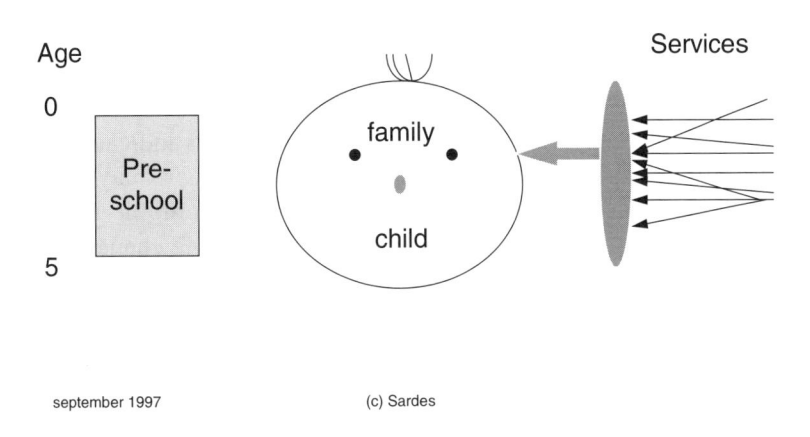

There are different models for the co-ordination or integration, for instance:

- a one stop model in which the client comes to one counter, talks about his or her needs and problems, and a professional leads the client to the most appropriate services; one of the weaker points of this model is, that clients need to take action to come to the counter themselves, in other words they have to be aware of their problems and of which services might offer them help;

- a neighbourhood network of youth care professionals with inter-professional consultation and co-ordinated action, in which, for instance, the leader of a pre-school playgroup observes certain problems, talks them over with colleagues from other services, and offers help to the family involved;

- a contact mother from the same neighbourhood and background as the families at risk, visits them, helps them to express their problems and needs, and suggests possible solutions with the help of certain services.

In all these examples, forms of case management are extremely important. These forms of interprofessional co-operation tend to occur especially for a certain age group, like pre-school or school age. One might argue that these models can bring about at best forms of horizontal integration. It is a great step from the usual way of service delivery if after some years of trial and error a form of horizontal integration is reached.

But if we keep in mind the need for a longitudinal approach, the question becomes is that all there is?

Integrated services: the longitudinal approach

The answer is no. Horizontal integration is not all there is. What we also need is vertical integration: an integration of services corresponding with the development of youngsters. Keeping in mind the goal of identity formation, we need a service delivery focused on the prevention of drop outs. What we need to build is a safety net, a chain of responsible institutions. The Dutch sociologist C. Schuyt has elaborated this concept (Schuyt, 1995).

His point of departure is the biography of a young person. One can make an inventory of problems which are encountered in the course of a young person's development, and chart the range of problems by examining the successive linkages of a young person's biography.

"A central consideration is that the vulnerability of certain young people's positions in our society comes to light at countless times during their lives. These individual moments form a series of links, which together form the biography. An analysis of those moments indicates what can go wrong at any time and what different and differently directed help and support may be needed. In addition, there are moments of transition from one linkage to another, or from one institution to another, for example, from school to work. These are crucial moments for the life chances of this group of young people: if something goes wrong during the transition from one linkage to another, then the chances are that it will also go wrong in the later linkages. Therefore, responsibility for one linkage is not enough, regardless of how well that responsibility is usually shouldered by a particular body, for example the school. The overview of moments and linkages should ensure that the policy for the group of marginalised youngsters is itself connected to form a responsible chain." (Schuyt, 1995, p. 27)

Professor Cees Schuyt identifies ten linkages:

- family situation;
- relationship family and school;
- at school;
- after school;
- dropout
- vocational training;
- to work;
- at work;
- life without work;
- participation in society.

In the OECD study we divide the biographical development of young people into three areas: pre-school, school (primary and secondary) and work. Therefore we had two main transitions to look after: from pre-school to school, and from school to work. In this OECD model the transition from primary to secondary school is a minor one, although it can be argued that in many countries it is a transition crucial for children at risk because of the consequences of choices made along that transition. Irrespective of the amount of transitions that should be identified in the development of children and youth, thinking about the management of those transitions is the key priority. With all transitions what is crucial are interlinked responsibilities between the service delivery institutions concerned (see Figure 4).

Figure 4

Longitudinal approach: Transitions

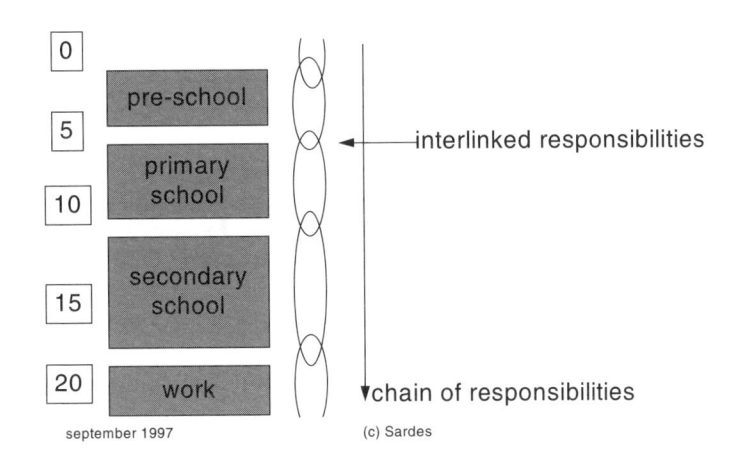

```
0
      pre-school
5
                        ← interlinked responsibilities
      primary
      school
10
      secondary
15    school

20    work           ↓ chain of responsibilities
september 1997        (c) Sardes
```

To quote Schuyt more extensively:

"Not every body or organisation has to be responsible for everything. Distinct responsibilities can be outlined for specific problems. This is the theory of linked responsibility: each linkage in the integral policy chain is responsible for a clearly defined problem area, without losing sight of the central objective, namely the acquisition of an identity of one's own. Central and local governments should then ensure that the overview of the entire chain is maintained. In fact, it amounts to:

- a precise and well-defined localisation of certain problems;

- localisation of the bodies which are respectively responsible for these problems;

- ensuring that good interfaces are developed and continue to exist between, on the one hand, problem and responsibility, and on the other hand, the different linkages.

The idea of linked responsibility is actually twofold. Firstly, there must be a permanent link between a certain (policy) body and a clearly defined aspect of the problem. Secondly, the succession of problems and their solutions and the mutual links between these problems and their solutions must be safeguarded by an umbrella organisation (see Figure 5).

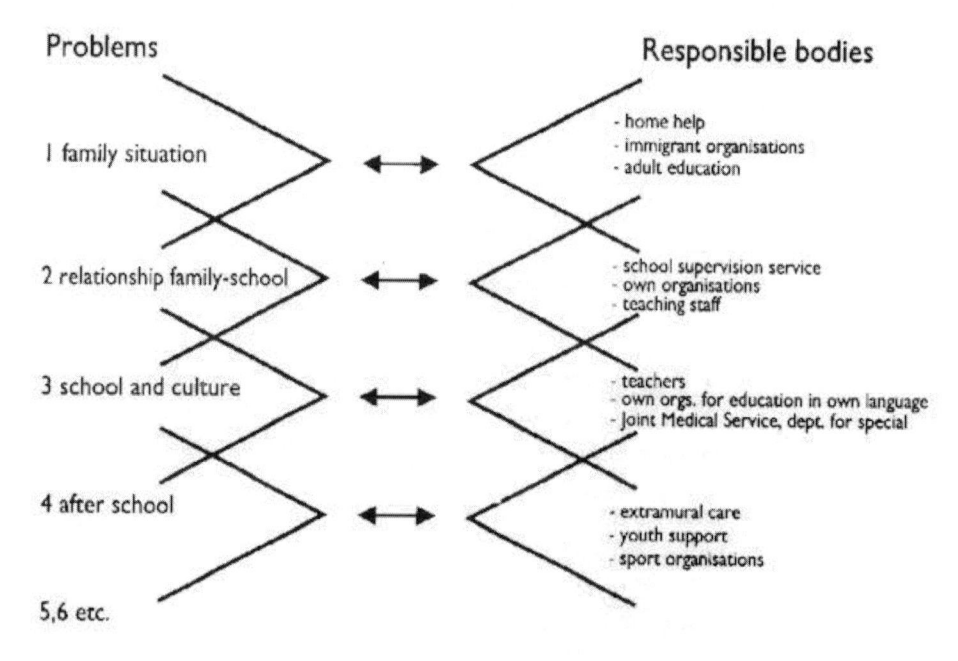

Figure 5. **Overview of (some examples of) links**

Problems	Responsible bodies
1 family situation	- home help - immigrant organisations - adult education
2 relationship family-school	- school supervision service - own organisations - teaching staff
3 school and culture	- teachers - own orgs. for education in own language - Joint Medical Service, dept. for special
4 after school	- extramural care - youth support - sport organisations
5,6 etc.	

In each case a link hooks onto the next link, both in the problem formulation and in the responsible bodies and organisations. A slight overlap of the links is no problem, it can actually work very well. The exact interpretation of these links will not be the same everywhere. The designation of the responsible bodies will differ from local authority to authority and (possibly) from problem to problem. The most important consideration when forming integral policy is that the government takes the initiative to chart out this linked responsibility. The government must be wary that the various problems are not claimed by too few and not by too many bodies accordingly. Responsibilities can be shifted or integrated where necessary." (Schuyt, 1995, pp. 50-51)

In combining horizontal and vertical integration we can build an even stronger chain, because both types of integration are complementary (see Figure 6).

Figure 6

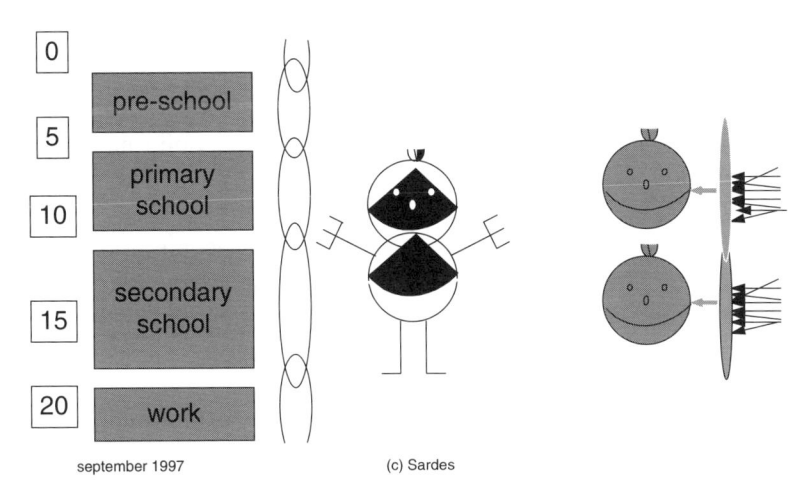

Horizontal + vertical integration

september 1997   (c) Sardes

Some strategic issues

It is one thing to argue that horizontal integration needs to be complemented with vertical integration, and quite another to put those ideas into practice.

In the OECD study many examples of especially horizontal integration were analysed, and the general suggestions for implementation that can be subtracted from those examples are also relevant for vertical integration. Those suggestions might function as a checklist for someone who would like to implement a co-ordinated or integrated approach.

- *Vision*: a clear vision is needed of where you want to be say four years from now, a vision that can inspire you and your colleagues.

- *Put children first*: since co-operation is an "unnatural act of non-consenting adults" you would like to avoid gate-keeping and other bureaucratic politics -- fights between institutions and/or departments within those institutions; by putting children first you focus on the one theme that can unit people instead of the many things that separate them; we have to think in terms of outcomes for children and once we agree on them we can talk about how we can bring those outcomes about co-operatively; we need to rethink our ownership of problems.

- *Training*: an essential part of the implementation process, both pre-service and in-service.

- *Community*: strive for community involvement.

- *Empowerment*: strive for empowerment of the families at risk; make sure policymakers as well as professionals are willing to share power with families and communities.

- *Change agents*: think about who can act as agents, in professional organisations as well as the community itself.

- *Stakeholders*: you need stakeholders at every level from community through professional organisations to policy agencies, from public and private agencies; the needs of children and youth need advocates.

- *People*: in short, we need dedicated and inspiring people, those who can bring about changes in the culture of an organisation, for instance by starting something new and involve a growing number of others; the necessary change of structures sometimes need other people and sometimes follow on cultural changes.

- *Small steps*: take one step at a time, be sure all the (institutional) incentives are pointing in the right direction; for instance: Co-operation and networking might be a condition for financing, or: money follows the families and not the institutions.

- *Success*: nothing succeeds like success, so share success experiences with all involved, including the community.

- *Evaluate*: evaluation can be a way of learning (both for individuals and for organisations or communities); you are allowed to make mistakes as long as you are learning from them.

- *Learn*: do not reinvent the wheel but learn from people elsewhere who have struggled with the same problems in bringing about more co-ordinated service delivery.

- *Time*: implementation takes time, often more time than politicians are willing to give; in turn, we can try to give politicians some small results regularly, keep them posted of all developments.

The checklist might give some readers a somewhat heterogeneous impression. A useful framework for structuring the list as well as finding more suggestions is constituted by three perspectives on preventive youth policies (Commissie OLPJ, 1997). A strategy can be focused on prevention of (societal) problems, on (individual) risks or on (individual) development.

The first perspective is focused on problems adults encounter and is therefore mainly concerned with the question "*What do we want to get rid of?*", for instance drug abuse, early school leaving or feeling unsafe on the streets. The perspective is negative towards youngsters and hence the objectives are stated in negative terms. Adults are at the centre, they have problems with youngsters and they want their problems to be addressed.

The second perspective focuses on risk factors regarding the youngsters and is therefore concerned with the question *"What would we like to keep as it is now?"*, for instance staying at school or staying healthy. Here the youngster is more in focus and adults are aware of the risks that threaten their situation. The viewpoint is positive inasmuch as adults want to safeguard circumstances that are positive for the development of the youngsters; the viewpoint is somewhat negative inasmuch as the adults only look at risks.

With the third perspective we move a step further: the youngster is really at the centre and taken seriously as someone who can contribute to solutions; the question is here *"Where do we as adults and youngsters want to go from here?"* For instance, how can youngsters take initiatives, or how can youth and adults together make our neighbourhood safe for children. The viewpoint here is fully positive and directed towards development and empowerment.

The three perspectives are complementary, and need to be distinguished carefully. Cities and communities tend to start with the first perspective, professionals tend to advocate the second perspective, and only recently, some people are also favouring the third perspective. However in implementing a more co-operative and integrated service delivery all three perspectives are relevant.

Together they could contribute to a new political framework for the place and future of youngsters in our society – a vision or framework that is badly needed.

Conclusions

This contribution started with the question whether is was correct to characterise the present situation of children and youth at risk and their families in the Western World as "hopeless but not serious". It is my conviction that the situation is indeed very serious, but it certainly is not hopeless. On the contrary: the OECD study can reinforce our hopes for a better future for groups at risk, and national dissemination can lead to discussions on the ways and means by which co-ordinating and integrating services can make a difference in that respect. Against that background I have been offering a conceptual framework of horizontal and vertical integration, which might be of help in your work for the groups at risk.

The aim was to enlarge the model of integrating services for one age group by introducing a longitudinal approach that follows the development of a child into adulthood. Special attention was asked for the transition between different developmental phases (mainly pre-school/school/work). Those transitions need to be managed very carefully, and it was suggested that the concept of interlinked responsibility be used to do that. The concept addresses the crucial question "How can responsibilities be divided in a way that builds a strong chain?" The combination of both horizontal integration (for one age group) and vertical integration (the longitudinal approach) can build such a strong chain in a way that offers fruitful perspective on more co-ordinated and integrated services for youngsters at risk.

Integrating services is not an end in itself. It is of course a tool towards the goal of integrating children and youth at risk and their families within our communities and society. The (OECD) concept of "at risk" is about making your contribution to active society, and you need to participate in society in order to be able to make such a contribution. We have expanded the concept here by emphasising identity formation and capacity building as important for both participation and contribution. Integral policies should have clear, unambiguous and realistic aims. For example, helping as many "youth who may become at risk" as possible to acquire a distinct identity of their own.

To summarise, policies of integration comprises a double task: to promote social integration through the integration of policy (Schuyt, 1995, pp. 36).

It is not for children to adapt to the way in which services are delivered. It is for all adults involved in service delivery, to adapt to the needs of children. We need to co-operate in order to be able to break the cycle of disadvantage, deprivation and underachievement.

Member states are challenged to use the framework as a tool when they try to disseminate and implement the results of the OECD study.

Implementation is known to be the crucial phase in processes of renewal and improvement, so the national, regional and local job is not going to be easy. Because if there were easy solutions to the problems we are dealing with, they would have been implemented already on a very large scale. But since there are no such magic bullets, we have to combat the at risk factors with all the institutions and people involved. In doing so we do not start from scratch, we can build on good (and bad!) experiences elsewhere. The OECD reports show us a path which is worthwhile considering when we strive for a co-ordinated service delivery which is both effective and efficient. The reports could prevent us from reinventing the wheel, and allow us to concentrate on making the "car" of service delivery "roll and work". In other words, we know better where to concentrate our efforts and invest our hopes -- as one of the great poets of the Romantic Age, Samuel Taylor Coleridge put it:

> "Work without hope draws nectar in a sieve,
> And hope without an object cannot live."

REFERENCES

Bernstein, B. (1970), "Education cannot compensate for society", *New Society*, 26 February, pp. 344-347.

Commissie OLPJ (1997), *Jeugd op de agenda: In gesprek over een politieke agenda voor kinderen en jongeren*, Zoetermeer [Committee on the Development of Local Preventative Youth Policy]

OECD (1995), *Our Children at Risk,* Paris.

OECD (1996a), *Successful Services for our Children and Families at Risk,* Paris.

OECD (1996b), *Integrating Services for Children at Risk,* Paris.

OECD (1998), *Co-ordinating Services for Children and Youth at Risk -- A World View,* Paris.

Schuyt, C.J.M. (1995), *Vulnarable Youth and their Future: A policy recommendation based on literature research*, Amsterdam.

TRANSITION TO PRE-SCHOOL: BRITAIN AND FINLAND

by

Jennifer Little
Lethbridge School District

The transitions from home to pre-school and pre-school to formal school are major events in any child's life. It is particularly important that children considered to be "at risk" for a variety of reasons have opportunities to experience pre-school settings that promote continuity between such transitions. Many countries in the western world provide early intervention programmes that aim to combat conditions that could result in social, emotional, physical and intellectual handicaps, in an attempt to maximise the progress for each child and promote a higher degree of success in life in general.

Often researchers tend to describe such programmes as an attempt to build stronger foundations for future learning for "disadvantaged children" who come from low socio-economic backgrounds. But all children from low SES families are not "disadvantaged" in the sense that they need compensatory education. It is, therefore, those children who fit a number of identifiable criteria that are categorised as "at risk" and who are thought to be best be served by programmes aimed at providing support, both to the family and the child.

Rather than describe these children as "disadvantaged", the term "at risk" is becoming more commonly used since it implies the distinct possibility of reducing the risk factors which may cause difficulties in the future.

> *The term "at risk" emphasises future prospects. It is a predictive concept which assumes that children and pupils "at risk" have certain characteristics which allow them to be identified but that these characteristics only become a problem when they meet events and conditions that have yet to occur* (OECD, 1995, p. 18).

With the recognition that there is a future for children considered to be "at risk", comes the clear implication that the school, the family and the community must work together to ease the transition between home and school by attempting to reduce the effects of identified risk factors for these children.

Government ministries, generally Education, Health and Social Services are attempting, in many countries, to provide various forms of early childhood programmes that are designed to alleviate or reduce difficulties that may be experienced by children "at risk", since these conditions may be seen as a hindrance to the optimal learning opportunities of children. Examples from Britain and Finland illustrate how some areas in the two countries attempt to ease the transition from home to school for children considered to be "at risk".

Britain

Nottinghamshire

Until recently, Local Education Authorities (LEAs) in Britain allocated education funds for nursery provision based primarily on the needs of children "at risk" in each authority. For example, the Nottinghamshire LEA has typically funded nurseries in the city centres with the intent of combating the perceived effects of low socio-economic status. Few nurseries were funded in the outlying areas, since children in these areas were considered to have more advantages than those living in the crowded city and town centres. Many of these nurseries operate within the guidelines of the High/Scope Perry Pre-school Project, a programme developed in the USA and designed to ease the transition to school for children "at risk".

Currently (1998), the British government is pursuing an early years initiative, focusing on an integrated approach to preschool care and education. LEAs are required to establish Early Years Development Partnerships and Plans. These are intended to lay the foundation for the government's long term vision of comprehensive and integrated services for young children in order to ease the transition to school. LEAs, in co-operation with families, Social Services and Leisure Departments, as well as providers from the voluntary and private sectors, will develop early years provision that promotes positive, developmentally appropriate learning experiences for preschool children. The intent is to ensure government funded nursery places for all four year old children (should their parents so desire) by the 1998/1999 school year, with the probability of introducing similar provision for three year old children the following year (1999/2000).

Bristol

The home is often seen as an important factor in children considered to be "disadvantaged" and likely to experience failure at school. Since it was becoming evident that many children of young mothers were experiencing developmental delays in the early years, the Bristol Child Development Programme was initiated to offer support for teenage mothers and attempts to alleviate projected difficulties long before the children begin schooling. Although these mothers are recent recipients of parenting themselves, they may not be mature enough to actually transfer those skills to their own situations (Hudson and Ineichen, 1991) or, having come from disruptive families, may not have had adequate parenting models in their own lives.

Since the programme has identified a lack of proper nutrition and a lack of stimulating play as the two major reasons for the poor development of some babies of teenage mothers, it focuses on the pre-school child's development and the under-developed capacity of the mother to foster it. Young mothers are linked with health visitors who provide support and information about early cognitive, social and language development and nutrition to assist them in developing parenting skills. The intent is to build up the mothers' sense of achievement, bolster their self-confidence and empower them to become more involved in enhancing their children's development, thereby increasing the children's opportunities to experience success once they begin school.

The main results of the programme have been positive (Hudson and Ineichen, 1991). The young mothers have shown an increase in parental responsibility for their children in the areas of general health, nutrition and language, cognitive and social development. The incidence of child abuse in the programme families has decreased due to an increased understanding by the mothers of their potential as effective parents. Still, there continues to be a need for more comprehensive and co-ordinated services from the ministries of Health, Education and Social Services that would provide continuity for these young mothers and their children as they move through the pre-school years.

Mid Glamorgan

The Link-Up programme, offered by many schools in Mid Glamorgan for children before they begin nursery school, is meant to ease the transition from home to nursery and, in the words of a teacher from Mid Glamorgan, to provide opportunities "for getting to know the parents before the child starts school, building up mum's trust in the school and building up the child's confidence that something nice and friendly goes on in this big noisy building". But the intent of the programmes clearly goes beyond just "familiarity" with the school. As the head teacher of one Mid Glamorgan school offering a Link-Up programme explained "The whole idea of Link-Up is that there is this bridge between home and school."

The Link-Up programmes are generally located in schools that have the space and resources to support them. Parents must attend with the children and actively participate in the activities that occur. In fact, where LEA funding is not available to employ qualified nursery nurses, parent volunteers are encouraged to set up the equipment and run the programme themselves, although school personnel take an active part in facilitating the programmes. Those programmes that are able to staff the Link-Up programmes with nursery teachers or nursery nurses attempt to teach the parents skills that they can use at home. For example, as much as telling stories and singing familiar nursery songs are for the enjoyment of the children, the Link-Up leaders also use these to model to parents how they, too, can read and sing to their children. Whilst the children are playing with the large equipment or manipulatives, the Link-Up leaders demonstrate language interactions, asking questions and responding to initiations by the children. As the Link-Up leaders observe the children playing and interacting with their parents and peers, feedback is provided to the parents in order to help them understand how young children develop.

Finland

There is not a separate pre-school system in Finland. "Pre-school education is a natural part of the day-care system" (Central Union for Child Welfare, 1995), with day-care coming under the auspices of the Social Welfare Services. In 1996, government legislation guaranteed a day-care place for all children under the compulsory school age of seven. The Child Day-Care Act legislates the educational aims of the day-care system, involving play, work and teaching based on Froebel's philosophy. Children with special needs are integrated into the regular centres, but with special care and in smaller groupings. Staff/child ratios are very small: 1:7 for children between the ages of three and six, and 1:4 for children under the age of three. All staff is trained, including university training for kindergarten teachers and vocational training for other staff. It is expected that one out of three staff members should be a kindergarten teacher.

Kiiminki

Kiiminki is a large village surrounded by a rural and sparsely populated area. For that reason, almost two thirds of the children using day-care services are in family day care. Social Welfare Services provides support to families requiring day-care or family care for their children and a home care allowance is an alternative to day-care placement for children under three.

There are three types of day-care available in Kiiminki. Play activities are offered twice a week for two hours and provide pre-primary instruction to the pre-school group (commonly the six year olds in Finland). Day-care centres serve approximately one third of the children in the area in three centres. The most widely used Family Day-care is offered under three settings: in the child minders' homes, in the children's homes or in a group family day-care for 10-14 children whose parents are shift workers. The centre serving Kiiminki was located in a large building, similar to a multi-family dwelling, within which several groups of children were facilitated. Since the family day-care groups are comprised of children of various ages and attempt to meet their varied needs, the pre-school groups must seek the activities of a larger peer group elsewhere, typically in the play activity groups.

When a child begins family day-care, the parents are involved in a collaborative process, with day-care personnel, of developing an individual care and education plan based upon the holistic needs of the child. A great deal of the learning takes place through play and interaction between the child and the environment. Emphasis is placed on the development of language and communication skills and a positive self-esteem. Regular evaluations of each child's programme determine the quality of the learning experiences, set new or continuous goals and ensure that the transition to school is smooth.

A recent evaluation (Kiimingin Kunta, 1995) of early childhood education and pre-primary teaching in Kiiminki offered positive feedback from parents and resulted in the following visions for the future:

- universal access for children in spite of regional or social differences;

- diverse and flexible programme development based on the needs of the locale;

- increased collaboration amongst all groups providing early childhood education;

- development of a co-operative network, both regionally and internationally.

The programmes described are attempting to ensure smooth transitions between home and care and educational settings. In many cases, these programmes attempt to reduce the certain costs of providing remediation in the later years of school, costs which escalate as the child advances in years. Notwithstanding the importance of the quality of pre-school education, transition programmes in the early years are more likely to be successful when there is effective parental involvement (Fuerst and Fuerst, 1993; Ball, 1994; Cleveland and Krashinksy, 1998). In addition, the earlier educational provision is begun, the more lasting and influential the benefits will be (Sylva and Wiltshire, 1993; Fuerst and Petty, 1996).

It is this recognition, backed by substantial research that must be addressed and accepted by governments. Although research has tended to concentrate on the advantages of early intervention programmes to children considered "at risk" for any number of reasons, to isolate these children from their peers in society and provide specialised programmes only for a particular group may foster racial and economic segregation, unacceptance and unawareness of multicultural diversity and unequal opportunities for all children, regardless of their status in society.

The most effective transition programmes appear to be those that begin with a holistic view of the child, that are monitored for quality and developmental appropriateness and that integrate all the available community components which provide services designed to meet the complex needs of the children and their families. As Evans (OECD, 1995, p. 141) stresses:

> "It is clear that the problems are more than can be handled adequately by education systems working alone: a coherent, systems orientation is needed. The implication of such an approach requires the development of new arrangements which may cut across existing departmental or ministerial boundaries and budgets."

Education, Health and Social Services must work together with families "...placing the child and not the system at centre stage" (OECD, 1995, p. 27). Only with such an integrated and early approach can all children, and particularly those "at risk", be assured of educational provision that will maximise their progress and enhance their chances of success in the future.

REFERENCES

Ball, Sir Christopher (1994), *Startright: The Importance of Early Learning,* RSA.

Central Union for Child Welfare (1995), *Day-care and Early Childhood Education in Finland*, Co-operation Committee for Early Childhood Education, Helsinki.

Cleveland, G. and Krashinsky, M. (1998), "The Benefits and Cost of Good Child Care: The Economic Rationale for Public Investment in Young Children", Childcare Resource and Research Unit, University of Toronto, Toronto.

DfEE (1996), *Nursery Education Scheme,* Department for Education and Employment, UK.

Fuerst, J.S. and Fuerst, D. (1993), "Chicago experiment with an early childhood programme: the special case of the Child Parent Center Program", *Educational Research,* Vol. 35, No. 3, Winter, pp. 237-253.

Fuerst, J.S. and Petty, R. (1996), "The Best Use of Federal Funds for Early Childhood Education", *Phi Delta Kappan,* June.

Hudson, F. and Ineichen, B. (1991), *Taking It Lying Down: Sexuality and Teenage Motherhood,* Macmillan Education Ltd, London.

Kiimingin Kunta (1995), "Early childhood and school programmes in Kiiminki", prepared for Childhood Education -- International Perspectives conference, Municipality of Kiiminki, Kiiminki, Finland.

OECD (1995), *Our Children at Risk*, Paris.

Sylva, K. and Wiltshire, J. (1993), "The Impact of Early Learning on Children's Later Development", *European Early Childhood Education Journal,* Vol. 1, No. 1, pp. 17-40.

AFTER SCHOOL CHILD CARE

by

Marjorie McColm
Ministry of Education and Training - Ontario

Once a child starts school it is assumed that the child is cared for all day. However, many children can spend as many hours in out-of-school programmes as in school, particularly children of working parents. Because of the temporary and patch work nature of out-of-school programmes their role in supporting the development of children is often overlooked and discounted. The challenges presented by Children and Youth at Risk (CYAR) cannot be met by schools alone but by a co-ordinated effort of all community agencies including before and after school child care.

The history of the development of school-age child care in Ontario

Since the turn of the century in Ontario, school officials have been concerned about care for low income children outside of school hours. It was school officials along with other community leaders who were instrumental in the establishment of the early Crèches and supervised playgrounds. In addition many communities established clubs for children such as Boy Scouts, Canadian Girls in Training and in rural communities 4-H Clubs. In the City of Toronto the board of education, the playground associations and the Crèches worked to-together to provide after school clubs for children who attended inner city schools. These programmes were established to provide school-age children with the opportunities for skill development and promote citizenship and community spirit (Young, 1994). It was recognised that school alone could not provide all opportunities for development and Teaming, particularly for children at risk.

During the Second World War, 42 school age child care centres were established with funds from the federal government, to care for children while their fathers were overseas and their mothers worked to support the war efforts. These centres were all closed in 1946. At this point the Ontario Ministry of Community and Social Services was given full responsibility for child care. Child care was classified as a welfare service and there was very limited supply. In 1966 federal funds were made available to share the costs of child care for low income families. However, even though most mothers of school age children were working outside the home (Lero, 1992), there was no real expansion in school age child care until the 1980s.

At this point schools once again were to play to a critical role. The Ministry of Education directed school boards to provide supervision or the lunch hour (with no additional funding) and a number of boards were allowing agencies such as the YMCA to set up-child care in vacant class rooms. The Ministry of Community and Social Services gave small start up grants to agencies and parent groups to start these centres. In 1987 the government passed legislation which positioned child care as an essential community service and required that all new schools be built with child care centres. The result of these of initiatives is that one third of licensed child care is now located in schools.

Currently, regulated child care only serves 8 per cent of children who require care. For most families in Ontario, child care arrangements are informal unregulated care, self care, sibling care, and patch work of "after-four" clubs and recreation programs.

The current government has frozen all Ministry of Education and Ministry of Community of Social Service capital and start-up programs. Child care expansion in Ontario has come to a halt.

Current issues for after school care in Ontario

- The dilemma of increasing demands for child care for school age children and shrinking resources to meet the need.

- There is no one level of government or department responsible for out of school programs, therefore, parents are left to try and determine what is available and how to access the service. Many parents of children at risk do not have the motivation or the skills to put a programme together.

- Perception that the regulated system is unnecessarily expensive and therefore unaffordable for most families.

- The regulations for school age children are inappropriate and promote programmes that do not meet the developmental needs of children, particularly the 9-12 year olds.

- The lack of flexibility in regulated child care isolates children from their community because they do not join in community activities such as sports, clubs, etc.

- The dollars spent on child care, recreation, social services and education programmes would go further if there were co-ordination and co-operation among the agencies.

- Subsidies for low income families should be used for a wider variety of programmes other than regulated care.

The government has just undertaken a review of child care in Ontario and released a document for public consultation. The recommendations include the development of more flexible and age appropriate standards for programmes for school age children and allow child care subsidies to be used in programmes other than licensed child care.

After school care and children and youth at risk

We know that for children and youth at risk, out of school programmes are necessary not only for recreation and stimulation but for safety and nutrition. We know that many low income families do not have enough food, children come to school hungry and stay hungry and at the end of the day there is no full refrigerator to lure them home. If they go home and their parents are at work there is nothing for them to do, and they are often afraid to play outside in what may be a dangerous neighbourhood. The parents often work in jobs where they are inaccessible by telephone, so no one knows if they have arrived home safely or what they are doing. Even if the mother is at home, research indicates that in many cases the care received is detrimental due to the poor emotional and mental health of the parent. For children at risk, quality after school programmes can be a source of social and emotional support.

The Spadina West solution for after school care

The Spadina West Community, located in the City of Toronto, has for many decades been the home of new immigrants. It has been described as the most culturally diverse community in Canada. Over 50 per cent of the families do not speak either official language (English or French) and the area has the highest proportion of adults who have not completed high school in the Metropolitan Toronto area. Consequently, the school serves a high number of CYAR. The community's social agencies and the elementary school have been working to co-ordinate out-of-school programmes for children since the turn of the century. Today the school, the child care programme and local agencies are continuing to respond to the needs of the community. They are currently developing a comprehensive, co-operative plan for harmonising out of the classroom programmes for school age children. The Spadina West children's services workgroup include:

- Alexandra Park Community Centre -- provides recreation activities for young children, youth and adults.

- George Brown College's Fashion District Child Care Centre -- licensed child care

- Ryerson Community School/Toronto Board of Education -- Junior Kindergarten to grade eight and provides after-four enrichment programs

- Scadding Court Community Centre -- recreation activities for young children, youth and adults including swimming.

The central goal of the working group is to provide high quality out of classroom activities that meet the needs of the families and children of the community.

These community agencies are currently collaborating on a number of services. The child care centre and the school jointly manage and staff the school breakfast and lunch program. The school takes children to the Scadding Court community centre for swim programmes and the Toronto Board pays for swimming instruction as part of the school's after school programs. Alexander Park uses the school gym for youth programmes in the evening. The agencies want to increase the number of children served in the existing programmes and develop new programmes in response to community need.

The Ryerson Community School plays a pivotal role mainly because of its legislated mandate and its access to the community's families. The school is interested in supporting the participation of the children in out of classroom activities in the belief that the children will acquire attitudes and skills that will support and enhance their academic performance. By working with the school the agencies hope to raise the communities awareness of activities available for children and to increase the participation rate of the children in the programs.

The school and the agencies are working towards:

- developing a shared mission statement for all out of classroom programmes for children and youth.

- a framework for programme responsibility that meets the needs of children and their families.

- developing consistent policies regarding child safety and risk management *i.e.* recording enrolment and attendance.

- developing a joint human resources strategy.

- developing a joint advocacy strategy.

- co-ordinating all funding applications and the development of new services.

- developing a three year funding strategy.

The workgroup has recently submitted to the Metro Task Force on Services to Young Children and Families, for their consideration as a pilot project, a model for collaborative after school care.

There is no question but that to improve the educational outcomes for CYAR, schools and agencies must take a holistic approach which puts the needs of the child in the centre.

Figure 1. **PARTNERSHIP RENEWED: A STRATEGIC PLAN FOR HARMONISING COMMUNITY PROGRAMMES FOR CHILDREN**

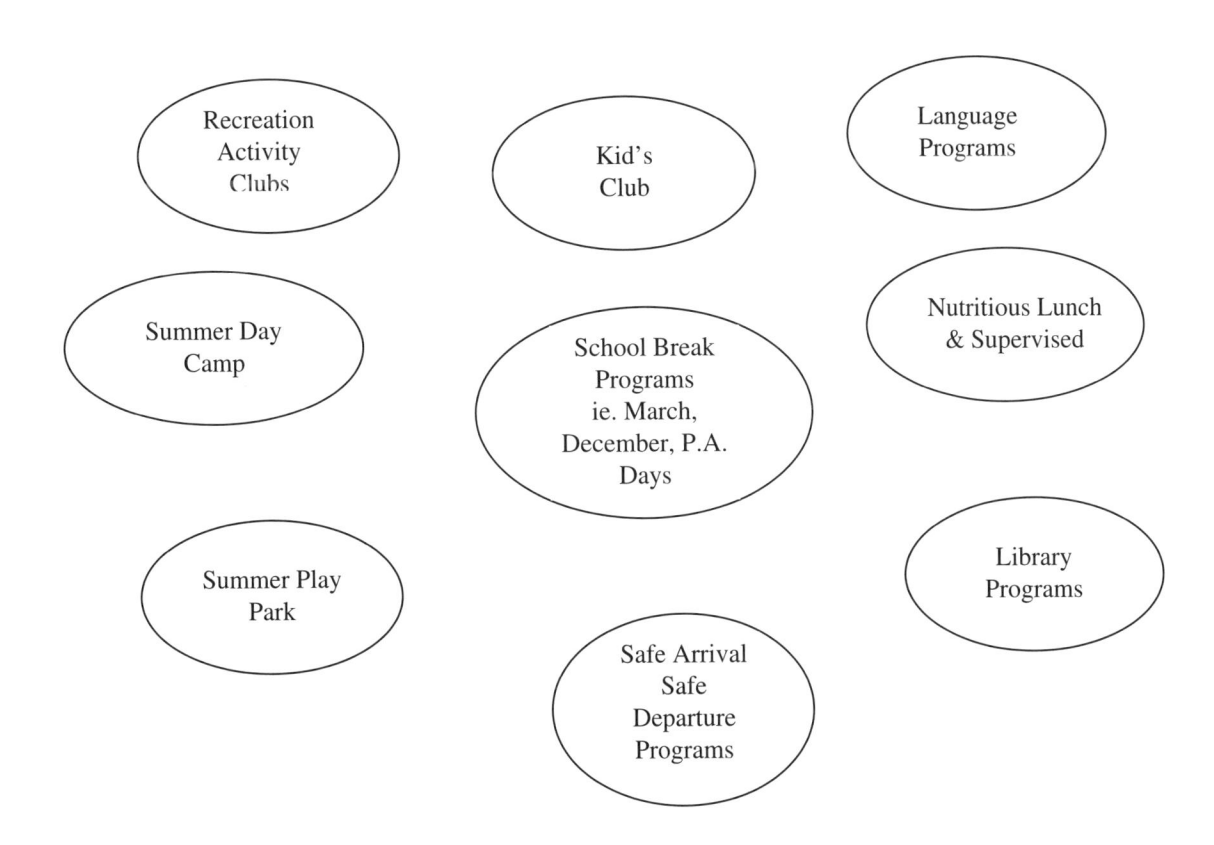

- Recreation Activity Clubs
- Kid's Club
- Language Programs
- Summer Day Camp
- School Break Programs ie. March, December, P.A. Days
- Nutritious Lunch & Supervised
- Summer Play Park
- Safe Arrival Safe Departure Programs
- Library Programs

Dundas West, Children's Services Workgroup
Alexandra Park Community Centre, George Brown College, Ryerson Community School, Scadding Court Community Centre

REFERENCES

Doherty-Derkowski, G. (1995), *Quality Matters. Excellence in Early Childhood Programs,* Addison-Wesiev, Don Mills.

Harms, T. and Clifford, R.M. (1994), *School Age Child Care Environmental Rating Scale*, Teacher's College Press, New York.

Kyle, I. (1991), "Ontario Report", in Allan Pence (ed.), *Canadian National Childcare Study: Canadian Childcare in Context,* Statistics Canada, Ottawa, p. 370.

Lero, D. (1992), *Parental Work Patterns and Child Care Needs: The Canadian National Child Care Study,* Statistics Canada, Ottawa.

Moss, P. and Pence, A. (eds) (1994), *Valuing Quality in Early Childhood Services,* Teachers College Press, New York.

Musson, S. (1994), *School Age Childcare. Theory and Practice,* Addison Wesley, Don Mills.

Offord, D. (1989), *Ontario Child Health Study: Children at Risk,* McMaster University, Hamilton.

Park, N. (1992), *A Comparative Study of School Aged Child Care Programs,* Queens Printer, Toronto.

Vandell, D. and Ramanan, J. (1991), "Children of the National longitudinal survey of youth: choices in after school care and child development", *Developmental Psychology*, Vol. 27 (4), pp. 637-643.

Young, N. (1994), *Caring for Play. The School and Childcare Connection,* Exploring Environments, Toronto.

Young, N. (1996), "Partnership Renewed: A Strategic Plan for Harmonising Community Programmes for Children", Report to the Spadina West Children's Services Workgroup.

Government Reports:

Province of Ontario (1996), "Improving Ontario's Child Care System", *Ontario's Child Care Review*, August, Queens Printer.

Metropolitan Toronto Task Force on Services to Young Children and Families, Submission to the Ministry of Community, and Social Services, Pilot projects for restructuring school age child care in Metro Toronto, June 1996.

TRENDS IN YOUTH EMPLOYMENT AND SCHOOL-WORK TRANSITIONS IN CANADA

by

Doug Giddings
Human Resources Development Canada

Introduction

It is widely believed that the long term job prospects of young persons are declining and that youth will face increasing difficulty finding satisfying and rewarding work. This generation of youth is believed to be doing much worse in many dimensions of social and economic life than the earlier generation of "Baby Boomers". Qualitative and anecdotal sources suggest that young persons share a sense of hopelessness and are uncertain about their futures. The paper outlines the scope and severity of youth unemployment in both quantitative terms and qualitative terms. The paper explores the factors that contribute to youth unemployment and the difficult challenge youth face in their search for stable employment and economic security.

Qualitative evidence

Human Resources Development Canada (HRDC) frequently employs qualitative research methods as a complement to traditional quantitative analysis. In the past few years HRDC has sponsored numerous focus groups on the issues of youth employment and school-to-work transitions. In early 1996, Ekos Research Associates, in support of the Ministerial Task Force on Youth, was employed to conduct a series of focus group sessions with youth and employers of youth. Price-Waterhouse conducted another series of focus groups in the same year as part of the developmental phase of a new longitudinal survey of youth and school-work transitions (sponsored by HRDC and conducted by Statistics Canada). Price-Waterhouse conducted 21 focus groups in six cities across Canada. This round of consultations focused specifically on issues of school-work transitions. One set of groups was composed of youth from 14 to 20 years of age. A second set was composed of parents who had children in the target age group of 14 to 20 years.

The focus group sessions confirmed that both youth and parents were very anxious about the labour market prospects facing today's youth. It was perceived that the job market facing today's youth was much more difficult than it was for their parents. It took longer to find a good job and many post-secondary graduates were unable to find employment. Even though higher education was no longer seen to guarantee a good job, most participants believed that getting a good education was crucial. Young persons are preoccupied with jobs and access to post-secondary education. With university tuition fees escalating, both groups were very concerned about issues of student financing. Parents and youth agreed that it was very important to get a job you liked. Many participants questioned whether or not a high school education was sufficient preparation for work. Both youth and parents wanted to know what courses of study would provide good jobs.

Quantitative evidence

How do the impressions gathered from qualitative analysis compare to the quantitative evidence on youth employment and school-to-work transitions? An examination of time series data on earnings, unemployment rates and graduate outcomes shows that the current pessimism about the prospects of today's youth appears misplaced at least for the well educated.

Historic youth unemployment rates

Youth unemployment has consistently exceeded that of the adult population. The patterns of youth unemployment compared to adults over the last twenty years can be seen in Figure 1. Not only is the unemployment rate of youth much higher than that of adults but the gap also appears to widen during periods of recession. However, the duration of unemployment spells for youth have traditionally been shorter than those of adults.

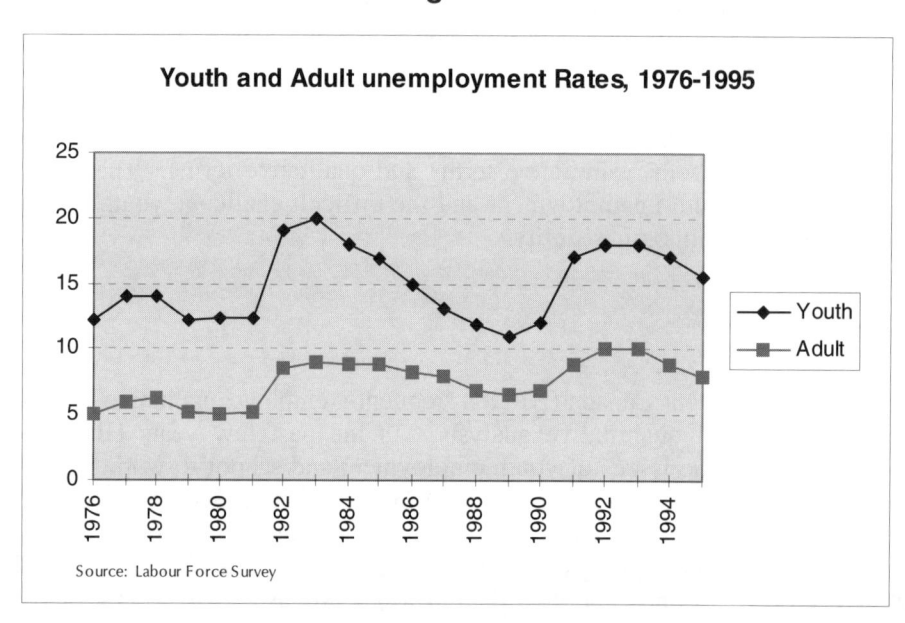

Figure 1

Youth and Adult unemployment Rates, 1976-1995

Source: Labour Force Survey

Highly educated young persons have much better employment prospects than their less educated peers (Figure 2). Specifically, youth with university degrees are just as well off now as they were 20 years ago, since their unemployment rate remained relatively stable from 1976 to 1995 (8.6 per cent in 1976 and 1995). However, the unemployment rate for those with some high school or a high school diploma rose dramatically from 10.3 per cent to 18.0 per cent over the same period. For those youth with a post-secondary certificate, the unemployment rate rose by over 2 percentage points from 8.4 per cent to 10.8 per cent over the same 20 year period.

Figure 2

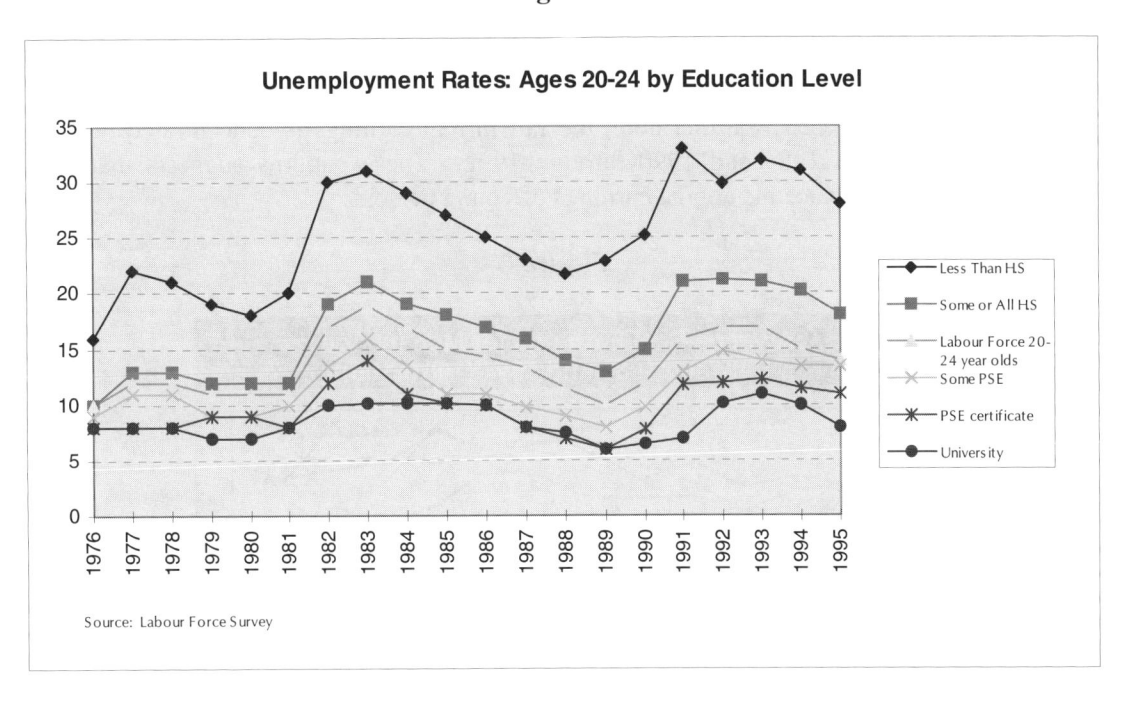

Unemployment Rates: Ages 20-24 by Education Level

Source: Labour Force Survey

Data from the National Graduates Survey over the past decade provides further evidence that the prospects of the more educated youth remain stable (Table 1). Looking at three cohorts of graduates (1982, 1986, 1990 cohorts) working full time two years after graduation, their employment record has changed very little. For example, 1990 trade/vocational graduates were more likely to be working full time in June 1992 (64 per cent) than 1982 graduates were in June 1984 (60 per cent). 1990 graduates with a bachelors degree were just as likely to be working full time (73 per cent) as 1982 graduates (73 per cent); and 1990 graduates with a masters degree were only slightly less likely (75 per cent) to be working compared to 1982 graduates (76 per cent). University graduates in specific fields in the humanities and such areas as the biological sciences have, nevertheless experienced greater difficulties finding good jobs than graduates in such fields as engineering.

Table 1. **Percentage of graduates working full time two years after graduation**

	Class of 1982 in June 1984	Class of 1986 in May 1988	Class of 1990 in June 1992
Trade/Vocational	60	69	64
Career/Technical	77	82	76
Bachelors	73	74	73
Masters	76	76	75
Doctorate	85	87	87

Source: National Graduates Survey, Statistics Canada.

Earnings

As shown in Figures 3 and 4 the average earnings of youth, men and women alike, have declined substantially from 1981 to 1993. During this period, the gap in earnings between 17-24 year olds and all other age groups increased. Furthermore, the fall in real earnings is concentrated in periods of recession -- 1981 through 1984 and 1990 through 1992. These patterns suggests that economic slowdowns inordinately reduce the annual earnings of young persons.

Figure 3

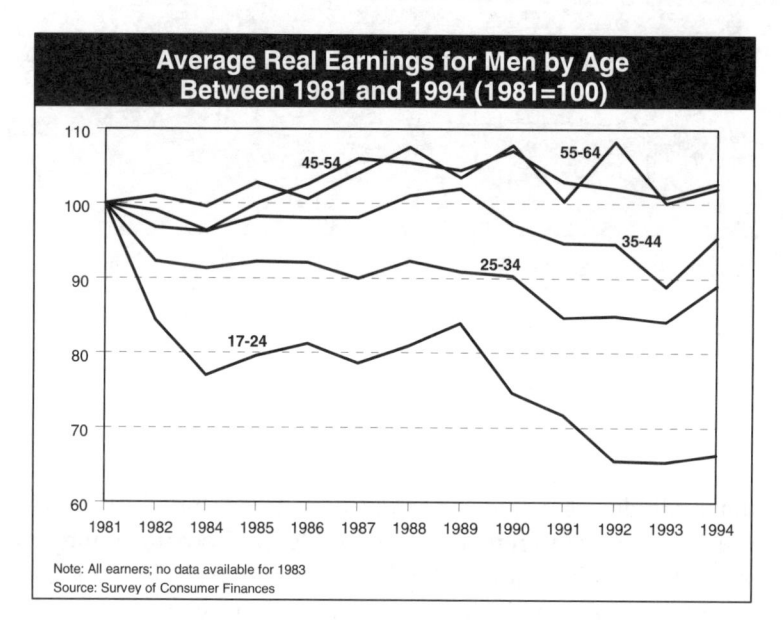

Figure 4

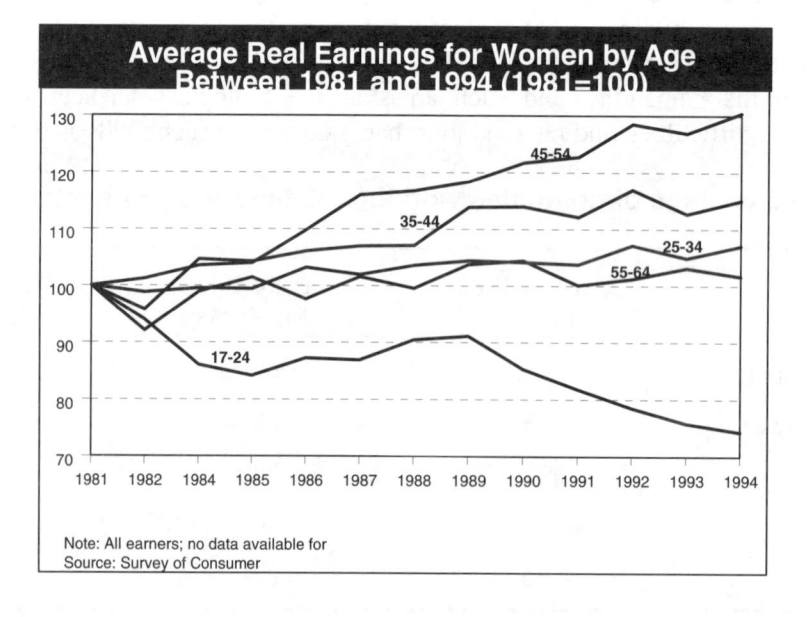

50

The increased incidence of part-time and part-year employment is in large part responsible for this trend. For women, no less than half of the increase in the earnings gap between the 17-24 and the 45-54 age groups (age premium) is attributed to the growing incidence of part-time and part-year employment for the young. For men, almost four-fifths of the increase in the age premium can be explained by the growth of non-standard employment.

Figure 5

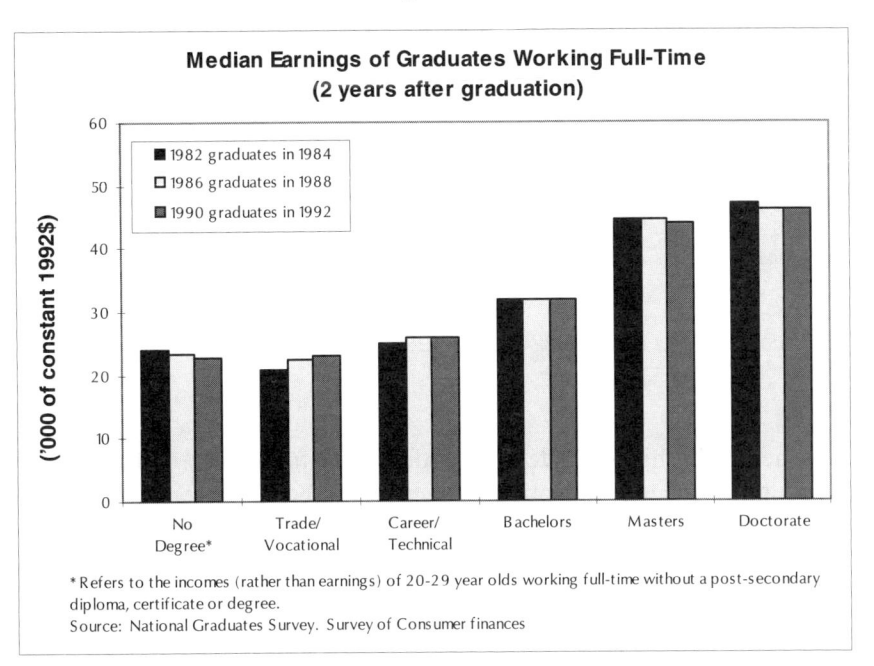

**Median Earnings of Graduates Working Full-Time
(2 years after graduation)**

[Bar chart showing median earnings in '000 of constant 1992$ for 1982 graduates in 1984, 1986 graduates in 1988, and 1990 graduates in 1992, across categories: No Degree*, Trade/Vocational, Career/Technical, Bachelors, Masters, Doctorate]

*Refers to the incomes (rather than earnings) of 20-29 year olds working full-time without a post-secondary diploma, certificate or degree.
Source: National Graduates Survey. Survey of Consumer finances

Data from the National Graduate Surveys show that highly educated youth have faired better. As shown in Figure 5, the median earnings of 1982, 1986 and 1990 graduates (that is all graduates ranging from trade/vocational certification to doctorates) who are working full-time two years after graduation have remained relatively stable or risen somewhat. In constant 1992 dollars, the median earnings of 1990 graduates with a bachelors degree ($32 000) working in 1992 were essentially identical to those of 1982 graduates ($31 900 in 1992 dollars). For those with a career/technical diploma, earnings rose to $26 000 for 1990 graduates from $25 000 for 1982 graduates. The median earnings for youth working full-time with no post-secondary education fell from $23 900 (constant 1992 dollars) in 1984 to $22 600 in 1992.

Demographic changes and educational supply

As is seen in Figure 6 the youth population has been declining since the early 1980s for those 15-19 years of age (with small increases since the early 1990s) and since the, mid 1980s for those youth 20-24 years of age. These demographic changes combined with increased school retention account for the declining numbers of young persons leaving high school and entering the labour market.

Figure 6

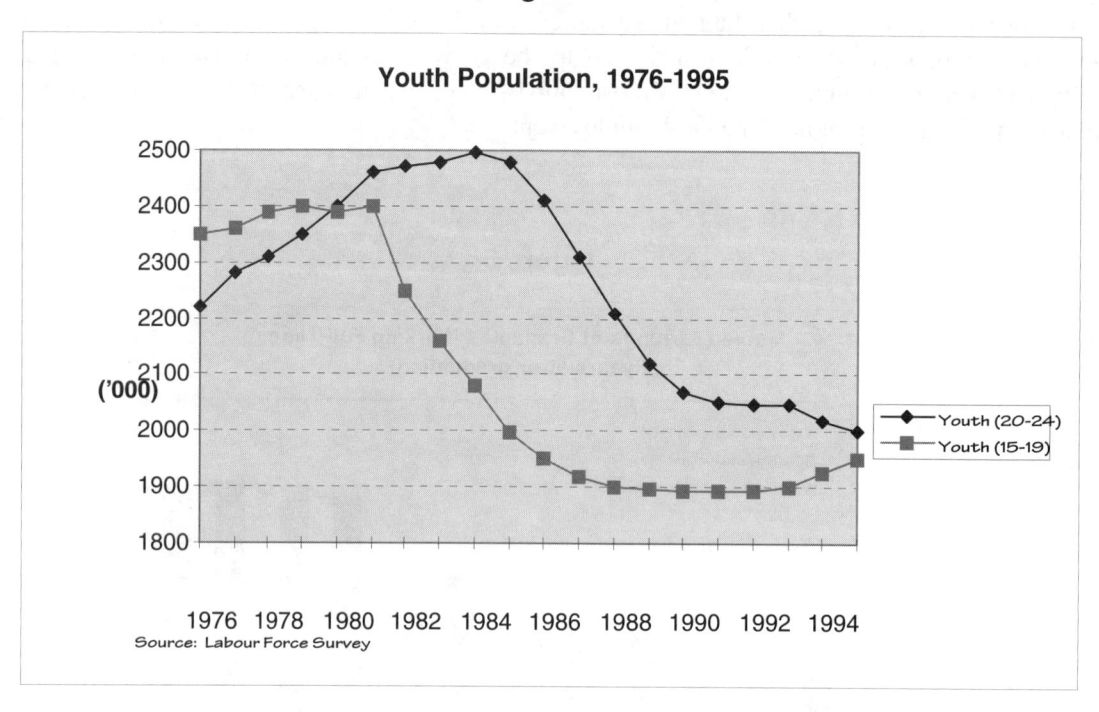

Youth Population, 1976-1995

Source: Labour Force Survey

Canada now has one of the highest rates of participation in tertiary education among the OECD nations and is becoming a high education society (Figure 7). Since the early 1980s, full-time enrolment has increased from just under 40 per cent to over 56 per cent in 1994. For the 15-19 age group, enrolment has levelled off at just over 80 per cent. Enrolment continues to climb for the 20-24 age group, more than doubling since the early 1980s (32.6 per cent today).

The recent School Leavers Follow-up Survey shows that most youth will receive some post-secondary education. According to the survey 85 per cent of youth will complete high school. Among high school graduates, 40 per cent will attend university within five years of completing high school and 30 per cent will attend college.

Not surprisingly, the probabilities of finishing high school and attending post-secondary education are highly related to family structure and socio-economic status. Two-thirds of those who do not finish high school are in what can be classified as a high-risk group (based on family structure, marital status, dependent children, disability and parental education and income). The fact that fully a third of those in the high-risk group completed high school shows that other factors such as parental attitudes to education, good teachers, good role models and individual initiative, determination and motivation are involved.

Over 60 per cent of those who did not complete high school have a grade 10 education or less. The majority of the non-completers have a full two years less formal education than those who enter the labour market after completing high school.

There are significant changes by gender. Young women are much more likely to complete high school and a quarter of young women who leave high school before completing do so for what are described as family reasons. Women are more likely to attend post-secondary education. According to the School Leavers Follow-up Survey 45 per cent of female high school graduates attended university compared to 39 per cent for male high school graduates.

The increased share of students in the youth population is of considerable importance for the interpretation of labour market outcomes for youth. Students are more likely than other youth to be employed part-time, out of the labour force, and working in clerical, sales and services occupations or in personal services or retail trade industries. By this token, students also earn less than their non-student counterparts. A portion of the decline in youth participation rates and in earnings can be attributed to the increased rates of education participation.

What is noteworthy is that due in part to rising rates of participation in post-secondary education, the supply of persons entering the labour market with these qualifications continued to increase in the 1990s.

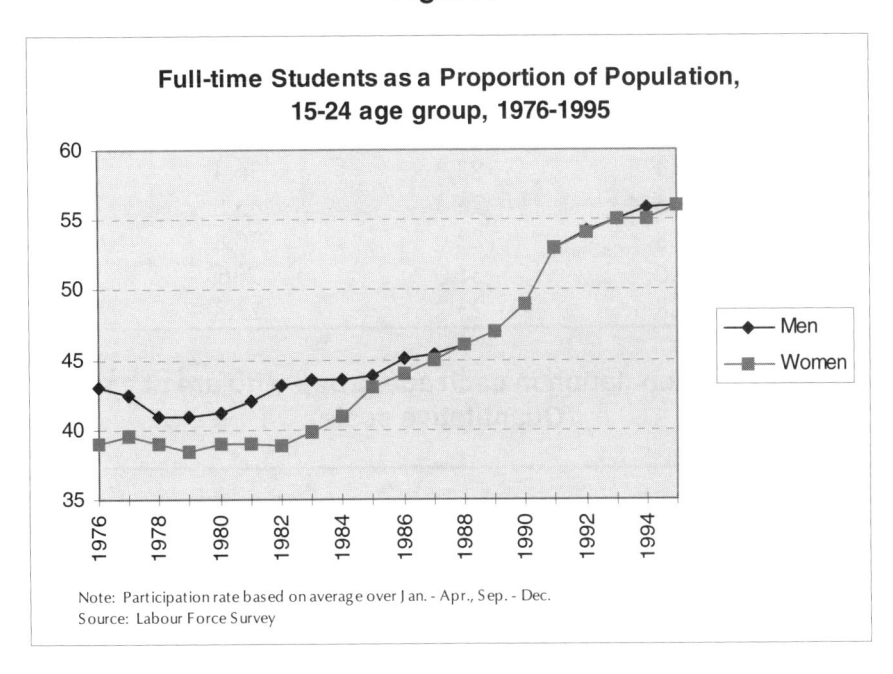

Figure 7

Full-time Students as a Proportion of Population, 15-24 age group, 1976-1995

Note: Participation rate based on average over Jan. - Apr., Sep. - Dec.
Source: Labour Force Survey

Due to rising rates of participation in post-secondary education, the supply of persons entering the labour market with these qualifications continued to increase in the 1990s.

Despite concerns about the quality and relevance of the public education system today's youth are more highly educated than preceding generations both in terms of completed years of study and in terms of scholastic achievement. This is evident in the following tables on the Canadian results of the International Adult Literacy Survey. However, many young persons continue to enter the labour market without the foundation of general skills. Of the seven countries in the study, Canada had more young persons at the lowest level of all the three dimensions of literacy measured.

Table 2. **Proportion of population in each age group who are at each literacy level, (Prose scale)**

Age	Level 1	Level 2	Level 3	Level 4/5
16-25	10.7	25.7	43.7	19.9
26-35	12.3	28.5	33.1	26.1
36-45	13.3	18.6	36.8	31.3
46-55	20.6	30.2	30.9	18.4
56-65	37.6	26.4	28.0	8.1

Table 3. **Proportion of population in each age group who are at each literacy level, (Document scale)**

Age	Level 1	Level 2	Level 3	Level 4/5
16-25	10.4	22.3	36.4	31.0
26-35	13.5	25.3	33.8	27.5
36-45	13.8	22.0	36.8	27.4
46-55	23.0	31.0	236	2.4
56-65	43.8	23.7	23.8	8.7

Table 4. **Proportion of population in each age group who are at each literacy level, (Quantitative scale)**

Age	Level 1	Level 2	Level 3	Level 4/5
16-25	10.1	28.6	44.6	16.7
26-35	12.0	25.5	35.1	27.5
36-45	11.9	22.4	35.6	30.1
46-55	23.9	32.2	24.8	19.0
56-65	39.7	21.5	31.4	7.4

Source: International Adult Literacy Survey, 1995.

Changing patterns of education and work

Today's youth combine work and education to an unprecedented extent. According to the recent School Leavers Survey, most high school students are very familiar with the part-time labour market before they leave school. Over 60 per cent of high school leavers held jobs in their final year of high school. The effect of part-time jobs on high school completion has been the subject of considerable debate. It is generally agreed that as evident in the School Leavers Survey, excessive part-time work is associated with non-completion. It is also appears that young persons who do no work at all in high school are less likely to finish high school than students overall. There is less agreement about the value of the skills and work attitudes acquired in part-time jobs.

School-work transition in Canada

Canada's structures of school-to-work fit what has been called the North American model. The emphasis of the education system is on higher level general skills rather than vocational skills. The transitions to work are informal. Formal apprenticeship in Canada has not been a vehicle of school-to-work transitions in the manner of the German apprenticeship system. The program is relatively small with about 130 000 registered apprentices and is concentrated in relatively few industrial and construction trades. In Canada the time that lapses after leaving high school and starting apprenticeship is eight years on average. Over one-half of apprentices had three or more jobs before entering the program and the average age of entrants is twenty-seven.

Another important feature of the Canadian system is the degree of choice. Students face important choices beginning in early high school. Decisions about which course options to take in high school (particularly higher level mathematics and science courses) have important implications for the types of post-secondary options available to them. There are important post-secondary choices such as college versus university and choice of field of study.

Parental involvement in these choices diminished as the students grew older. Beginning in high school youth are making key decisions about their future (Price-Waterhouse). Nevertheless the support and encouragement of parents remains very important. The focus groups also confirmed another key component of the Canadian system: the need for comprehensive information on courses and careers.

Canadian youth have high expectations (Krahn, 1996) concerning post-secondary education and careers. Whether or not these expectations are realistic depends very much on individual motivation and ability. However, the desire to obtain a post-secondary education is clearly rational in terms of its benefits.

With the prevalence of part-time work beginning in high school and traditional full-time summer jobs, students will likely have several jobs before completing their studies. This period could last a decade or more. With the trend to more and more education, transitions are completed later in life. It is more difficult to say on the basis of quantitative evidence that youth are experiencing relatively greater difficulty or hardship in making the transition. According to the National Graduate Survey of 1990 graduates, over eighty-per cent of university graduates were employed within six months of graduation.

In recent years there have a number of initiatives to improve the connections between high school and work. First is the growth of internship and work-study programs. These programs range from traditional forms of co-operative education based on short periods of work experience to more occupationally focused and intensive models of internship and apprenticeship. The New Brunswick Youth Apprenticeship Program is a good example. The Youth Internship Program of Human Resources Development Canada is another. Youth Internship has three streams: the school-based, the community-based and the sector-based streams.

It is generally agreed that business is working more closely with high schools. School-business partners are now commonplace. The Conference Board of Canada established the Business-Education Partnerships Forum to promote business-education co-operation. In addition to developing a framework of ethical guidelines, the Forum recognises and promotes exemplary practice through its national awards.

Another recent trend in Canadian high schools is a restructuring of vocational and technical education. High school vocational programs in Canada were in steady decline since the late 1970s and Canada's community colleges emerged as the focal point of technology education. In some provinces vocational education in specific trades such as automotive repair are being replaced by more generic technical programs combined with academic study. A more recent approach resembles what is sometimes called "tech-prep" in the United States. Academic and career courses in senior high school are linked to advanced courses in community colleges.

The movement to a greater emphasis in curriculum on learning outcomes, expectations and standards in broad areas of literacy, communication and employability skills promises greater coherence between what students learn in high school education and the skills required in the workplace and in life. The Employability Skills Profile developed by the Conference Board of Canada has inspired educators to identify cross-curricular skills such as communication skills and problem-solving skills as an integral element in specific curriculum areas such as mathematics, social sciences and languages and in the high school experience overall. There is a trend to a greater integration of computers and technologies into the curriculum and instruction. Finally, work-study programs have become an accepted component of high school curriculum ranging from school-based activities to intensive forms of internship.

Changing skill requirements

With technological change and the globalisation of markets (Figure 8) the workforce is necessarily becoming highly educated and skilled. In the period from 1991 to 1995, employment of those with university education increased substantially while plummeting for those with grade 8 or less.

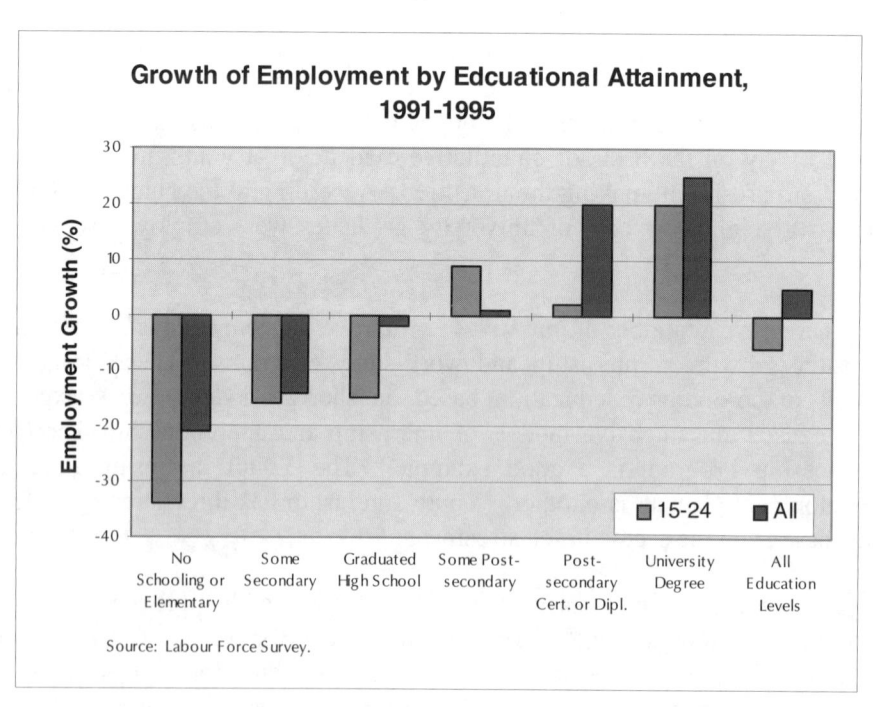

Figure 8

Growth of Emloyment by Edcuational Attainment, 1991-1995

Source: Labour Force Survey.

Projections from the Canadian Occupational Projections System for the years 1990 to 2000 show that 54.9 per cent of the net change in jobs by skill level will be in jobs that require more than 16 years of education and on-the-job experience. The proportion of these highly skilled jobs in the Canadian labour market is increasing dramatically.

However, much job growth will continue to be in jobs that require less than 12 years of combined education and training. As seen in Figure 9, jobs requiring less than 12 years of education comprised 45.1 per cent of the labour force jobs in 1991. Even though jobs requiring less than 12 years of education and training make up 39.7 per cent of job growth, the labour market share of these jobs will decline.

Figure 9

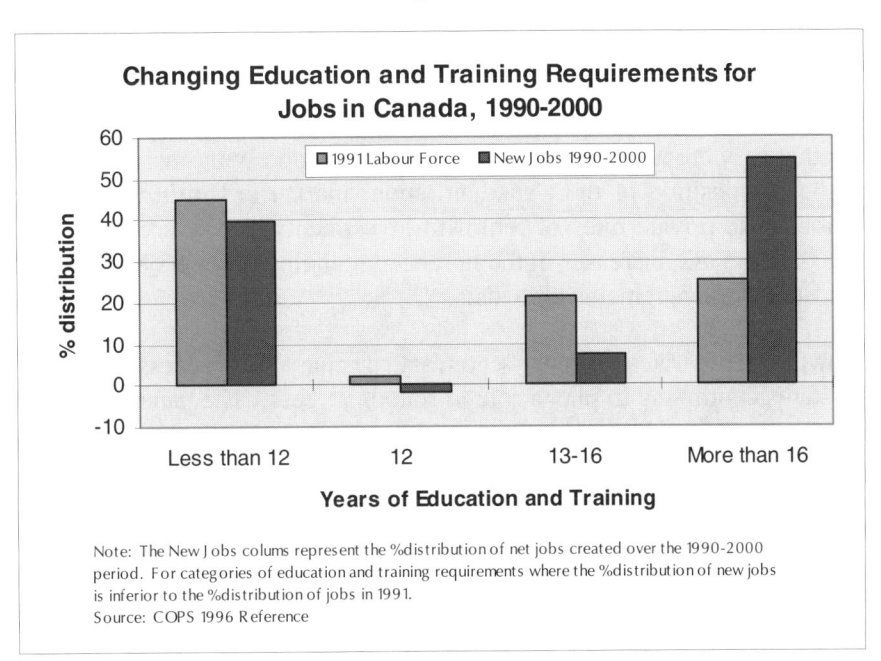

Changing Education and Training Requirements for Jobs in Canada, 1990-2000

Note: The New Jobs colums represent the %distribution of net jobs created over the 1990-2000 period. For categories of education and training requirements where the %distribution of new jobs is inferior to the %distribution of jobs in 1991.
Source: COPS 1996 Reference

While a large proportion of the job growth will be in these jobs requiring less than 12 years of combined education and training, their relative share in the labour market will decline. Jobs requiring 12 years of combined education and training will decline in both absolute and relative terms. A small proportion of the job growth will be in these jobs requiring 13 to 15 years of combined education and training. Over half of the new jobs will require 16 years and more of education and training.

Part-time and contractual work will play a greater role in the labour market of the future. Non-standard jobs have accounted for close to half of the total job growth over the past twenty years. The importance of these jobs in the economy increased from 24 per cent of all employment in 1976 to 29 per cent in 1994. The stability of a full-time permanent job may prove elusive for many young persons. More graduates are working on a term or contract basis.

Traditionally, less educated young persons have tended to enter the labour market in low skilled occupations, often in service areas, and progressed as they accumulated job experience to more highly skilled occupations, often in the goods producing sector. Will this pattern continue when there is little or no job growth in the medium level skill categories?

Summary

Despite a declining youth population many young persons are experiencing a difficult transition to the world of work. Education does matter. The data on employment and earnings leads to the conclusion that it is those young people with high school education or less whose position has worsened dramatically over the past 20 years. While there is anecdotal evidence of the problems faced by university graduates, the data do not support that their employment situation is any different from 20 years ago and their income situation is no different from cohorts of eight years earlier. However, graduates from some fields, especially in the arts and humanities but even in some science disciplines, are experiencing difficulty in finding good jobs. Overall, what has likely changed is a growing sense of insecurity leading to concerns about finding and keeping a job, the ability to buy a house, and to save for the future. The complexity of choice and informal nature of school-work transitions and career progression adds to this uncertainty and creates a desire for better information.

It would appear that the views and attitudes of the parents and youth in the focus groups concerning education were reasonably realistic and well founded. The increased participation in tertiary education shows that they are acting on these convictions. Underlying this drive to higher education is the fact that the composition of the Canadian labour market is shifting to jobs requiring higher levels of education. The private rates of return to investments in post-secondary education remain high, and despite the dramatic increases in the numbers attending post-secondary education, the wage premium for educated workers remains high also.

Despite the growth in the rates of post-secondary participation, access remains an issue with socio-economic status continuing to play a role in school success. The paper did not address whether or not the concerns of youth and parents about escalating tuition fees and student debt were based on fact and what implications this might have for post-secondary enrolments and access.

It was thought that the best way to help youth was to ensure that they completed high school. Canada now has a high rate of high school completion. However, the results of the International Adult Literacy Survey show that many high school graduates lack these basic literacy skills. Many youth continue to enter the labour force without the necessary foundation in basic skills and without vocational preparation. These youth face a difficult and uncertain future.

REFERENCES

Anisef, P. and Axelrod, P. (1993), *Transitions: School and Employment in Canada,* Thompson Educational Publishing, Toronto.

Ashton, D. and Green, F. (1996), *Education, Training and the Global Economy,* Edward Elgar, Cheltenham, UK.

Betcherman, G. and Leckie, N. (1997), *Youth Employment and Education Trends in the 1980s and 1990s,* Canadian Policy Research Networks, Ottawa.

Bloom, M. (1990), *Reaching for Success: Business and Education Working Together,* Conference Board of Canada, Ottawa.

Canadian Youth Foundation (1997), *Help Wanted: How Can the Private Sector Improve Employment Prospects for Young Canadians?,* Canadian Youth Foundation, Ottawa.

Centre for Policy Studies in Education, University of British Columbia (1993), *The Changing Role of Vocational and Technical Education and Training: Canada,* Council of Ministers of Education, Occasional Paper No. 1, Toronto.

Conference Board of Canada (1993), *Employability Skills Profile,* Conference Board of Canada, Ottawa.

Corson, D. and Lawton, S.B. (Eds.) (1993), *Education and Work,* Proceedings of the International Conference Linking Research and Practice, OISE, Toronto, 2 volumes.

Ekos Research Associates (1996), *Reconnecting Younger Canadians: Problems and Solutions from the Labour Market,* Human Resources Development Canada, Hull.

Human Resources Development Canada (HRDC), Ministerial Task Force on Youth (1996), *Take on the Future: Canadian Youth in the World of Work,* HRDC, Hull.

HRDC and Statistics Canada (1993), *Leaving School,* Results from a national survey comparing school leavers and high school graduates 18-20 years of age, Statistics Canada, Ottawa.

HRDC and Statistics Canada (1995*a*), *Adult Education and Training Survey -- 1992,* Statistics Canada, Ottawa.

HRDC and Statistics Canada (1995*b*), *School Leavers Follow-up Survey: Background Paper,* Statistics Canada, Ottawa.

HRDC and Statistics Canada (1996a), *After High School: The First Years,* The first report of the School Leavers Follow-up Survey -- 1995, Statistics Canada, Ottawa.

HRDC and Statistics Canada (1996b), *Reading the Future: A Portrait of Literacy in Canada,* Statistics Canada, Ottawa.

HRDC and Statistics Canada (1996c), *The Class of 86 Revisited,* A compendium of findings of the 1991 Follow-up of 1986 Graduates Survey with comparisons to the 1988 National Graduates Survey, Statistics Canada, Ottawa.

Krahn, H. (1996), *School-Work Transitions: Changing Patterns and Research Needs,* Discussion Paper prepared for Applied Research Branch, Human Resources Development Canada, Hull.

Lavoie, C. (1996), *Youth Employment: Some Explanations and Future Prospects*.

Leckie, N. (1996), *On Skill Requirements Trends in Canada, 1971-1991,* Canadian Policy Research Networks, Ottawa.

Marquardt, R. (1996), *Youth and Work in Troubled Times: A Report on Canada in the 1990s,* Canadian Policy Research Networks, Ottawa.

National Council on Education (1995), *Matching Education to the Needs of Society: A Vision for All Our Children,* The Conference Board of Canada, Ottawa.

OECD (1996a), *Education at a Glance: OECD Indicators,* Paris.

OECD (1996b), *Education at a Glance: Analysis,* Chapter 3: "Transition from school to work", Paris, pp. 41-53.

OECD (1996c), *Lifelong Learning for All,* Chapter 4: "Improving pathways and transitions in lifelong learning and work", Paris, pp. 123-161.

OECD (1996d), *Pathways and Participation in Vocational Education and Training,* Paris.

Reid, A. (1996), *Shakedown: How the New Economy Is Changing Our Lives,* Doubleday Canada, Toronto.

Riddell, W.C. (1994), *Human Capital Formation in Canada: Recent Developments and Policy Responses,* Discussion Paper No. 95-04, UBC, Centre for Research on Economic and Social Policy.

Statistics Canada (1997), *Focus Groups with Youth and Parents in Preparation for Future Surveys on Youth and School-Work Transitions,* Final Report prepared by Price-Waterhouse and sponsored by Human Resources Development Canada, Ottawa.

PART TWO

COMMUNITY INVOLVEMENT

MISSOURI'S CARING COMMUNITIES

by

Marilyn Knipp
Associate Director - Missouri Department of Social Services

Every day in every community across Missouri, the well-being of Missouri's 1.3 million children and their families signal the need for change. According to the Annie E. Casey Foundations Kids Count, Missouri ranks 33rd out of the 50 states in a national composite as determined by ten indicators of the condition of children.

A critical gap exists between the opportunities that are available to Missouri's children, and the opportunities Missourians want for their children. Too many young people have limited success in school. Too many youth leave school unprepared to enter into productive adulthood. Often their parents do not have sustained employment or sufficient wages to provide more nurturing and healthy home environments. The cost in human and economic terms is unacceptable.

Many public and private, federal, state and local programs address these problems. Funds are diminishing. Accountability is focused on inputs and activities, not results. Programs are not yielding acceptable results for children and families. Demands and requirements of one program may directly contradict those of another serving the same family. Missouri's Caring Communities is changing all that.

In 1993, Missouri's Governor Mel Carnahan established the Family Investment Trust (FIT), by executive order, to change how state government and communities work together to improve results for Missouri's children and families. The Governor called for changing fundamental practices in the delivery, financing, and governing of services. These changes have one aim, a shared vision for children to have strong families and communities where parents are working, children are succeeding in school and growing up healthy and safe, and youth are prepared to enter into productive adulthood.

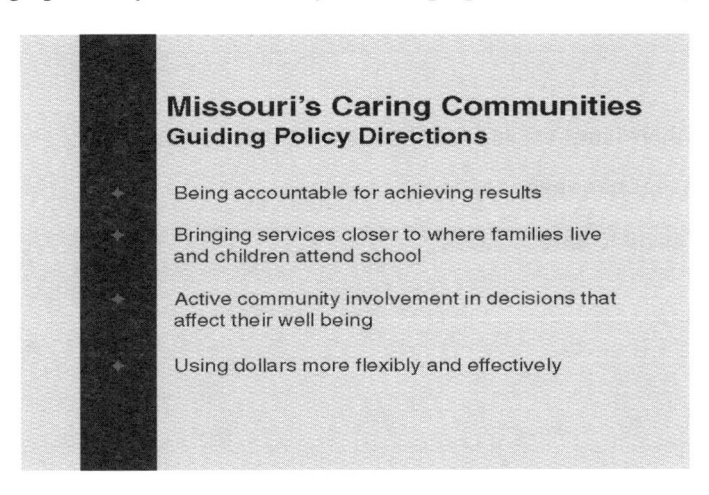

Missouri's Caring Communities
Guiding Policy Directions

- Being accountable for achieving results
- Bringing services closer to where families live and children attend school
- Active community involvement in decisions that affect their well being
- Using dollars more flexibly and effectively

FIT's Board of Directors includes corporate and civic leaders, and the directors of seven state departments: Corrections, Economic Development, Elementary and Secondary Education, Health, Labour and Industrial Relations, Mental Health, and Social Services. It is financed through public and private support. As it was created by executive order, is guided by public-private leadership, and is jointly financed, it represents a new way of doing business.

Community Partnership Spending
Source for Caring Communities

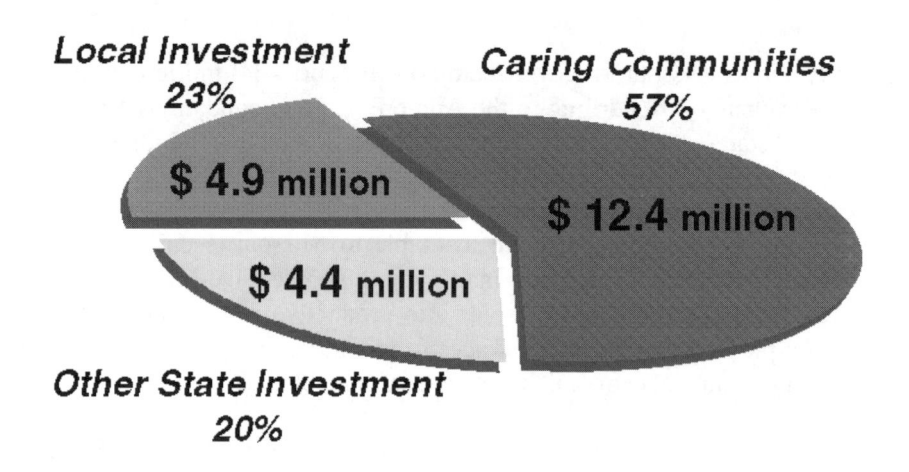

- Local Investment 23% — $ 4.9 million
- Caring Communities 57% — $ 12.4 million
- Other State Investment 20% — $ 4.4 million

Source: FY97 Community Plans and Summaries

Another unique aspect of FIT is the continued financial and technical support of several national and state foundations, including the Danforth Foundation, Greater Kansas City Community Foundation, Ewing Marion Kauffman Foundation, Annie E. Casey Foundation, Edna McConnell Clark Foundation, Kraft Foods, Inc., and the Robert Wood Johnson Foundation.

FIT worked with communities and state agencies to develop what has come to be called "Caring Communities." FIT assisted Caring Communities in establishing six core results:

- parents working;
- children safe in their families, and families safe in their communities;
- healthy children and families;
- young children ready to enter school;

- children and youth succeeding in school;
- youth ready to become productive adults.

and 18 benchmarks to measure their success:

Missouri's Caring Communities Benchmarks

Parents Working
- Employment rates
- Earnings
- Retention of employment

Children Succeeding in School
- Achievement levels
- Grade retention
- Grades

Children & Families Healthy
- Preventable hospitalizations
- Out of home placements for psychiatric reasons
- Immunization rate at kindergarten enrollment
- School absences

Children Ready to Enter School
- Kindergarten readiness test scores

Children & Families Safe
- Substantiated child abuse/neglect
- Out-of-home placement for abuse/neglect
- Hospitalizations due to injury
- Delinquency and habitual delinquency
- Suspensions/expulsions

Youth Ready to Become Productive Adults
- High school graduation
- Teen pregnancy

FIT is responsible for setting the vision, mission and values for the Caring Communities sites. It is also responsible for strategic planning, technical support, evaluation and communications for the state agencies and communities.

With guidance from FIT, Caring Communities are making three fundamental changes in how Missouri's systems work:

Caring Communities is changing the way decision are made by involving neighbourhood residents and community stakeholders in decisions that affect their well-being.

- Community Partnerships are county or multi-county local governance structures responsible for developing the overarching strategies to achieve the six core results. They enter into partnerships with state agencies and share accountability for results.

Caring Communities is changing the way services are delivered by integrating and locating them in the neighbourhoods where the children go to school and their families live.

- Caring Communities is a process whereby neighbourhoods design and monitor integrated systems, based at or linked to schools, to improve results. A school/neighbourhood council facilitates the process and accepts responsibility for results.

Caring Communities is changing the way services are financed by combining funds more flexibly across state agencies and communities, and by tying program funding to the results they produce.

- A cross-agency budget, a first in Missouri, supports local governance, service delivery, capacity-building, and evaluation. Additional private and public resources are combined at state, community, and neighbourhood levels.

Eighty-six Caring Communities sites within 14 Community Partnerships, encompassing 16 Missouri counties are serving over 42 000 children, including some of the highest risk populations in the state. This number will continue to grow as Caring Communities is expanded.

Each site's implementation plan has been designed and directed by a site council, and assisted by a site-based co-ordinator. The Community Partnerships facilitate co-ordination, networking, training and reporting by the sites.

The Community Partnerships are citizen-driven community collaborative involving efforts by the state to work with neighbourhood, business, civic and labour leaders to restructure traditional human services and employment programs and improve the lives of children and families in Missouri.

Each Caring Communities program is tailored to meet the needs and strengths of its citizens. Through Caring Communities, a wide range of services and supports are available. Some of the services are new; some already existed. The difference is that services now connect to each other and to the neighbourhood school. All services and supports are focused on achieving Missouri's vision for children and families.

Tutoring, health screenings, immunisations, mentoring, counselling, parent support and resource centres, neighbourhood watch programs, summer enrichment, job fairs, job readiness training, job search, family events and after-school clubs are some of the typical services offered through Caring Communities.

The place where services are delivered is also changing. Family support workers, child protection staff, nurses and employment counsellors are increasingly being located at the schools, giving families easy access to services. Nurses are available in schools for health screenings and care. Service providers are even contributing to more flexible service delivery by being available in the evening and on weekends. In addition to school-based programs, services are also being delivered in homes, community centres, churches, and other neighbourhood sites.

Missouri's Caring Communities
SHARED DECISION MAKING
Community Engagement

State Agencies — Community Partnerships — Site Councils

Caring Communities is working. We are achieving better results for children and families:

- Substantiated child abuse decreased 7 per cent in Caring Communities neighbourhoods and 5 per cent state-wide;

- New commitments to the Division of Youth Services increased state-wide, but decreased 20 per cent in Caring Communities neighbourhoods;

- Recidivist adolescent delinquency decreased 45 per cent;

- Hospital treatment because of injuries decreased 3 per cent state-wide, but 6 per cent in Caring Communities neighbourhoods;

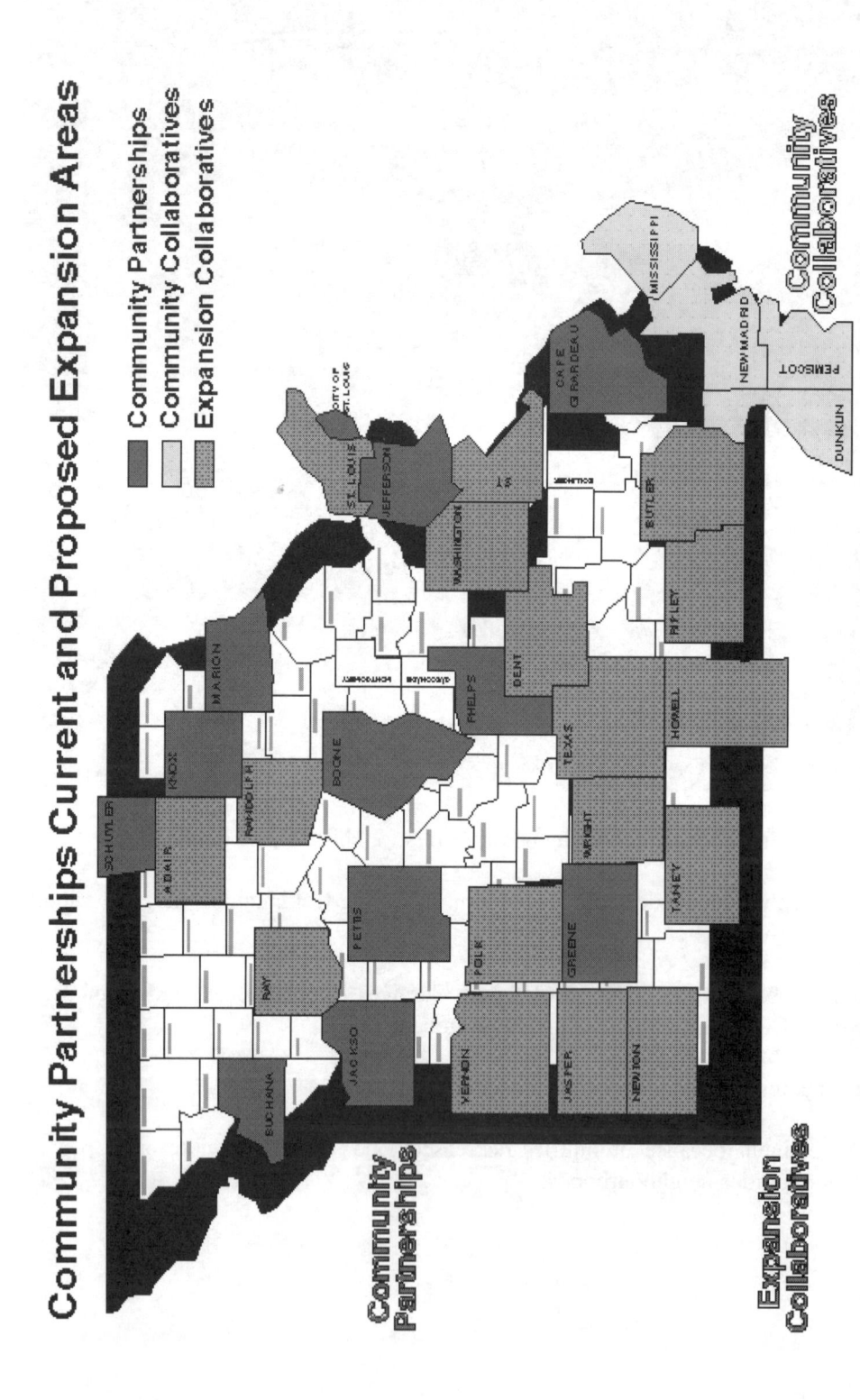

Community Partnerships Current and Proposed Expansion Areas

- Community Partnerships
- Community Collaboratives
- Expansion Collaboratives

These geographic areas represent 64% of the state's population.

- Preventable hospitalisations decreased 16 per cent state-wide, but 24 per cent in Caring Communities neighbourhoods;

- Out-of-home placements due to abuse or neglect decreased 6 per cent;

- Parental employment has increased through innovative programs; for example, 1 456 individuals moved into jobs with earnings over $7.50 an hour through a wage supplementation program in Jackson County;

- Family support centres bring together formal service delivery and informal "natural helping" networks;

- Parent voices are requested and valued;

- Engagement of individuals with diverse backgrounds, interests, and outlooks increased;

- Schools stayed open well beyond regular hours for community activities and services;

- State agencies engaged in joint strategic planning, budgeting, capacity-building and evaluation; and

- Federal, state and local dollars were leveraged to support reform, for example, a disjointed system of early childhood care and education is becoming a co-ordinated system.

Informal surveys of Caring Communities sites has also revealed promising results:

- Far more parents and neighbours volunteer their time as tutors, mentors, and activity leaders than was the case prior to Caring Communities.

- Parent involvement with their students and the schools has increased dramatically, as evidenced by parent/teacher conference attendance and participation in regular school events.

- Children with special academic, social or family needs are receiving specialised attention through such programs as counselling, tutoring and remedial classes, and self-esteem building activities.

- To deal with the challenge of working parents, several sites have created before and after-school child care programs, providing children with opportunities to learn, grow, and avoid being alone during crucial hours before and after school.

- Many sites have created school and neighbourhood health centres. Through these facilities and co-operation with area health care organisations, children, parents and neighbours have immediate access to primary health care and screening.

- Site councils and on-site staff have leveraged Caring Communities funding by attracting the no-cost participation of other community agencies and securing donations of dollars and materials from local businesses.

Below is a list of a few tangible outcomes achieved by individual school and neighbourhood sites for each of the six core results.

Parents working

- A "Treat Yourself Right" program offers support for 35 working mothers through skills classes, opportunities for networking and support.

- An ongoing computer training class offers basic computer skills.

- A job placement and assistance training program assists parents and residents in finding employment.

- A "Work Net" job search satellite has been created, which allows adults to search for employment available in the community.

Children safe in their families, families safe in their communities

- Family activities are provided once a month; a family resource centre is open daily during school hours and one evening a month.

- Suspensions due to incidents on school buses have decreased from 38 during the period September-December 1996 to only four during the same time period in 1997.

- 83 per cent of all families participated in at least one parent support or safe neighbourhood event such as Safety Day, Dinner Playhouse and Chili Night.

- Due to the efforts of clinical social workers, a suicide pact among students was discovered and disbanded.

- School suspensions have decreased by 26 per cent from 1996-1997, due to implementation of a student recovery room.

- A gang awareness program was presented to 125 parents and residents in response to a growing local problem.

Healthy children and families

- All kindergarten, first, third and sixth graders had vision screenings. Fourteen received free eyeglasses donated by Lens Crafters.

- A review of immunisation status of 475 students, during the 1996-97 school year found 23 students in need of further immunisations. A review in 1997-98 found only 7 needing immunisations.

- During 1997, over 1 700 individuals visited a school-based health clinic. The centre performed 34 Health Children and Youth screenings (EPSDT) and 321 immunisations. Additionally, 114 members were served by the nutritionist.

- School nurse provided health screening and blood pressure tests for 350 residents at a neighbourhood carnival.

- Students received dental screenings and oral care kits from the Department of Health and Kansas City Free Health Clinic.

- All 501 students in one elementary school received dental screenings by a dentist. 65 received follow-up services including, fillings, exams, cleanings, extractions and root canals. Dental sealants were offered to all second grade students.

Young children ready to enter school

- Through a health fair and personal contact, all the students in an elementary school in Jackson County were immunised prior to the start of the 1997 school year.

- Twenty 3 and 4 year-olds receive early childhood education and care at an Early Childhood Centre.

- Through efforts of a local health centre, 100 per cent of kindergarten students were fully immunised prior to the start of school in another elementary school.

- Family School Liaisons make personal visits to families with children about to enter kindergarten. Kindergarten attendance is up 3 per cent.

Children succeeding in school

- 15 parents have signed pledges to spend one hour per month at school reading with and tutoring students.

- 100 per cent of parents attended parent/teacher conferences, as compared to only 73 per cent the previous year. 105 students completed a drop-out prevention/alternative suspension program. Of these, 60 per cent improved their school attendance and half, a reduction in behaviour requiring disciplinary action.

- 59 students are being tutored in math and 54 in reading skills. The completion rate for the tutoring program is 95 per cent.

- 84 students participate in the HOSTS program (Help One Student to Succeed), a mentoring program that improves reading, writing, vocabulary and study skills. This program has received national recognition.

Youth prepared to enter productive adulthood

- Eleven adult males and 14 boys completed a 7-week "Boys to Men" curriculum. Five men are now volunteering in the classroom.

- "Men on the Move," a volunteer group, have started a Cadet Corps with students, focusing on academic success, leadership and community service.

- A full-time job developer has made classroom presentations and assisted over 200 students in preparing resumes, and over 300 in conducting job searches.

- 150 volunteers from government agencies serve as mentors for students.

- Volunteers from the business community, medical field and other professions provide career education to expose students to non-stereotypical careers.

- High school students serve as mentors and tutors for elementary students. Adult mentors also work with students, through the "Youth Friends" program.

- Middle school students are teaching computer skills to elementary children.

Conclusions

An independent evaluation that looked at the core results and benchmarks found that Caring Communities are available in the neighbourhoods with the highest needs, in the schools with the highest needs, and working with children and youth with the highest needs. This suggests that Caring Communities have been targeted where they are most needed. The benchmarks indicate that problems are greater in some neighbourhoods than in others, and greater among program participants than among others in the schools.

Caring Communities has not only achieved better results for children and families, it has become a process, the way state government and communities do business. Missouri is utilising the community partnerships to address policy issues such as welfare reform and child welfare. By bringing the full range of players to the table, from the state level down to the neighbourhood level, results are being achieved. This innovative approach to service delivery blends funding streams, breaks down historical barriers and achieves results that communities select.

We are proud of the success and growth of this program. Today, nearly 64 per cent of Missouri's children and families are reaping the benefits of the unique collaboration between seven human service state agencies and their local partners. At a recent legislative hearing a Kansas City business leader said, "The Caring Communities funds are the glue which can hold, mend, and bind together communities and neighbourhoods in which our children and families live. We believe that every community and neighbourhood has assets that have not been fully tapped. Small amounts of funds well spent in a neighbourhood, decided upon by citizens, can often do more than the most massive well-funded government plan or program."

REDESIGN OF SERVICES FOR CHILDREN AND FAMILIES

by

John Lackey
Commissioner of Services for Children and Families

Introduction

This document provides highlights on the Redesign of Services for Children and Families taking place within the Province of Alberta, and milestone activities from November 1994 to September 1996.

Background

In 1993 the Government of Alberta appointed a Commissioner of Services for Children with a mandate to design a new, integrated, more effective and community based system of support for children and their families. In an extensive consultation process, more than 3 300 Albertans from 65 communities provided their views on how the present system of Children's Services could be improved to better serve and protect children at risk and their families.

A consensus from the consultations was that the system of services for children had to change. More specifically, the following messages were heard:

- People need to be able to find help;

- Parents and youth don't want to be "labelled";

- We need to take a "child in the family" approach;

- We need more prevention and early intervention services;

- We need to integrate services;

- Leadership and responsibility should be returned to the community; Aboriginal communities should have the opportunity to meet their own needs by providing services to their own people;

- Programmes should be funded only if they are successful;

- Communities need stable and flexible funding for services.

The Commissioner reported (Focus on Children) that parents and communities want an active role in the redesign of services and in the responsibility for the well being of their children. He noted that communities best understood the problems and issues experienced by local children and families and could determine the best ways of responding to them. Government programmes were not designed for this flexibility and had overlooked the positive role communities could play in protecting and helping children.

The Commissioner's report also pointed to the lack of success in improving the health and well being of Aboriginal people who make up almost 50 per cent of the children in the care of Child Welfare.

New direction

On November 30, 1994, the Minister of Family and Social Services, announced a plan for a new approach to delivering children's services. A Regional Steering Committee would be appointed to co-ordinate a community planning process to develop a service plan for the region over a three year time frame. Based on the Service Plan, Child and Family Services, authorities would be established to administer the new system in the region.

Four key areas of action were identified to effectively redesign children's services.

- **Integrated Services:** Planning and service delivery was to be integrated at the community, regional, and provincial levels, to facilitate barrier-free access to holistic services for children and families.

- **Community Based Services:** Communities support the principle of participation and access for all. The role of natural helpers, support networks and cultural groups would be integrated and expanded within the professional delivery of service.

- **Improved Services to Aboriginal People:** The responsibility for planning and delivering services for Aboriginal children and families would be transferred to Aboriginal communities. Planning and service delivery will reflect the values, beliefs and customs of First Nations, Metis, and other Aboriginal people in a respectful, collaborative way.

- **Focus on Early Intervention:** Regions would provide an array of timely, accessible services to assist/support children and families in developing skills to build on their strengths, and reduce the need for crisis intervention. To begin the development of the early intervention, the Government has allocated $20 million for early intervention programmes over three years to community groups and agencies who submit proposals and meet a set of qualifying criteria. Projects are to reflect community involvement in planning and delivery. Learnings will be integrated into regional service plans.

Alberta's vision for children

The Commissioner's report identified a vision that had emerged from the consultations which will serve as a reference point for service plans:

- safe and stable, healthy environments for children that promote learning and development;

- efficient and effective services that are community based and managed;

- services that are culturally appropriate;

- mutual support networks of communities, friends and families to solve problems.

Guiding principles

The following principles focus on what is best for children and families, and will help guide service planning:

- your first priority is the safety and healthy development of children and families;

- parents and extended families have the primary responsibility for their children;

- when working with the family, focus on the child's needs and the ability to meet those needs within the family and community;

- success is measured by positive outcomes;

- services are community-based and integrated to remove barriers in meeting children's needs;

- people who use children's services will be involved in all decisions that affect their lives.

Service plans and business plans

The planning process is divided into three phases:

Phase 1: Preliminary Service Plan

The responsibility of the Regional Steering Committee is to develop a preliminary plan which:

- determines vision, goals, outcomes and action plan for the region;

- builds on the four key areas of change, community delivery, early intervention programs, aboriginal services and integrated services;

- assesses the current services available; establishes the needs of children and families; and identifies gaps between needs and existing services;

- ensures community involvement has taken place at all levels of service planning including: who was consulted; how communities were consulted; the feedback and recommendations received; what effect this consultation had on the plan.

Phase 2: Service Plan

Upon approval of the preliminary plan in principle, the Regional Steering Committee will develop a service plan which:

- builds on the Preliminary Plan and the four key areas of change;

- describes the provision of services to children and families;

- ensures compliance with provincial requirements and governing legislation;

- co-ordinates children and family services between regions;

- co-ordinates children and family services with other authorities providing human service, *e.g.* Regional Health Authorities;

- is feasible within anticipated resources.

Phase 3: The Business Plan

The business plan is the responsibility of Regional Authorities. It will outline the details of how the service plan will be implemented. Therefore it will cover the following components:

- types of services and programmes and projected outcomes;

- budgets;

- human resource planning;

- training;

- organisational structures;

- facilities plans;

- specific implementation plans including contract management;

- client involvement and ongoing community input;

- detailed evaluation procedures including outcome measurements.

Structures

Community Working Groups

- These are locally based groups which develop a preliminary service plan for their communities, reserves, settlements within each of the 18 regions. The process can be taken on by existing groups or new groups that become established for one purpose.

Steering Committees

- Steering Committees, appointed by the Minister of Family and Social Services, are responsible for developing the service plan for their regions.

- Steering Committees must establish working relationships and communication processes with the working groups that keeps the development of plans as open as possible and continually weaves together the work of the groups and communities so that a regional plan evolves. The Steering Committee must ensure groups are working within a framework of the Service Planning Handbooks, legislation and government requirements.

Community Facilitators

- The facilitators are employees of the Commissioner of Services for Children and Families. Their role is to support the total planning process within a region. This includes assisting co-chairs and members of Steering Committees and community work groups in developing service plans.

Children and Family Services Authorities

- Upon approval of a Regional Service Plan, a Regional Authority will be established to assume responsibility for developing business plans, allocating funds, inviting and evaluating service delivery proposals, managing overall services and maintaining community involvement in identifying priorities and refining the planning processes.

Provincial Committees

The following committees have been established to develop provincial frameworks, provide support, advice and facilitate the planning process:

- Deputy Ministers and Assistant Deputy Ministers Committee.

- Integration Sub-Committee.

- Council of Regions.

- Funding Model Committee.

- Standards Advisory Committee.
- Technical Support Services Advisory Committee.
- Support Services Co-ordinating Committee.
- Early Intervention Provincial Programme.
- Legislative Development Project Working Group.
- Protocol Working Group.
- Monitoring and Evaluation Co-ordinating Committee.
- Communications Advisory Committee.
- Transition Team.
- Early Intervention evaluation Mentoring Project Committee.

REFERENCES

Publications of the Government in Alberta:

Focus on Children (Nov. 1994)

Finding a Better Way (Nov. 1994)

Handbook #1: *Laying the Foundation -- An Overview of the Service Planning Process* (June 1995)

Handbook #2: *Putting the Plan Together* (May 1996)

Early Intervention Programme Funding Guidelines, Part 1 and 2 (May 1995), Revised in 1996

Child and Family Services Authorities Act (May 1996)

Provincial Requirements for Regional Services for Children and Families (May 1996)

Focus on Children and Families Newsletter

Getting to Know Your Community Baseline Information (July 1995 -- August 1996)

New Ideas and Approaches (July 1996)

Annex

MILESTONES: November 1994 -- August 1996

The following are key activities that have taken place since the plan for the Redesign of Child and Family Services was announced in November 1994.

- The Commissioner of Services for Children and Families is mandated to redesign services which are based on four key areas of change: Integrated Services; Community Based Services; Improved Aboriginal Services; Focus on Early Intervention.

- $50 million for EIP was approved over a three-year period.

- Seventeen Planning Regions are established with the same boundaries as Regional Health Authorities.

- A series of public meetings across the province explains the redesign initiative and invites public participation in the planning process.

- Steering Committee co-chairs are appointed by the Minister for the 17 regions; there is at least one Aboriginal co-chair in each region.

- Members of Regional Steering Committees are appointed; half of whom are Aboriginal.

- A Council of Regions is established in October 1995 to provide advice to the Commissioner concerning the redesign of children's services. There is representation from each of the 17 planning regions. The Council meets bimonthly.

- Enabling legislation to provide for the establishment of Child and Family Services Authorities was prepared in consultation with partnering departments and Steering Committees and received Royal Assent in May 1996.

- May 1996, Region 4, Calgary Rockeyview Preliminary Plan is submitted.

- May 1996, Provincial Requirements for regional Services for Children and Families was approved and distributed to regions.

- May 31, 1996, Minister without Portfolio, Responsible for Children's Services is appointed within the portfolio of Family and Social Services.

- By June, 1996, over 10 380 people are involved in a total of 345 Working Groups, Focus Groups and 17 Steering Committees.

- June 1996, A framework for evaluation of EIP programs has been approved for implementation across the province.

- July 1996, Region 17, Preliminary Plan is submitted.

- Sept-Dec 1996, Training networking workshops for community EIP monitoring teams, to introduce indicators to measure what is happening for children and families.

- November 1996, regions 1, 2 and 7, Preliminary Service Plan is submitted.

- As of December, 1996, approximately 3 600 information or consultation meetings have been held across the province to let people knew about the planning process and to seek their input.

- December 1996, Regions 6 and 13, Preliminary Service Plan is submitted.

- January 1997, Region 5, Preliminary service Plan is submitted.

- March 1997, metis Settlements become Region 18.

- March 1997, regions 3 and 9, preliminary Service plan is submitted.

- As of March 31, 1997, 235 projects have been approved for funding under the Early Intervention Program across all regions of the province.

- April 1997, Region 14, Preliminary Service Plan is submitted.

- May 1997, Region 10, Preliminary Service Plan is submitted.

- May 1997, Region 4, Service plan is submitted.

- May 1997, Region 11, Preliminary Service Plan is submitted.

- June 1997, Region 8, Preliminary Service Plan is submitted.

- June 1997, Region 15, Preliminary Service Plan is submitted.

- November 1997, Region 7, Service Plan is submitted.

- December 1997, Calgary Rockyview Child and Family Services Authority is established.

- February 1998, Region 16 Service Plan is submitted.

- February 1998, Regions 1, 2, 3, 8, 9, 10 Draft Service Plans are submitted.

PARENTAL INVOLVEMENT IN PRE-SCHOOL EDUCATION IN FRANCE

by

Josette Combes
Association Collectifs Enfants, Parents, Professionnels

France has a long-standing tradition of public funding of schools. Until 1983, the system was highly centralised and budgets were managed by the Ministry of Health and Social Affairs in the case of *crèches* and by the Ministry of National Education via its education districts in the case of primary and secondary schools and further training institutions. Following the 1983 Decentralisation Act, the full implementation of which took several years, local authorities were given new responsibilities and appropriate budgets. For *crèches*, a contribution is paid by the *Caisse Nationale Des Allocations Familiales* (National Fund for Family Allowances) through its local offices, while families also pay a means-tested contribution and municipalities cover the rest. For primary schools, teachers' salaries are still paid by the central government budget, but municipalities pay maintenance costs and the salaries of other staff. Primary school is free of charge for all pupils, except in the case of private schools. But most private schools receive government subsidies provided they sign a contract with the government that requires them to teach the national curriculum, which is in principle the same for all schools. Under this highly uniform education system, families have traditionally been excluded from participating in decision-making and the organisation of schools, regardless of the type of institution or their children's age -- infants in child-care facilities such as *crèches*, children from age three in nursery schools, children from age six in primary schools or older ones in secondary schools. Associations representing parents are tolerated in schools and are able to participate through highly formal procedures. They are often run by quite small groups of people who rarely change, as election methods virtually guarantee that they will be re-elected automatically. In *lycées*, which teach pupils for the last three years of secondary school, parental participation is nearly non-existent.

In the 1970s, a variety of different movements called educational practices into question, particularly regarding teaching methods and the participation of users (parents or pupils) in a number of decisions. At this time, many so-called alternatives schools sprang up, which tried to develop a different model of learning and applied different educational principles (Freinet, Montessori, Decroly and Steiner can be mentioned as some of the important educators who inspired these movements). Most of these schools, unlike denominational schools, found it very hard to survive, as the government was unwilling to help fund them since they used methods and taught curricula different from those recommended by the Ministry.

At the same time, because of the lack of satisfactory day care for infants with working parents, parents began to organise among themselves to meet their own needs. The pioneers of these initiatives followed the example of what was being done in other countries, such as Quebec with its non-profit day care centres, Sweden with its *crèches* self-managed by parents, the United Kingdom with its play groups or Berlin with its children's communes. They also drew inspiration from research on children's development and the writings of authors such as Brazelton and Winnicott, and Françoise Dolto in France.

These pioneering experiments initially relied on a great deal of voluntary work by parents and on underpaid professionals who had little training but were enthusiastic and gained solid on-the-job experience that they would later turn to good account. In 1980, ten or so of these so-called "unofficial" or "parallel" *crèches* grouped together to defend and promote this new system with a view to obtaining government funding and to operating more effectively. ACEP (*Association des Collectifs Enfants Parents*) was established in February 1981 -- an additional "P" was added in 1990 standing for "Professionals", who were also partners in this form of co-operative *crèches*. In August 1981 the Ministry of Social Affairs officially recognised these *crèches*, entitling them to receive government contributions like traditional *crèches*, but of a lower amount, since the voluntary service of parents enabled them to operate at lower cost.

ACEPP's role initially consisted of:

- promoting these new *crèches* across a broad public, in particular by providing technical support and information to parents or professionals wishing to set up a new centre;

- defending the interests of parental *crèches* vis-à-vis decision-makers, in particular in dealings with the physicians who grant the official authorisation that makes *crèches* eligible for public funding, and also by keeping local authorities informed, since after the Decentralisation Act they became directly responsible for developing child care;

- improving the standard of services by encouraging parents and professionals to receive training and become more proficient in running this novel type of co-operative *crèches*.

The crucial feature of the system was the involvement of parents, and especially fathers, as essential partners in education. The challenge was to gain recognition that this involvement was of great benefit to children, families and the community. But the teaching profession as a whole was highly sceptical about the value of any "intrusion" of users in developing and running the services of which they were the recipients. The entire system resisted a practice that it classified under the heading of "social innovation", and it must be admitted that many alternative schools failed to survive because they did not receive enough support from their official partners.

The parental *crèches* developed quite spectacularly, since their numbers soared from some 20 in 1981-82 to more than 1 300 at present, encompassing approximately 20 000 families and over 3 000 professionals. These are not necessarily full-time *crèches*, and include child care centres open on a part-time or temporary basis or centres that provide day care before or after school. But they all have in common the fact that they operate under the supervision of a parents' assembly, and parents are generally actively involved in educational tasks.

The reasons behind this development may be summarised as follows:

- the real and pressing needs of families;

- the interest that authorities funding child care ultimately took in these initiatives, since they saw that they were a less costly way of increasing the number of *crèches*;

- ACEPP's role as the political representative and the organiser of the network.

In 1986 ACEPP received the assistance of the Bernard van Leer Foundation and was finally able to launch a pilot project for the creation of parental *crèches* for disadvantaged children. Although the first pioneering *crèches* had been set up by middle-class parents with a relatively high level of education, it seemed obvious that the parental *crèche* could also meet the needs of poorer families provided that support could be made available at all stages from initial planning to the actual start-up.

The basic principles of this project were:

- to enable all children, whatever their social and cultural background, to have access to high-quality education which protects and develops their physiological, emotional and intellectual potential -- in other words, to have access to a basic civil right;

- to foster better knowledge on the part of parents, and especially mothers, of the child's needs and the resources at their disposal to meet these needs. When parents are able to participate regularly in the routine activities of *crèches*, talk with professionals, see other parents become involved and take the time to participate in group discussions of problems, they escape the isolation of the poorly planned large housing estates built in the 1960s and the cultural marginalisation flowing from their lack of familiarity with the language and culture of the country in which they have settled.

In these housing estates, which initially represented an improvement in the living conditions of many blue-collar workers, large numbers of foreigners have been re-housed fairly systematically, without steps to preserve the networks of solidarity that existed formerly. The lack of the amenities of normal city life (public services, adequate transport, cafés, recreational areas, green spaces and informal meeting areas) has had a dehumanising effect on these areas in which large numbers of people are concentrated. In addition, because of the high proportions of foreigners, some residents may feel that they have been "overrun", which may lead to problems of xenophobia. In some neighbourhoods over 30 per cent of the population is of foreign origin (the national average is only 9.6 per cent), unemployment rates are between 25 and 30 per cent (compared to the average of 10.2 per cent), 14 to 20 per cent of families are headed by single mothers, etc.

Consequently, the third objective of this project was to create places in these neighbourhoods where families of very different socio-cultural backgrounds could meet and come to know each other, in order to dispel family attitudes of suspicion and withdrawal which are key factors in determining children's behaviour when they later go to school. To promote tolerance within neighbourhoods, to encourage women to join literacy or training programmes, to provide greater access to information on social benefits and health care -- these were the objectives that these parental *crèches* hoped to achieve.

After a three-year experimental period, the funding of the project was renewed with a view to expanding this type of service, developing further training of the professionals working in the centres and assisting women with social reintegration and finding jobs. More than a hundred centres have been created, reorganised so as to meet local needs more fully, or provided with pedagogical or organisational assistance.

One of the main tools used to achieve these goals was the training of professionals in a multicultural approach, which should be an integral part of their initial training but is in fact given very little emphasis in the ordinary curriculum.

At the same time, nursery schools were approached to encourage teachers there to continue the dialogue between parents and professionals initiated in the parental *crèches*. It must be admitted that the difficulties have often been insurmountable, since most teachers seem to think that, although parents may be useful to help accompany field trips, they definitely do not have a necessary and desirable contribution to make to the education process itself. Nevertheless, as part of the ZEP programmes (Priority Education Areas) launched in France in 1981 and then reinforced in 1990, some ties have been established between the *crèches* and primary schools. These have encouraged schools to take the family backgrounds of children more thoroughly into account and have promoted better mutual understanding between teachers and families. But in general, active parent participation in school is not really planned and organised, and despite a number of official circulars issued under different ministers, about the obligation of schools to open up to families, is left to the initiative of schools.

The fact of the matter is that parental *crèches* are one of the few examples of an educational approach that integrates parents and professionals as partners in the education process. ACEPP has been a leading supporter of parental participation. Its efforts to promote and publicise these issues has helped change official attitudes towards families. For example, the obligation for *crèches* to create a council in which parents are represented dates from 1983. This was an important step, and although as implemented it often only resulted in highly formal quarterly meetings in which parents have only advisory status, it has changed the attitudes of professionals and families by recognising parents' right to have a say in their children's education. These councils have enabled parents and teachers to exchange views and information and in the end this has no doubt helped parents to take a greater interest in their children's education.

Conclusion

I would like to stress two main aspects that the emergence of parental *crèches* has helped to promote.

Firstly, the interest of organising services based on consulting with users and involving them in providing services. This is the most effective way of keeping funding requirements down while achieving better results in terms of quantity and quality. In other words, it is more cost-effective.

Secondly, the comprehensive, integrated approach that can be built up. The parental *crèches* not only deal with young children but also assist their mothers in becoming integrated into society and self-supporting; what is more, they help build a living democracy by establishing channels of communication between social groups and official decision-makers. All this helps keep citizens better informed and enables them to establish a direct dialogue with government, something that is usually quite difficult to achieve.

In recent years, a great deal of research and discussion in the social field has focused on what are known as "neighbourhood services", which combine government funding with the voluntary participation of users. Associations organise services to meet people's needs that are seen as being too costly at a time of budget cuts because they are "unproductive", even though they do much to improve the quality of life of citizens. These kinds of services are no doubt the way of the future and a sound compromise between full funding by government and the complete relinquishment of its social responsibilities. Citizens' participation also makes it possible to adapt services to the socio-cultural, geographical and economic setting in which they are provided. It ensures that services are used by those who need them and that they meet people's needs effectively because they are tailored to those needs and directly involve individuals who are producers at certain times and consumers at others. These services create social ties and cohesion because they are so solidly grounded in the place in which they are provided. Lastly, they encourage individuals and communities to take responsibility for themselves, which is no doubt one of the best forms of social regulation and of combating underachievement in school and delinquency among idle adolescents unable to find jobs.

Finally, they are means of implementing early-prevention strategies which avoid the labelling of groups at risk that occurs when they are targeted by specific programmes.

To conclude, in response to what was said in the discussions, I shall venture the following view. While it is true that identifying risk factors is the responsibility of researchers and also of policy-makers, since economic and social management plays a key role in how these factors evolve, this approach raises problems when it comes to practice in the field. The fact of the matter is that educators must above all identify the factors for success:

- Those that are inherent in the personality of each child;

- Those that can help optimise existing means and resources;

- Lastly, those that must be added by finding new solutions and by making a more convincing case to decision-makers that the funding they provide will be cost-effective.

- Any programme that focuses too narrowly on a specific group of children is potentially self-defeating. An education system should be able by itself to provide equal opportunities for all and, although all children will not achieve the same academic success, schools should at the very least ensure that all are respected as individuals and treated with dignity.

- More than programmes targeting certain groups of children at risk, a comprehensive policy of high-quality education will enable all children to take full advantage of their educational opportunities.

PROFESSIONAL SOCIAL WORK: EDUCATION AND SERVICE INTEGRATION ROLES

by

Mary R. Lewis
LMSW-ACP, Ph.D., Professor
University of Houston, Graduate School of Social Work

Purpose and scope

Professional social work education prepares graduates to perform roles in service integration in a variety of settings and at different levels of responsibility. This paper will discuss the general nature of social work practice and the curriculum requirements of the Council of Social Work Education (CSWE) in the United States for accrediting Bachelor's and Master's level social work degree programmes in colleges and universities. There is a voluminous literature, delineating and describing the roles and functions of social workers, that is used in social work education. Some, with a generalist approach, that have been frequently used in academic degree programmes include Compton and Galaway (1994), Connaway and Gentry (1988), DuBois and Miley (1996), Johnson (1995), Pincus and Minahan (1973), Siporin (1975) and Zastrow (1995). In addition, there are books that focus upon the roles of social workers in different settings, such as schools (Allen-Meares *et al.*, 1996). However, none of the traditional textbooks portray the rapidly changing nature of school-based social work that includes the wide variety of integrated services being developed by other public and private agencies as portrayed in this paper.

The roles of social workers in many other countries and the requirements for their professional education are very similar to those in the United States, for example, in the United Kingdom, Australia, New Zealand, Canada, Sweden and Finland.

General nature of social work

Social workers provide direct services to children, youth, and families through individual, family, and group methods. Through a variety of counselling approaches, they may help clients identify their concerns, consider solutions, and find resources. Social workers must have assessment skills which enable them to see beyond a client's statement of a need to comprehend the family, social, and community context in which the client has experienced a problem. They must have a knowledge base and interviewing skills that enable them to consider physical, social, psychological, environmental, and systemic issues that may be relevant to a client's problem. They must be well informed about the public and private service networks, available resources and eligibility requirements. Often, providing information to clients needing services is not sufficient to empower them to seek and obtain them. Clients or their families may need assistance in understanding and accepting the meaning of an assessment or diagnosis and the nature of additional services that could be helpful. If clearly motivated to receive additional services, they still may need help in accessing appropriate ones. Consequently, social workers must have negotiating, brokering, and advocacy skills with both clients and personnel in agencies and organisations that provide needed services.

Social workers are employed in a wide variety of types of public and private agencies, such as health care, mental health, child welfare, gerontological, family service, substance abuse or criminal justice agencies, and in schools. Often they are members of multi disciplinary teams that co-ordinate to provide an array of needed services to an individual or family. Some work in employee assistance programmes of private corporations to assist workers with job-related pressures or personal problems that affect the quality of their work. Some social workers have a private practice in clinical social work and psychotherapy or organisational consults.

Social workers become middle and senior administrators in all of the types of agencies mentioned above, serving as supervisors, programme managers, and agency executives. They focus upon policy and planning issues, helping to develop programmes to address issues such as child abuse, homelessness, substance abuse, poverty, and violence. They help to raise funds and write grants to support these programs. They conduct research on and analyse policies, programs, and regulations and make recommendations for changes that would enhance service delivery. Some help to formulate government policies and advocate policy positions in government agencies, research institutions, or on legislators' staffs. A few enter politics successfully. Those who attain doctoral degrees usually accept teaching, research, or consulting positions.

Since 1993 in the United States, all States and the District of Columbia have had licensing, certification, or registration laws regarding social work practice and the use of professional titles. Beginning and advanced levels of education and proficiency are recognised in these professional regulations of social work practice as they are with other professions. Social workers held about 557 000 jobs in the United States in 1994. Nearly 40 per cent were in government agencies, primarily in departments of human resources, social services, child welfare, mental health, health, housing, education, and corrections. Most in the private sector were in voluntary social service agencies, community and religious organisations, hospitals, nursing homes, or home health agencies (US Department of Labour, 1996, p. 133).

There is no single source for identifying how many professional social workers in the United States are employed in school settings or in school-based or school-linked services. Allen-Meares, Dean of the School of Social Work at the University of Michigan, and David Kupper, Assistant Professor in charge of the school social work concentration at the University of Illinois, Urbana, are conducting a national survey of school social workers in the United States to learn more about what they believe are the most important knowledge components in traditional school social work practice and the degree of complexity in these knowledge components. Through state education agencies and other salient sources, they were able to get a population list of more than 11 000 social workers employed by public schools to invite to participate in their survey (Personal communication with David Kupper, Oct. 16, 1996).

However, this paper will show that other organisations and community-based coalitions, in addition to schools, are creating school-based or school-linked service integration programs. Social work professionals are among the leaders of these efforts.

Curriculum components in professional social work education in the United States

The fundamental purpose of social work education is to prepare competent professionals who are committed to practice that includes services to economically and socially disadvantaged people and who seek ways to alleviate poverty, oppression and discrimination. Two levels of social work education are accredited in the United States by the Council on Social Work Education (CSWE) for social work practice competence: the baccalaureate and the master's. There are approximately 383 BSW and 117 MSW accredited academic degree programs. The baccalaureate level prepares students for generalist social work practice and the master's level prepares students for advanced social work practice in an area of concentration. The two levels of education differ from each other in the depth, breadth, and specificity of knowledge and skill that students are expected to synthesise and apply in practice. The professional foundation curriculum that includes the common body of knowledge, values, and skills of the profession is included in both levels. This foundation content is transferable across settings, population groups, and problem areas. The master's level goes beyond the foundation content to include an identifiable area of advanced practice for which a student gains knowledge and skills. The master's level requires the equivalent of two academic years of full-time study.

Entering the master's level does not require the completion of a BSW degree. Some MSW programmes allow BSW graduates to enter with advanced standing, reducing the amount of additional education that is required to attain the MSW degree. One of the strengths of the profession is that it is based upon and values the liberal arts educational preparation. A college graduate with any type of bachelor's degree is eligible to apply for admission to a master's degree program. Educators and leaders in the profession believe that this practice enriches the profession.

The professional foundation curriculum

The Commission on Accreditation of the CSWE specifies the following content that must be included in the professional foundation curriculum of accredited social work degree programs.

- The profession's Code of Ethics and its practical implications.

- Appreciating cultural, ethnic, racial, class, gender, religious, ability, age, and other types of diversity that affect the concepts of the needs of the populations served and appropriate professional practices.

- Principles of social and economic justice, including attention to the causes and effects of institutionalised forms of oppression and discrimination and strategies of intervention to combat them.

- Populations-at-high-risk of disadvantage or need.

- Concepts and theories of human bio-psycho-social development.

- The types of social environments and social systems in which individuals live (families, groups, organisations, institutions, communities) and ways in which they can promote or deter people in maintaining or achieving optimal health and well-being.

- The history, mission, and philosophy of the social work profession.

- Historical and current patterns of provision of social welfare services and the role of social policy in helping or deterring people in maintaining or attaining optimal health and well-being.

- Political and organisational processes that influence policy formulation.

- Frameworks for analysing social policies in light of principles of social and economic justice.

- A generalist approach to social work practice emphasising professional relationships characterised by mutuality, collaboration, and respect for the strengths of client systems of all sizes.

- Practice skills including defining issues, collecting and assessing data, planning and contracting, identifying alternative interventions, selecting and implementing appropriate courses of action, monitoring and evaluating outcomes, applying appropriate research based knowledge, and termination dynamics.

- An understanding and appreciation of a variety of scientific and analytic approaches to building knowledge for practice and for evaluating service delivery, and the ethical standards accompanying these approaches.

- A field practicum of at least 400 hours (BSW level) and two totalling 900 hours (MSW level) supervised by an instructor with an MSW degree plus two years of practical experience. Some field practice settings are in agencies staffed primarily by social workers, such as child welfare and family service agencies, but the work always involves interagency aspects. Many field placements are in settings where another profession is the dominant one, such as mental health, health, and public schools, where social workers are members of multi disciplinary teams.

Master's level advanced concentrations

Each graduate programme in social work designs its own framework for advanced practice concentrations to be anchored in the liberal arts and the professional foundation, to be consistent with the purpose of social work and to have curricular coherence and logic. Frameworks that are frequently used by programmes include fields of practice (*e.g.* child welfare, mental health), problem areas (*e.g.* health care), populations-at-risk (*e.g.* ageing), intervention methods or roles (*e.g.* casework, group work, community organisation), and practice contexts (*e.g.* schools). Programmes determine and clearly state the expected educational outcomes for each concentration offered (Commission on Accreditation, 1994).

Doctoral level education in social work

There about 60 doctoral degree programs in social work located at colleges and universities throughout the United States (Casebolt, 1998) but they are not under the jurisdiction of the Council on Social Work Education. They must meet the requirements set by the universities, states, or other university accrediting bodies for doctoral degrees. There is an informal organisation named Graduate

Association for Doctoral Education in Social Work (GADE) that holds annual meetings of chairpersons of doctoral programs in social work.

Roles for social workers to link services with schools

Social workers who are in direct service, supervisory, or administrative roles in any agency or context crave more effective service integration because they are acutely aware of the detrimental effects on clients of service fragmentation and confusion in the service systems. Their professional education has oriented them to facilitating access to services and reducing system barriers. They are family and community-focused in assessment and service delivery strategies. Yet their ability to bridge system boundaries is often constrained by the roles and positions defined for them within the agencies where they are employed.

As this OECD project focused on service integration for educationally disadvantaged children and youth, examples will be provided of roles for social workers related to school-based or school-linked services. The examples will be drawn from the Greater Houston (Texas) metropolitan area and from the work of the Children's Aid Society of New York City.

The many faces of school-based service integration involving social workers in Houston, Texas

Throughout the United States, there is increasing momentum for locating health, mental health, social, and other services at schools rather than relying altogether on referrals from schools to community or agency based services. The city of Houston is the fourth largest (Famighetti, 1996) and its greater metropolitan statistical area is the tenth largest (US Bureau of the Census, 1995) in the United States. The developments in Houston would be similar in some respects to developments in other large American urban areas. However, the patterns emerging in Houston are also influenced by factors which may be unique to Houston and Texas. The school-based models are in both the public and the private, non-profit sectors. Over 100 professional social workers were identified in 1996 as being employed by public sector agencies in Houston, including 70 employed directly by school districts. At least 33 additional social workers are employed full-time by a variety of private, voluntary organisations to provide school-based services, but primarily by Communities in Schools, Family Service Center, and DePelchin Children's Center. The expansion of school-based social work practice in Houston has influenced the field curriculum of the University of Houston's Graduate School of Social Work. Now one third of its first year master's level students have school-based field placements. The major models of service integration utilising social work personnel will be described.

Traditional school social work practice

Traditional school social work practice, the model that appears most frequently in existing social work literature (Allen-Meares *et al.*, 1996), has evolved slowly in Texas, but is gaining momentum. This is a model which envisions a social worker in every school. Where the work focuses upon a target group of pupils, such as the disabled, a social worker may be assigned to work with such pupils across a number of schools. In rural areas, a social worker may serve several schools. The social worker is usually a member of the pupil personnel services team, which typically includes the Principal or his Associate, a nurse, a guidance counsellor, an educational psychologist, and possibly other professional specialists besides teachers who are employed at a school. Teachers, administrators, and others refer children to the social worker whose needs can not be met by services within the school, who seem to be at high risk of dropping out or have unexplained absences, or who need crisis intervention. Social workers make many home visits, provide information and referral services, develop parent education and parent involvement programs, facilitate parent/teacher conferences, provide liaison with other agencies in the community, and may be the school's key link with other organisations in the community who want to provide volunteer services in the school. Time and case load constraints usually limit the duration of their therapeutic interventions. Some of them reach more individual students by organising groups focused upon specific goals, such as social skills or anger management. The role of the social worker in this model is influenced by whether the state education agency or the school district has an appropriate job description and personnel classification scheme that incorporates the unique educational qualifications and professional contributions that social workers can make. The principal's view of the role of a social worker is another major determinant of the professional use of social workers in schools. The role is also influenced by whether there are professional social workers in higher supervisory and administrative positions within the educational system who can provide the professional support needed by the direct service workers.

Public schools in Texas have a short history of employing professional social workers compared to states such as Iowa, Wisconsin, and Illinois where this profession is well-established in schools. The first law to certify social workers in Texas was enacted in 1981 (Act of June 1, 1981) and the legislation was strengthened in 1993 when the licensing of social workers was required (Texas Professional Social Work Act, 1993). It was not until 1989 that the Texas Education Agency (TEA) added "social worker" to the Texas Education Code compensation list which outlines the different professionals that a local school district may choose to hire with state dollars. Before that, some social workers were employed in schools, but in other positions, such as guidance counsellor. Although the 1989 ruling indicated that social workers could be included as members of pupil personnel services, it did not prescribe that only licensed social workers could fill these positions. The state legislature provided the needed title protection in 1995 (Act of May 30, 1995) clarifying that people employed in social work positions in public schools must be licensed social workers. Also, the wording of the law meant that social workers could be employed throughout the education system, not just in pupil personnel services. Momentum increased also for employing school-based social workers in 1991 when the Texas legislature mandated that all public schools must utilise site-based management (Act of May 27, 1991). As a result, principals had more discretionary money in their budgets and some employed social workers even if the profession was not well integrated into a school district's administration or system of personnel classification.

Much of the legal pressure for obtaining professional social work personnel has come from numerous streams of federal legislation that target the needs of children and youth who are disabled or at high risk of dropping out of or failing in school, such as the Individual with Disabilities Act (P.L. 94-142). Medicaid (Title XIX of the Social Security Act) can provide funding to schools for social work services that can be classified as part of the Early Periodic Screening, Diagnosis, and Treatment (EPSDT) Program. The Improving America's Schools Act (IASA) of 1994 (P.L. 103-382), re-authorising the Elementary and Secondary Education Act, authorised numerous ways of helping low income, educationally disadvantaged or homeless children, and for fighting drug abuse. It also authorised the local use of available funds for pupil services. Numerous other sources of federal legislation that could be used by states or localities to fund school social work positions have been documented by Hare and Allen (1996).

The Houston Independent School District (HISD), which serves the inner city area employs about 50 school social workers, most of whom work in the traditional roles described above. However, several work full-time with pupils in special education or alternative schools and their families, or in the district office's psychological services. Seventy-eight per cent of the pupils served by HISD are from minorities of colour, many of whom live in concentrated poverty areas. About 30 social workers are employed in the traditional roles by seven other school districts within the Greater Houston Metropolitan area.

Community Youth Services (CYS)

Community Youth Services is a unique public sector organisation that developed through joint planning by the county's child protective service agency, the juvenile court, some public school districts, and in some areas, the police, to identify and serve status offenders on a voluntary basis and divert them from the Court. CYS began in 1970 at the Harris County Juvenile Probation Department, using federal funds from the US Office of Juvenile Justice and Delinquency Prevention. These funds had been designated for deinstitutionalising juvenile status offenders and differentiating court and service procedures for status offenders and youth charged with committing crimes. After the federal grant expired, CYS obtained county funds under the auspices of the Harris County Children's Protective Services Board. These funds were and continue to be matched on a 50/50 per cent shared funding arrangement through contracts with 11 participating school districts. Officially, CYS is now part of Harris County Children's Protective Services, but by agreement with the juvenile court and participating school districts, it is the designated Harris County programme to work with runaway, homeless, or truanting pupils, and other status offenders. School-based services provided by 52 CYS staff target primarily secondary school aged pupils and their families who have been referred by school personnel. Among these are 26 professional social workers. Services include free counselling and generic casework services, and crisis intervention offered on a voluntary basis. Office space for the caseworkers is provided in schools. The mobility of CYS staff permits them to take services directly to families in their own homes. By networking and co-ordinating with existing non-profit, church sponsored, contract services, and public agencies, clients are assisted in resolving their problems without the loss of parental authority and the more costly intervention of the court system. During the 1994-95 school year, 15 628 youths and their families received services. Of these, 5 364 families were assisted in obtaining other social services, and 5 102 obtained assessment and treatment through contracts with community and therapeutic resources. These school-based and relevant contracted services cost $2 190 456 in the 1994-95 academic year. A federal grant supports anger management and conflict resolution training for some parents and youth. The Director of CYS and most of the senior administrative and supervisory personnel are professional social workers.

In addition to the school-based work, CYS has two other components. One is a reception Center and shelter for runaways and truants referred by law enforcement personnel. It also offers services requested on a voluntary basis to parents and teens in conflict. The other is a host family programme that provides an alternative to traditional shelter care and permits youth to remain in their own school and community while living away from home in another family. Also, family therapy is available to work toward restoring a family unit or preventing a placement outside the home. Psychological testing is offered to identify educational or treatment needs.

Social work leadership in other public sector service integration efforts

Professional social workers are employed also in key positions by other public agencies that provide services in schools in Harris County, which is a much larger metropolitan area than the city of Houston and which includes 24 different school districts. For example, the Texas Children's Mental Health Plan is an interagency collaboration involving ten state agencies and has its own line item in the Texas State budget. The Director of the Harris County part of the plan is a professional social worker who has considerable power in making decisions about how available funds are spent in Harris County. She gives priority to home and school-based service delivery strategies that have been developed in co-operation with neighbourhood-based coalitions of residents who help to define service needs and priorities in their areas (Personal communication from Patti Gray, Director of Harris County Children's Mental Health Plan, June 17, 1996). For example, she has a goal of developing preventive mental health services at four core school-based sites in one of the most disadvantaged inner-city areas served by one high school and the elementary and middle schools that feed into it.

Communities in schools

Conservative attitudes of Texans create substantial reluctance to adopt sweeping governmental solutions to social problems and generate some policies intended to create the maximum feasible participation of the private sector in the development and financing of school-based services. For example, in 1987, the State Legislature appropriated 2 million dollars, which became available in 1989, to support the Communities in Schools (CIS) model of bringing services to schools (Act of May 28, 1987). Legislative support for the CIS model has increased since then. The Houston Independent School District (HISD) and some other districts provide additional financial support for CIS services. These policies support models for bringing the social services to or near schools through the voluntary sector and community-based management of federal, state, and local streams of funding that could support service integration. In Houston, there are five different CIS programmes serving 39 elementary schools, 23 middle schools, 12 high schools, and 5 multiple level schools such as K-8th grade (*Fall Source Book,* 1995). About half of the financial support for them comes from the public sector and half from foundations, corporations, and other private sources. Altogether in Texas, there are 22 programmes that are affiliated with the national communities in Schools, Inc., the largest non-profit, voluntary agency in the United States that fights school dropout. It has been operating since 1977 and is growing steadily. The number of programmes in the nation has tripled since 1989.

The CIS model uses community-organisation approaches to creating coalitions that make community assessments of need related to the school dropout problem and who develop programmes to meet these needs. With sufficient local leadership and momentum, a Board of Directors is selected and a programme becomes incorporated as a non-profit organisation that can raise money for services. The Houston CIS director and staff work with school districts to locate the specific schools with the largest percentages of youth at risk of dropping out. CIS personnel then negotiate with the principal and staff of each school where they design the provision of services tailored to meet the constellation of most pressing needs of the children and youth there. The Houston CIS will not enter a school with a full-service program until it has raised $100 000 to support the effort. The CIS philosophy is also neighbourhood-based in the respect that CIS prefers to start work in a high school and then develop services at the elementary and middle schools in that high school's feeder pattern. This approach aims to maximise the impact that the programme can have on a specific neighbourhood.

CIS also develops innovative transition-to-work programmes known as Academies. They provide a free-standing facility or wing of an existing school in a corporation or other organisation that can offer hands-on work, training experiences, part-time jobs, mentoring or job shadowing opportunities, internships, scholarships, computer equipment and other incentives. For example, in Houston there is an academy at Burger King. Corporations sometimes loan executives to share business expertise with CIS.

The Director of the Houston CIS is a professional social worker and most of the other 18 professional social workers employed there are in management roles, such as Project Managers.

Schools of the future

Schools of the Future were initiated through the leadership and support of the Hogg Foundation for Mental Health at the University of Texas, Austin, and funded for five years in four Texas cities to demonstrate models of health and human service integration that could impact educational improvement and school reform (Holtzman, 1992, 1993). The four cities are Austin, Dallas, Houston, and San Antonio. At each location, needs assessments were conducted before the specific projects were developed in order to evolve locally appropriate governance structures and targeted services. The four project co-ordinators include three professional social workers and one who is not. A recent study of the co-ordinators' roles identified the knowledge, skills, and other characteristics that were viewed by key informants as being essential to the success of these four co-ordinators (Iscoe, 1995). Many of these are included in the requirements for social work education programmes listed above.

The Family Service Center (FSC) of Houston was chosen in 1990 to be the major administrator and fiscal manager of the Houston School of the Future project. FSC shares this responsibility with the HISD. Also, this School of the Future created a community-based Partnership Council whose membership reflects the major corporations and private foundations, and some social service agencies in Houston. The council consists of any person, business or organisation which supports the School of the Future, but it does not meet regularly as a group. However, the Executive Committee, consisting of key partners, serves as an Advisory Committee. The Project Co-ordinator is a social worker. Four other social workers are employed full-time in school-based activities, as well as several other professionals, and many volunteers. They provide a wide array of services in 16 different schools in the "Heights" area which has a predominantly Hispanic, low-income population. Assessment by the University of Texas at the outset had concluded that about 46 per cent of the parents and children had limited English proficiency and there were unacceptably large percentages of pupils who experienced drug and alcohol abuse, had been victims of child abuse or other family violence, and were involved in gangs.

Following are examples of the wide array of school-based services being offered in 1996:

- a family-focused violence prevention program;

- a family-based substance abuse prevention/early intervention program;

- school/home-based individual and family counselling sessions to teen parents;

- a health clinic;

- an Even Start literacy project;

- parent education;

- mentoring and tutoring for pupils;

- after-school programmes such as Boy Scouts, martial arts instruction, band and music instruction.

Information was provided about the additional financial resources, grants of money, and monetary and in kind contributions that have been received to support this rich and diverse array of school-based services. The School of the Future programme demonstrates the complex nature of developing such services from a community organisation approach and also the necessity of having professional leadership with managerial and community organisation skills .

The DePelchin Children's Centre School-Based Prevention Programs

DePelchin Children's Center, a multi-purpose voluntary, non-profit child welfare agency, has recently organised a Prevention Department that is developing school-based integrated services in nine different schools under professional social work leadership and in collaboration with other service agencies in Houston. Examples of the types of services offered include:

- social responsibility and social skills groups for children;

- consultations to teachers about classroom management dilemmas;

- school wide social skills and violence prevention training;

- a programme to assist children making the transition from elementary school to middle school;

- grief support groups for children who are facing the death or incarceration of a parent;

- parent education programmes and a job bank;

- support groups for pregnant and parenting teenagers, as well as individual and family counselling;

- pregnancy prevention programs;

- literacy, English as a second language, and citizenship classes;

- Family Resource Centres;

- family-oriented special activities such as "Sunday in the Park" and an annual "Dads' Conference". In a few of the schools, more therapeutically oriented home-based treatment programmes are provided. Both public and private sources of funding support these activities.

Full service community schools in New York City

The Children's Aid Society (CAS) of New York, one of the oldest voluntary, non-profit children's agencies in the nation operated under social work professional leadership, was included in the OECD site visits to the United States in 1994. It is achieving international recognition for its creative leadership in building three full service community schools in the Washington Heights-Inwood section of Manhattan. In 1989, CAS joined with the New York City School Board, School District 6, and other community-based organisations in a partnership to address the pressing needs of children and families in this area. A needs assessment conducted by CAS in 1987 had found that this part of New York City had the highest level of drug addiction and crime, including murder, of all city precincts. Two of every three new babies in the community were born to a mother between 15 and 19 years of age. 86 per cent of the students in the School District were Latino, the great majority of whom were recent immigrants from the Dominican Republic. The district had the highest number of students with limited English proficiency of any in the state and it ranked last among New York City's 32 school districts in students reading at or above grade level. At this time, none of the city's traditional youth organisations had a presence in Washington Heights-Inwood. CAS was considering opening a community Center, but when it learned that the NY City School Construction Authority was planning to build some new schools in the community, CAS forged an alliance with the public school authorities to create community schools that would contain both the educational programmes and the needed health and welfare services of a large social service agency under the same roof. The partnership between CAS and the School Board was created before the schools were built. Therefore it was possible for the vision of the full service school to influence the physical, administrative, and educational structures that emerged. The first one, a middle school, opened in March, 1992. Later, two elementary schools opened as community schools. These schools now provide a focal point in their community to which children and their parents can turn for education and all types of other services, such as health, mental health, dental, recreation, supplemental education, youth programs, parent education, family life education, and summer camping services.

For example, at the middle school, the facilities are open six days a week, 15 hours a day, year-round. The school now has a Family Resource Center that is operated by 25 trained parent volunteers, who also work in the school's health clinic, and are eligible to participate in a training programme to become dental assistants, secretaries, and receptionists, while receiving stipends.

The CAS provides a mobile health unit that extends its services to local Head Start Centres and other public schools in Washington Heights. It is a custom-designed van with a fully equipped paediatric and dental clinic. Van staff provide vision and hearing examinations, blood tests for lead poisoning and sickle-cell anemia, WIC certification, immunisations, booster shots, check-ups, screenings for developmental delays and disabilities, and complete dental treatment. Some of the medical and nursing staff of the school's clinic are provided through the professional education training programmes of the Columbia Presbyterian Medical Center and their School of Dental and Oral Surgery.

There is an extended school day programme operated by CAS, in consultation with the Principal and Assistant Principals and teachers, and employing many of the regular teachers. This extended programme can create a seamless day for pupils who decide to participate. There are both pre-school and after-school programs, such as sports, band, dance, English as a second language, fitness training, and business studies.

The curriculum of the middle school is divided into four Academies: Business Studies; Community Service; Expressive Arts; and Math, Science and Technology. Each one has its own Assistant Principal and teaching staff. Many of the ideas about programmes to offer in the extended school day programme grow out of the interests created through these four organising ideas. For example, three student-run businesses operate in the extended day hours:

- a catering company which prepares and serves food and beverages for parties and receptions in the school and the community;

- a T-shirt company, which designs, produces and sells T-shirts usually centred around a particular school event; and

- the SUMA Store Company operating within the school that sells 300 different items, such as school supplies, snacks, comics, posters, and books other than school textbooks.

Students are officers and staff of the store. In 1993, they voted themselves 20 per cent of the profits as stipends. They donated 10 per cent of the profits to the school and most of the rest of the profits were plowed back into the store.

There is a Saturday programme that offers gym, computer proficiency, and day trips to other CAS centres for swimming, barbecues, and excursions into the country. A summer program, beginning a week after the end of regular school, and running Monday through Friday from ten a.m. to six p.m., has two categories. One offers regular summer school for pupils who would not pass on to the next grade without these additional courses. But there are also frequent day trips to beaches, swimming pools, museums, parks, and to the CAS country camp where an Outward Bound type course has been designed. The second component offers shorter special programs, such as a two week business entrepreneurial "boot camp" for pupils who wish to intensify their studies in this area. Another example is a six weeks course in dance and creative writing offered in conjunction with the Alvin Ailey Dance Company.

In keeping with the goal of providing outreach and services to residents of all ages in the neighbourhoods around the community schools, programmes are being developed for older teenagers, senior citizens, and other groups not mentioned above (The Children's Aid Society, 1993*a* and *b*).

The Children's Aid Society created a Community Schools Technical Assistance Center that offers information and individualised assistance to individuals and organisations anywhere who have an interest in making their schools more responsive to the needs of children and families. This Center will offer training and guidance about all aspects of designing and implementing a community schools programme that suits the unique needs and strengths of individual communities. Consulting and training services may be targeted to elementary, middle or high schools, local school boards, community organisations, parent associations, policy makers, universities and research centres, and leaders in education reform.

Social work roles encountered in other OECD site visits

The OECD site visits to exemplary service integration programmes were organised, for the most part, by the educational authorities in the various countries. Often the site visitors met people in groups where the focus was not upon determining the professional identity of the various participants as much as understanding the total operation of the program. Therefore, the site visitors did not always identify who the social workers were. However, in most countries visited, it was obvious that they are utilised in direct service, middle, and senior management positions of both public and private organisations that participate in service integration efforts.

Summary and conclusions

This paper has provided general information about the nature of professional social work practice and roles in the United States. Also, a short outline portrayed basic components required in the curricula of accredited social work education programmes in higher education. Social work curricula prepare graduates with knowledge, skills, and readiness for service integration roles and positions. Examples of social work roles and organisations focused upon those involving school-based service integration because the most recent OECD project on children-at-risk emphasised linkages between public schools and other service sectors. First the traditional concept of school social work practice was illustrated. Additional examples were provided of school-based service integration programmes that were initiated and operated with professional social work leadership through partnerships among schools and other public and private social service agencies. By utilising examples from Houston, Texas, one of the largest cities and urban areas in the United States, it was possible to show the momentum, dynamic interest, and energy now being centred upon integrating social and health services with public schools in order to serve children, youth, and their families more effectively. Although the constellation of agencies and models vary from city to city, these illustrations are typical of the types of school-based service integration programmes now emerging throughout the nation. The comprehensive, full-service community school model developed through the initiative of the CAS of New York City provides another example of complete integration of education, health, and social services by one of the oldest professional social work agencies in the United States. Some of these programmes could be replicated in other countries. These models reveal how the public and private sectors can complement each other to provide a variety of approaches to linking services in schools in ways that are most appropriate for different neighbourhoods and target populations. A list of key informants who can provide additional information about the programmes described in this paper is appended.

The results of this study support a position that school social work practice should be conceptualised more broadly than services provided by employees of the public education sector. Contemporary federal and state funding patterns for health, education, and welfare services are providing opportunities for other public and private organisations to offer school-based services. Other avenues for basing services in schools provide creative opportunities for communities to mobilise, combine, and maximise public and private resources for these purposes. In states where traditional school social work is well-established, these patterns offer the promise of even more services for school children, youth, and families.

REFERENCES

Act of June 1, 1981, 67th Leg., R.S., ch. 776, sec 1, 50.001-50.033, Tex. Gen. Laws, 2923-2932.

Act of May 28, 1987, 70th Leg., R.S., ch. 1099, sec. 49, 11(d), Tex. Gen. Laws, 3745.

Act of May 27, 1991, 72nd leg., R.S., ch. 391, sec. 30, 21.931, Tex. Gen. Laws, 1846.

Act of May 30, 1995, 74th Leg., R.S., ch. 260, sec. 1, 21.003(*b*), Tex. Gen. Laws, 2259.

Allen-Meares, P., Washington, R.O., and Welsh, B.L. (1996), *Social Work Services in Schools,* Allyn & Bacon, Boston.

Casebolt, Ann Nichols (April 14, 1998), President, Graduate Association for Doctoral Education in Social Work, email message from acaseboi@saturn.vcu.edu to mrlewis@uh.edu.

Children's Aid Society (1993*a*), *A Unique Partnership, The story of a Community School,* New York.

Children's Aid Society (1993*b*), *Building a Community School,* New York.

Commission on Accreditation (1994), *Handbook of Accreditation Standards and Procedures*, Council on Social Work Education, Alexandria, VA.

Compton, B. and Galaway, B. (1994), *Social Work Processes* (5th ed.), Brooks/Cole Publishing Company, Pacific Grove, CA.

Connaway, R. and Gentry, M. (1988*), Social Work Practice,* Prentice Hall, Englewood Cliffs, NJ.

DuBois, B. and Miley, K. K. (1996), *Social Work, an empowering profession,* Allyn & Bacon, Boston.

Fall Source Book (Dec. 1995), Cities in Schools, Inc, Alexandria, VA.

Famighetti, R. (ed) (1996), *The World Almanac and Book of Facts,* Funk & Wagnalls Corp, Mahwah, NJ.

Hare, I.S. and Allen, K. S. (1996), "The Economic, Political, and Social World of School Social Work"*, in* R. Constable, J.P. Flynn, & S. McDonald (eds.), *School Social Work* (pp. 66-84), Lyceum Books, Inc, Chicago.

Holtzman, W.H. (ed.) (1992), *School of the Future,* Hogg Foundation for Mental Health, University of Texas, Austin, Texas.

Holtzman, W.H. (ed.) (1993), *Shared Opportunities for Schools and Communities,* Hogg Foundation for Mental Health, University of Texas, Austin, Texas.

Iscoe, L. K. (1995), *The Project Co-ordinators, A key to the school of the future,* Hogg Foundation for Mental Health, University of Texas, Austin, Texas.

Johnson, L. C. (1995), *Social Work Practice: A generalist approach* (4th ed.), Allyn & Bacon, Boston.

Pincus, A. and Minahan, A. (1973), *Social Work Practice Model and Method,* Peacock Publishers, Itasca, IL.

Siporin, M. (1975), *Introduction to Social Work Practice,* Macmillan Publishing Co., Inc, New York.

Texas Professional Social Work Act of 1993, 73rd Leg., R.S., ch. 605, sec. 1-43, 50.001-50.034, Tex. Gen. Laws, 2277-2298.

U.S. Bureau of the Census (1995), *Statistical Abstract of the United States: 1995* (115th ed.), U.S. Government Printing Office, Washington, DC.

U.S. Department of Labour, Bureau of Labour Statistics (Jan. 1996), *Occupational Outlook Handbook*, 1996-97 edition, U.S. Government Printing Office, Washington, DC.

Zastrow, C. (1995), *The Practice of Social Work* (5th ed.), The Dorsey Press, Chicago, IL.

PART THREE

IMPLEMENTING SYSTEM CHANGE

IMPLEMENTING SYSTEM CHANGE FOR EFFECTIVE CLIENT SERVICES

by

Alex Dingwall
New Brunswick Department of Education

The report *Successful Services For Our Children And Families At Risk* explores many ways that countries are moving towards the implementation of programs and services to meet the needs of children and families at risk. This review focuses on the interplay and roles of laws and policies; strategic level decision makers; service co-ordinators and the professional that implement services with the consumer/client. There is an acknowledgement that "successful services", those that are most effective and need fulfilling for the client, will have to move to an implementation model that features case management that is developed, co-ordinated, and communicated in an integrated fashion. Professional and non-professional services can no longer meet the complex and varied needs of communities, families and children in isolation from each other.

It is proposed that a multi-disciplinary structure will be better able to blend the educational, health, social, financial, recreational and psychological needs of families. This approach would recognise the dynamic interrelationship of societal needs and the individual growth and development factors that contribute to eventual the well-being and success of children and families "At Risk".

In a paper by Volpe (1996), it is described that children's services are usually less than a system involving co-ordination, co-operation between providers and families and are often a collection of competing, independent and specialised agencies; hard to manage in a cohesive and focused way; inefficient (in many ways); politicised and too rigid.

The vision of Integrated services is one of increasing effectiveness, of being more efficient and accessible, eliminating gaps in service, planning in more holistic way and increasing service to the consumer. His report reviews the perceived advantages and disadvantages of integrated services from the perspective(s) of the administrator, managers and professionals and clients.

Advantages of Integrated services may include: positive morale of staff; professional satisfaction; an increased understanding of the roles and perspective of other professionals; sharing of information; better relationships and communication with the community; enhanced outcomes for the client reduced cost; more consistently and quicker response; accessibility; and an improved knowledge of the consumer (parent and child).

Concerns or perceived disadvantages may include: increased bureaucracy; negative impact on other programs and services; professionals may request greater "equity in status" and remuneration; re-alignment and change of service structures, leading to a significant increase in workload; loss of professional identity by service providers; reduction in specialisation; funding reductions and job losses; and difficulty in developing inter-professional relationships.

BECHTEL MODEL OF CHANGE

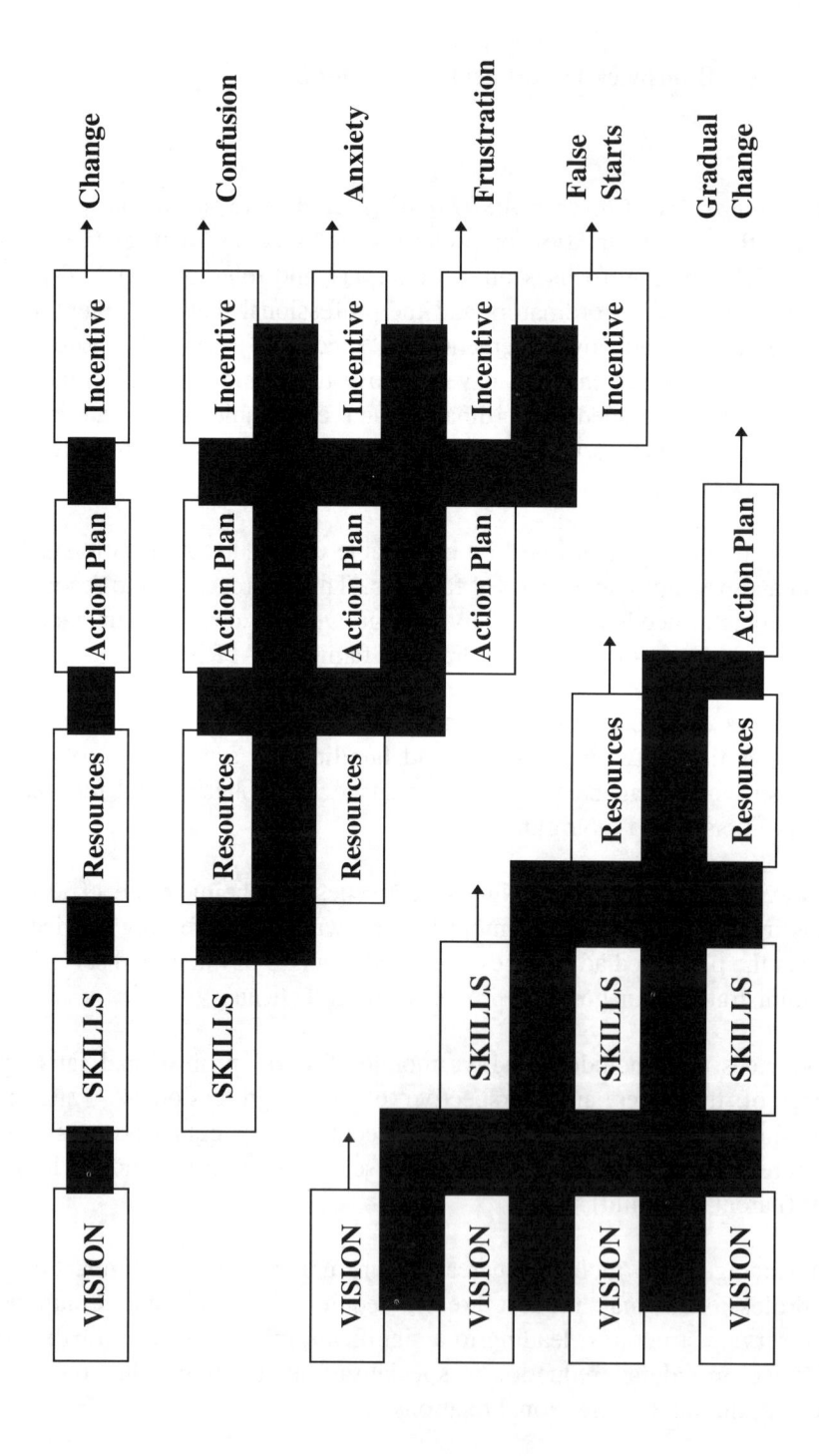

VISION	SKILLS	Resources	Action Plan	Incentive	→ Change
	SKILLS	Resources	Action Plan	Incentive	→ Confusion
VISION		Resources	Action Plan	Incentive	→ Anxiety
VISION	SKILLS		Action Plan	Incentive	→ Frustration
VISION	SKILLS	Resources		Incentive	→ False Starts
VISION	SKILLS	Resources	Action Plan		→ Gradual Change

108

Many of the perceived disadvantages would be expected when change and shifting paradigms occur in an organisational system. It has to be realised that to implement successful systematic change certain process components have to present. The most serious challenge is not in creating new systems of delivery but ensuring that all the factors are in place to enable a successful change process. These factors that are illustrated in Figure I have to be given proper consideration for the change process to be successful.

Change requires a *vision* that has been carefully developed and communicated among all those that are involved. The focus should be on effective service to the client.

Integrated services would require the development of *new skills* by all the service providers. Skills development itself requires a different approach to training (multi-disciplinary); and the allocation of significant resources and time. While it may be a saving in some areas; additional costs may be increased in other areas. System change requires the *allocation of resources* especially for the skill development of staff. While services integration is sometimes viewed as a money saving strategy, this is not always the case in the short term.

System change always requires a co-ordinated, well thought out *plan of action* that stipulates the when, how and who.

Finally, there should be a substantive reason or *incentive* for the change. If organisations are self evaluating, the need to change may be internally motivated and continual.

As proposed by Bechtel Engineering, if the above factors are in place, then the impetus to implement change will be more likely to occur in a meaningful way. If a component is missing then the implementation will cause frustration, anxiety decreased efficiencies and anger among all those concerned, including the client.

Adding to the complexity for change there is also the issue that inhibiting factors may come from many different levels within our hierarchical arrangements. For instance, in government structures, vision, incentive and support has to come not only from the but also from the legislation of the state. It has to be bold, dynamic, non-competitive, positive and communicated in many different ways so that all involved in the society (community) can clearly understand what the desired outcomes are and how best to achieve them.

It also is extremely important for resources to be defined so that they support or enable the co-ordination and integration of services and that they not be a barrier to success. The skill development and training should model integrated services in that they should be multi-disciplinary and co-operative.

There is an observation that integrated services seem to flourish under policies that encourage decentralisation, and feature a wide range of services functioning collaboratively with the community and the privatised sector. Most of the "Best Practices" reviewed in the report, *Successful Services for Children and Families at Risk*, occur in communities and seem to be part of strategies for innovation with supplementary funding from the mainstream systems. However, dynamic, inter-agency collaboration and integrated case management is still the exception in providing services to children. Implementing reform and change across all levels including laws and policies; strategic level decision makers; service co-ordination, program delivery, professional contact with the client is very complex.

When reviewing these issues surrounding the promotion of effective services for At Risk Youth, we should consider the following:

- The balanced development of children is increasingly seen as holistic. It is embedded in and emerges from a balanced social support system.

- The narrow categorical organisation of services is inadequate to meet either the extent or the nature of the present demands.

- There is definitive research on innovative practices. This should initiate substantive discussion towards future actions.

- Co-ordinated and comprehensive services to support and enable children to succeed in school has not been a focus.

- Most of legislation supports bureaucratic structures that have different mandates, rules and regulations and are isolated and rigid. Generally bureaucracies cannot focus on the individual client needs, and are unable to be dynamic and changing.

Conclusion

As a result of this and other research, it appears that integrated services is a highly desirable approach for the effective and efficient delivery of programs and services to youth. If so, we must recognise that the change process to establish a different model of support is complex and varied. Actions, strategies, can be formed to ensure that the process will be carried out in spite of the challenges that are inherent in moving to a new direction.

FROM PROGRAMMATIC TO INTEGRATED SERVICES IN NEW BRUNSWICK, CANADA

by

Alex Dingwall
New Brunswick Department of Education

New Brunswick is a province on the eastern seaboard of Canada, with a relatively small population of 730 000, located primarily in a rural setting.

The education system serves approximately 135 000 students with distinct Anglophone and Francophone programs. There is a highly centralised government structure with legislation and funding moving through the Department of Education to 18 school districts.

Since approximately 1985 Provincial youth policies have focused on ensuring that children are ready for school; able to achieve success during public school years and having the skills and qualifications to move into employment. In 1984 an Office of Government Reform working paper noted that "The education system cannot depend solely on teachers to provide students with the best possible learning environment. Availability and access to a variety of professional support services is essential to teachers, administrators and parents in order to enhance the learning process and to ensure a quality learning environment."

This statement preceded a tremendous change in the education act of 1986, allowing school age children with disabilities equal access to education within the regular classroom structure. Disabled (as well as gifted) children were described as exceptional in the new legislation and included those with learning disabilities, cognitive and physical disabilities, and behaviour disorders.

As a result, other government agencies that provided services to children with disabilities, or those "At-Risk", begin to focus on co-ordinated services supporting education. The vision was that enabling children to attain success in their public schooling will be the first step towards them later becoming contributing members of their community.

The government departments involved in partnership initiatives included Health and Community Services; Human Resources Development -- NB; Municipalities, Culture and Housing (Recreation and Sport); Advanced Education and Labour, Solicitor-General, Justice and the Federal Government Departments of Health and Human Resource Development.

One of the first formal programme developments for integrated services was an agreement between Health and Community Services and Education to provide professional support in the areas of Social Work, Psychology and Speech Language Pathology. This agreement was unique in that the provincial and regional policies on program delivery were co-managed between the two departments, Health and Education. Although the professional staff were employed and paid by Health and

Community Services, such issues as resource allocation, hiring and supervision, assessment and referral were joint responsibilities.

A Provincial and Regional Operations Committee comprised of senior management of Health and Education were charged with effective and efficient program management and delivery. Initially the management committees worked their way through a proposed policy and regulation structure that was initially developed by central bureaucracy. Specific resources were identified and in-service on the co-ordination of program delivery were made available.

After some familiarity with the system was achieved, management then went on to the establishment of program standards, assessment and prioritisation of service for social work and speech language pathology. An evaluation phase validated the extent of program delivery and its perceived effectiveness towards increasing the ability of the child to achieve success in school.

This implementation of the integrated services was facilitated by an inter-departmental arrangement that was innovative, collaborative, responsive and focused. This committee structure has just recently been expanded to include other government departments including Solicitor General, Human Resources Development -- NB, and Public Health. The focus has changed from the effective management of resources; to a broader aspect including the communication and organisation of general youth policies and programmes for all youth deemed At-Risk. These include:

- *Early Childhood Initiative:* Birth to 5 years of age; public health referral service, integrated day care, food supplement program and family support.

- *Youth Futures*: Transition programmes and At Risk youth services for youth age 14-24.

- *Inter-Departmental Agreement to Support Youth with Behaviour Difficulties:* Mental Health and Young Offender programs co-ordinated with education.

- *Youth Apprenticeship*: Focused transition programs with the co-ordinated support of federal and provincial departments and the private sector.

- *Star Program:* Return to school, age 16-18.

- *Youth At-Risk:* Physical Activity and Recreation programmes with an impact on the positive physical, social and cognitive development of youth.

- *Family Services:* Focus on the betterment of conditions that promote the healthy well being of all members of the family.

Over the past 10 years, New Brunswick has seen provincial departmental initiatives for youth significantly move towards a more comprehensive, co-ordinated and integrated process. The original vision that focused on ensuring that the child achieve success in school has necessitated increased communication, collaboration and sharing of resources among all the government departments that provide services to youth. The planning, policy development, program delivery and evaluation became a collaborative effort. This sharing requires the bureaucratic structures to be more sensitive to other opinions and professional viewpoints, and both flexible and adaptable to community needs and individual perceptions on how effective the program and services are.

ISSUES IN MANAGING AND SHARING INFORMATION FOR IMPLEMENTING SYSTEM CHANGE

by

Hermann Rademacker
German Youth Institute

The conceptualisation of services, their implementation, and the decisions regarding the necessary supply, need sound information regarding the quantity as well as the quality of the needs they are intended to respond to. When we talk about integrated services, and include the different forms of co-ordinated and co-operating services among the case studies of this OECD project (and in some fields of action as *e.g.* the transition from school to work) these must be recognised as a big advance on the traditional separation of services between schools, business, and different social welfare providers. We must also address the generating of necessary and useful information, and managing and sharing it with those involved.

This job is supported as well as complicated by the fact that those people and agencies needing and wanting the information are also the sources for a good deal of the relevant information. Usually, they are not just neutral and disengaged sources and providers of information but actors in the field. They may provide services, or as administrative or political agents in the field, they may be responsible for coping with the social problems to be overcome. This means that generating, collecting, managing and sharing the information, is not just empirical social research. It is also a very political job which needs political competence and support as well as expertise in collecting and processing empirical data.

Social reporting regarding children and youth in Germany

When considering the social reporting on the situation of youth and families in Germany certain political implications become evident. The most important reports on the federal level are youth reports, family reports and reports on vocational education and training. In addition to these federal reports, some *Länder* and even some communities have established similar reporting systems of their own. Finally, there are poverty reports for different regions which may be elaborated under the responsibility of governmental institutions but are also initiated by welfare organisations, the churches, the unions or through the co-operation of such groups.

The Federal Government is committed by law to submit a youth report to Parliament every four years, or once during each legislative period. The report is elaborated by a commission, whose chairperson as well as its members are nominated by the government but who then work independently. Despite the influence of the government on the composition of the group the reports maintain a certain independence and can often challenge established practices. It can take several months for the government to formulate its comments which accompany the report when it is given to parliament and made public. The fact that the commission represents the youth services and their various organisations has resulted in their relative independence from governmental expectations.

The youth reports are of great political and strategic importance for the development of youth services in Germany. For instance, the Eighth Report, which was prepared during intensive discussions for a new children's and youth services law in the 1980s strongly supported a holistic view of young people's development and the kind of support they needed. This idea had already been a conceptual element in many social services activities and projects, but the report strengthened the approach and provided a benchmark for professionals to work to. The first paragraph encourages the youth services and their administrative and political actors to intervene in other fields of society when necessary in order to realise positive conditions for the development of children and youth. And this, without doubt, goes far beyond the social influence and the power that youth services in Germany enjoy today and thus has a rather utopic quality. On the other hand it presents a challenging interpretation of the concept of integrated services which is far beyond the simple idea of just tearing down bureaucratic barriers between existing youth services.

Youth reports in Germany, which have been produced for some 25 years have become landmarks for the development of youth services in Germany. They serve both social and political roles, and also stimulate conceptual development. They are, however, elaborated under the sceptical eyes of professionals who tend to see society from the point of view of the disadvantaged and often from a non-capitalistic perspective. Nevertheless, the political process – from the constitution of the committee, the election of experts, the reaction of the government and the parliamentary and public debates following the publication of the report -- are necessary to make the report a political instrument for youth policies and for the development of youth services.

The Ninth Youth Report -- the first one after German unification which therefore deals with the special situation of youth and youth services in Eastern Germany -- is published and the Tenth, concentrating on the situation of children under 14 years of age, is almost finished.

Parallel to the Youth Reports there are also Family Reports in Germany. They are worked out in the same way as the Youth Reports but they are not necessarily produced in each legislative period. Five have been realised while the sixth is currently being prepared.

The annual reports on vocational education and training are produced by a totally different political process. They are elaborated in the Federal Institute for Vocational Education and Training in Berlin. The institute has been established and is working on the basis of the vocational education and training act. The report is elaborated in co-operation with the Federal Ministry of Education, Science, Research, and Technology. It is first discussed in a kind of governing board of the institute, the "Hauptausschuß", where the employers organisations as well as the trade unions, the Federal Government and the *Länder* (states) are represented. They comment on the report from their point of view and propose political action to be taken to overcome the deficits and problems the report identifies. There is strong emphasis from the participating groups to find a consensus regarding their statement on the report, since the pressure on the government to act according to their proposals becomes so much the stronger. But if no consensus can be found on certain aspects, minority votes are noted in the report.

The first such Report on Vocational Education and Training in Germany was published in 1975, the latest one in 1997. During these years the reports have developed to reflect actual developments such as the recently increasing problems in the transition from vocational education and training to employment (*Berufsbildungsbericht*, 1996)

Similar concepts of social reporting have been adopted by different authorities at the state or community level. Some produce reports on the situation of children and youth, and some on the situation of young people in the transition from school to work. The city of Duisburg which furnished one of the case studies in this OECD project has provided one of the most advanced examples of a regional report of the transition from school to work in their municipality. The latest one, published in 1997, reflects the situation of vocational education and training in Duisburg in 1996.

In this, as in most of the other cases, the motive is to initiate change and to mobilise resources to improve funding and opportunities. The commissioning of such reports, therefore, usually occurs at times of crisis or when there is a broad consensus on the necessity of reform.

Often, the function of these reports is to stimulate discussions in different groups which may have conflicting interests, such as businesses and trade unions, youth services and schools of vocational as well as general education and also governmental agencies on different levels. In Duisburg for example a permanent group of representatives of government and business was established to discuss a common policy to deal with the deficits of opportunities for vocational education and training in the region and to co-ordinate the contributions from the agencies involved.

This kind of social reporting is without doubt important. To be able to locate the limited resources available in the most effective way, information is absolutely necessary. But the use of that kind of information is mainly restricted to the political and the strategic level of action. In some cases, it might be also helpful on the managerial level but it is only of little relevance for the improvement of practical educational and social work in schools, companies, and other projects and agencies. It does not help -- and is not intended to help -- the exchange of information regarding project practice and, for example, to make the experience of examples of good practice available to other projects which may want to learn from them.

Case studies as a means of networking practice projects

In the European Union there are many programmes and initiatives in the fields of education and youth services which also aim at the improvement of the educational and social service practice by networking and exchanging information and experience within such networks. By the way -- the problematic assumption in these programmes seems to be that improvements and experience flow downhill from the comparatively developed northern and middle European countries to the economically less developed Mediterranean countries. The German Youth Institute has participated in some of these networks and the experience is that the results of that kind of exchange are often rather poor. It sometimes does not bring much more than a new kind of tourism for some civil servants and professionals -- which is not necessarily bad -- but does not meet the sophisticated objectives set.

After having accompanied this OECD project on some occasions and after using the study's methodology for preparing case studies (Volpe, 1996), I am sure this concept could be easily expanded not only to evaluate projects and programmes but also to be used as an excellent means to share and exchange information at the field level where the action takes place.

The basic idea is to make use of the interactive elements in the concept and to exchange the case studies within networks of projects. The questionnaire published (OECD, 1996, pp. 295-328) could be used as a structure for the exchange of information between projects in such networks. The description should be -- as in the OECD project -- supported by external experts. The criterion for a satisfactory description should be -- as in the CIPP[1]-concept – that there is an intensive feedback with the project described and – and this is going beyond the CIPP-concept – that other projects in the network get all the answers to the questions they have regarding the project described. This in general should also cover the question of how and why the project so described actually works and why it is successful or failing.

As each project has to co-operate in its own case study and has to answer the questions of other network members, the generation of the case studies leads to an intensive exchange of information and experiences within the network and by that process also improves the understanding of one's own project and its conditions for failure and success. It also helps to identify possibilities for change and innovation in ones own project which until then have been seen as normalities outside the ranges of development and change. That which had previously been taken for granted might be re-evaluated through discussion. The general philosophy of such a strategy might be called, *Learning from the different.*

The German Youth Institute has started to adapt the CIPP concept for this kind of work, to combine evaluation and exchange of experiences, at the field level, of projects supporting disadvantaged youth in their transition from school to work. We are working with two networks in northern EU Member countries. The experience thus far has been positive -- but it is a lot of work -- not only but also because of the different languages being used in the projects.

---

1.   CIPP -- Context, Input, Process, Product -- is a means of structuring case studies (Stufflebeam, 1971).

REFERENCES

Bundesministerium für Bildung, Wissenschaft, Forschung und Technologie (Hrsg.) (1996), *Berufsbildungsbericht 1996*, Bonn.

Bundesministerium für Bildung, Wissenschaft, Forschung und Technologie (Hrsg.) (1997), *Berufsbildungsbericht 1997*, Bonn.

Bundesminister für Jugend, Familie, Frauen und Gesundheit (Hrsg.) (1990), *Achter Jugendbericht*, Bonn.

Bundesminister für Jugend, Familie, Frauen und Gesundheit (Hrsg.) (1995), *Neunter Jugendbericht*, Bonn.

OECD (1996), *Successful Services for our Children and Families at Risk,* Paris.

Stadt Duisburg, Der Oberstadtdirektor Amt für Statistik, Stadtforschung und Europaangelegenheiten (Hrsg), *Berufsbildungsbericht Duisburg 1996* (Duisburg, August 1996)

Stufflebeam, D.L. (1971), "The relevance of the CIPP evaluation model for educational accountability", *Journal of Research and Development in Education,* Fall, pp. 492-501.

Volpe, R. (1966), "The CIPP model and the case study approach", in OECD, *Successful Services for our Children and Families at Risk,* Paris.

PREPARING PROFESSIONALS TO WORK IN A CO-ORDINATED SYSTEM OF SERVICES FOR CHILDREN AND YOUTH AT RISK

by

Phyllis R. Magrab
Georgetown University Medical Centre

Introduction

With the goal being economic and social well-being, OECD Member countries share the belief that a strong foundation in the early years of development is essential for helping citizens become productive members of society. Unfortunately, in most countries, there are groups of children who are vulnerable to poverty and other hazards that will lead to serious difficulties in their lifelong learning and ultimate employability. Thus, addressing the special needs of these vulnerable children and their families as early as possible is critical and represents a significant challenge for schools, social welfare services, and communities.

The current work in progress of the Centre for Educational Research and Innovation (CERI) intends to understand the educational and special service needs of these vulnerable children and youth, to identify risk factors in the various countries studied, and to examine strategies for providing services that are effective and well co-ordinated to these children. Because of the complex nature of the needs of these children and their families, no single professional discipline -- neither education, health, nor social work -- can alone solve the problems. How providers collaborate to achieve a co-ordinated system of services is a potent consideration in the effectiveness of services; yet, few professionals are trained to work in this type of context. Building on the findings of the current work, this paper addresses the training of educators and other professionals to function in an integrated service delivery system for children and youth at risk. The implementation of policies promoting integrated services provision in a large number of Member countries has created a significant need in this area.

The population of children and youth at risk

In the current CERI study in progress, children and youth at risk are described as "...those pupils from disadvantaged backgrounds who fail to reach the necessary standards in school, often drop-out, and as a consequence, fail to be integrated into a normally accepted pattern of social responsibility, particularly with regard to work and adult life". Because the technological advances of society require considerable skill for individuals to be productive, school failure and school leaving imply a broad range of economic consequences including costs to social security, health, and social services as well as lost tax revenues. For these children there are many other manifestations of a failure to integrate successfully into society which include health problems, substance and drug abuse, crime, early pregnancy, and unemployment that have further cost implications.

In studying Member countries, CERI has identified the following factors as associated with risk: poverty, ethnic minority status, family issues (including single parenthood, inadequate housing, home-school breakdown, and child abuse), type of school attended, geographical location of the school and community factors.

The prevalence of "at-risk" children is difficult to determine because most Member countries do not have a standing definition against which they collect statistical data. While there is variability in definition, the data that are available suggest that this group of children, with figures between 15 per cent and 30 per cent being quoted, represents a substantial problem to many Member countries.

The roles of multiple professions

The complexity of the underlying, contributing factors to "at risk" status and the way these manifest themselves requires input at the service level from a range of professionals including educators, social workers, physicians, and nurses. These professionals must understand the needs of these children and their families in the broadest possible framework. For example; teachers should be able to provide not only the appropriate and necessary learning for general education and specific skill building but do so with an understanding of the various external stresses these children are experiencing. Social workers, dealing with the various family stresses, must be knowledgeable about supportive community services and other resources that treat, for example, substance abuse, and especially, be in contact with the schools. Physicians and nurses who provide health supervision and specific services in relation to special health needs, such as early pregnancies and sexually transmitted diseases, must not be in isolation from teachers and social workers.

All of this points to the need at the service level for these professionals to work as a team. Shared information, co-ordinated planning and decision-making, and co-operative service development produce more effective services to children and youth at risk and their families.

The importance of service integration

The importance and need for co-ordination is best and first understood through the eyes of the family. Families, in their efforts to raise healthy, educated, socially responsible children, should receive services in a dignified, culturally sensitive manner. Receiving conflicting information and advice, experiencing lack of communication among service providers, and not having a coherent system of supportive services is frustrating and ineffective. For service providers, lack of knowledge of each other's goals; lack of understanding of the totality of resources in the community; and, at times, unresolved or incompatible differences in education, social service, and health approaches to care, impact negatively on how services are delivered to children and their families. The concept of a team approach to planning and decision-making, which can take many forms, has evolved slowly but represents the most promise for reducing fragmentation and enhancing good communication among professionals and with the families they serve. Working in teams can range from convening around the needs of a particular child to meeting regularly for planning and developing new policies or programs.

Importantly, the best intended service providers cannot effectuate co-ordinated approaches to care without the understanding and support of supervisors, program planners, and policy makers. Policies for implementing the educational and human service systems must reflect these same concerns of reducing program fragmentation and increasing co-operation and collaboration across all agencies to promote change at the service level.

Clearly if service integration is to be achieved, steps must be taken at all levels of the service delivery system. Practitioners and teachers, program planners, and policy makers must have a common goal of providing services to families in a coherent, co-ordinated way that allows for maximum communication and understanding. Policies developed at the national level have critical implications for how individuals at the local level can implement programs. Both vertical and horizontal co-ordination are essential to have a smooth functioning system for children and youth at risk and their families.

Why focus on training to achieve service integration?

The role of training is critical to achieve system development and system change that incorporate the goals of service integration. The training of professionals to work in a co-ordinated delivery system includes developing values, attitudes, and specific skills whether these professionals are preparing for direct service or teaching roles, service planning careers, or policy development positions. The interaction between training and outcomes in service delivery is complex. Persons trained in new approaches can influence the system in positive ways as they become employed in it or they can become frustrated by systems unwilling or reluctant to change. On the other hand, an enlightened set of policy makers and service planners can influence training curricula by creating the demand for a new type of trained individual with skills that currently are not taught and support positive changes at the direct service level.

Professional expectations and values

If there is agreement that service co-ordination is an important goal for achieving appropriate and effective services for children at risk, then it is extremely important to establish professional training mechanisms to accomplish this. Individuals select careers based on their expectations of having particular roles and responsibilities in the work force that require utilising a set of skills usually acquired during their professional training. The initial training for the human service and education professions not only develops these skills but sets the tone for the professionals' expectations of their roles in the service delivery system. If the concepts and skills needed for effective co-ordination are not embraced as part of professional training in each of the disciplines, then these future professionals will not have the expectation that effecting co-ordination is part of their responsibilities.

Pre-service training, particularly, has a strong influence on the belief systems of the professionals trained. If values of respecting families and culture and collaborating with other professionals in the decision-making process are not a part of the initial training of professionals, it is difficult to establish these at a later time. The attitudes professionals hold towards service co-ordination are strongly influenced by training experiences.

The impact of professional skills on service integration

One of the established roles of training is the preparation of individuals to perform specific functions in their jobs. In this case, it is essential that professionals be trained in specific functions that they can perform to support appropriately co-ordinating services for the family. There are related attitudes, knowledge, and skills that can be incorporated in professional training such as learning how to work in teams, understanding the roles of other professionals, and learning how to co-ordinate services for families. Pre-service training of the various professionals including teachers, social workers, physicians and nurses often lacks mechanisms for including this in the various curricula.

Training is our most important vehicle for creating a work force that is compatible with the goals of integrated and co-ordinated services for children at risk and their families. In all the professions, there is a need for curriculum development as well as formal and informal training opportunities at the pre-service and in service level to attain the goals of service co-ordination for these children and their families.

Specific elements in training professionals for service integration

At the heart of training professionals to serve children and youth at risk and their families is establishing a framework that incorporates developmentally based, family-centred, culturally respectful principles of care and that values a co-ordinated system of services. Such a framework includes training at several levels: awareness and orientation to concepts, knowledge and skill development, and skill application and transfer. There is a definable content, as noted above, that can form a concrete curriculum applicable to all the disciplines involved with children and youth at risk and their families. Whether there are specific training implications for educators as opposed to health and social service professionals is a further issue that can be addressed. At minimum, key curriculum and training elements for implementing a co-ordinated system of services for children and youth at risk include the following:

- knowledge of concepts of service integration at all levels (policy, programme, and practice);

- knowledge of the roles of the various disciplines who serve children and youth at risk;

- preparation for functioning as an effective team member (at the service as well as the planning level); and

- preparation for co-ordinating services.

Knowledge of service integration (policy, programme and practice level)

To develop an understanding of service integration at policy, programme and practice levels includes an appreciation that diversity exists among families with children at risk as well as among the programmes and agencies who serve them. Within the service system, there can be differences in mission, scope, eligibility, and expertise of personnel. Understanding the implications of this at all level, policy, programmes and practice is basic to learning about service integration.

How agencies set goals, share information, plan joint programmes, and develop common procedures and policies are important areas for training. Effective service integration models can be studied. This includes understanding policies at both the national and local level that support co-ordination, the role key individuals and groups play, and the specific programmatic methodologies utilised. Appreciating the relevance of domain similarity, task specialisation, and inter-unit communication in these models is another important element of training. The difficulties that arise in relating to achieving co-ordinated or joint efforts, including issues of confidentiality, incompatible data sets, and regulatory policies, can also be examined.

Knowledge of the role of the disciplines serving children and youth at risk

At the programme planning and service level, developing an understanding of the vital roles of the various disciplines which serve children and youth at risk and their families is critical. Training should address both the unique contributions of each of the disciplines, in particular, education, social work, medicine, and nursing, and the overlapping capabilities. In training, identifying one's own discipline's role in the prevention and intervention process and using other disciplines by appropriate referral are necessary skills to be developed.

Preparation for team memberships

Preparation for team membership has implications at both the planning and service level. Whether we are speaking about a team of professionals who are working towards agreeing on a common service plan for a child at risk and his or her family or about a group of policy or program planners from various agencies who are working towards agreeing on a common action plan for developing and implementing services, the basic skills of effective team membership apply. The goal in training is to prepare individuals to function as part of a group of professionals who co-operate in decision-making and implementing the decisions made.

Building cohesion, commitment, and respect in such groups or teams form the underlying elements of the training needed. This training requires a knowledge of how groups work on their task and an understanding of the interrelationships among group members. Co-operation, consensus building, and conflict resolution are key skills. There are existing models that can be incorporated in training for developing theses skills. Such models train in facilitating communication, problem solving, and implementation of decisions. Through these models, skills can be developed for sharing information, active listening, engaging in group problem solving, and giving and receiving feedback. Behaviours that impede group work such as competition, interpersonal conflicts; lack of leadership, changing group membership; lack of commitment, unilateral decision-making, and territoriality (unwillingness to acknowledge the roles and responsibilities of others) can be understood. Importantly, preparation for leadership of such teams is included as well.

Preparation for co-ordinating services

Family level

Learning how to co-ordinate services for children and youth at risk and their families, often called "case management", begins with recognising that families are partners in this process. For this reason the term, "case management", in some localities; is dropping out of use. This change in name implies a change in philosophy as well. A family-centred approach to co-ordination implies that families are no longer "managed" but, rather, participate in decisions and, as needed, are assisted by professionals with accessing and co-ordinating services. The professional's role in co-ordination of services in this context builds on family strengths and acknowledges family preferences. It may change as the needs of the family change.

Preparation for a role in service co-ordination is not limited to any single discipline. All professionals working with children and youth at risk can develop skills in assisting families to identify their concerns, priorities, and resources and learn to co-ordinate the services needed. Based on the particular circumstances, different professionals may be called upon to play this role to a greater or lesser extent.

Service co-ordinators need to know about the assessment and evaluation possibilities of the various disciplines (their purpose, cultural appropriateness, etc.), resources available, how to co-ordinate resources, and how to deal with transitions, such as from school to work. Preparation for working with families to co-ordinate their services must include learning how to negotiate the infrastructure of services available for children and youth at risk and their families. Models exist that demonstrate how services can be co-ordinated, monitored, and evaluated.

Organisational level

Training efforts for multi-disciplinary co-ordination should address issues arising at management levels in order for children, youth, and families to be served holistically, flexibly, and sensitively by direct service workers. Supervisory styles, methods of assigning workloads, methods of pooling funds, developing management information systems, and confidentiality issues are a few examples of topics that could be addressed in multi-disciplinary and multi-agency training for managers to enhance their ability to support and encourage service integration.

Community level

In the community, agencies, programs, and individual service providers must work together to develop and implement a co-ordinated system of services for children at risk and their families. To achieve this, typically, key groups will come together to share information, determine needs, and plan services.

Training support to these individuals to establish commitment, to define goals, and to implement appropriate co-ordination strategies, often, is an effective mechanism to further the goal of service integration.

Settings and strategies for training professionals in service integration

There are multiple strategies for training professionals to function in an integrated service delivery system for children and youth at risk and their families. Some of these approaches involve teaching within individual disciplines and others involve joint training possibilities; some are at the pre-service level and others, at the in-service level, some are didactic and, importantly, some should be experiential. The general teaching elements described above form the basis for such training.

Pre-service training

Perhaps the single most important issue at the pre-service level is getting disciplines to recognise the need for establishing a curriculum in service co-ordination. But this alone does not guarantee inclusion of this curriculum in overall training programs because there are so many competing demands. Until this is accomplished in all the disciplines serving children and youth at risk and their families -- education, social work, medicine, and nursing -- we will not have an adequately trained work force to achieve a co-ordinated service delivery system.

At the pre-service level, such a curriculum can evolve through didactic teaching and practical experiences. This implies faculty preparation to teach the essential content areas and the participation of other disciplines and families in this teaching. In particular, successful existing models for such training incorporate joint training opportunities across disciplines and interdisciplinary training modules.

To develop joint training requires leadership and administrative support within the higher educational system. For example, in teacher training and educational administration programs, this involves reaching beyond the professional boundaries of Schools of Education and taking leadership at administrative levels to bring together other professional training programs in social work, medicine, and nursing in order to explore common training goals and develop joint activities. This implies an identified commitment at the highest levels of administration within each of the higher education entities, which is sometimes difficult to achieve.

In-service training

There are at least two important reasons to establish in-service training opportunities related to service co-ordination. First of all, there is a timeliness issue for service systems, the need to rapidly develop a capacity for co-ordinated service delivery through utilising the existing work force. To achieve this, professionals in the system must develop new attitudes as well as expanded knowledge and skills in service co-ordination. A second, equally compelling reason for in-service education is that service systems for children and youth at risk are constantly evolving. Delivery must stay abreast of these changes as well as their implications for co-ordination.

In-service training can be either formal or informal. It can take the form of on-site in-service opportunities, professional association conferences and workshops, or multi-disciplinary conferences and workshops. The specific elements for training may be addressed systematically or in parts. For those professionals who have neither an appreciation of the importance of service co-ordination nor the skills to achieve it, a well-organised continuing education experience may be very useful. The leadership issue of how to initiate such opportunities remains a question.

A further strategy for assuring training in service co-ordination, perhaps in a more generic sense than specifically for children and youth at risk, is to include this content area as a certification requirement or as an area in professional licensing examinations as appropriate to each discipline. For example, teacher certification could require evidence of training in service co-ordination or medical licensing examinations could include questions in this area if it were viewed as a priority. These types of requirements are concrete relocations of how successful we have been in effecting change in training programs to achieve service co-ordination.

What is the status of training for service integration in OECD Member countries?

In order to understand the status of training for service integration (co-ordination) in the various professions in OECD Member countries, CERI is proposing to invite Member countries to gather information about their current training capabilities for service co-ordination in education, social work, medicine, and nursing and about the outcomes of such training. Jointly, the participating countries and CERI will establish a process to identify the relevant information to be gathered and the methodology to accomplish this. Information from the participating countries will form country reports to be synthesised into a common report and presented to all OECD members.

INNOVATIVE STRATEGIES TO PROVIDE INTEGRATED CHILDREN'S SERVICES: GOING TO SCALE IN ONTARIO, CANADA

by

John H. Lewko, Laurentian University
Michael Shea, Useful Research & Consulting, Inc.
Richard Volpe, University of Toronto
Cynthia Lees, MCSS North Bay Dan Salhani, University of Regina

Introduction

Faced with sometimes drastic restructuring of economies, human services delivery systems are undergoing dramatic changes throughout the world. These changes along with concerted efforts to reduce fragmentation and correct inequities have made service integration an important area for research. Although the concept of inter-professional teamwork has enjoyed widespread acceptance in the field of child abuse, its implication as part of integrated service delivery remains largely unexplored. This is especially true for understanding the unique problems of providing services for children in remote and inaccessible areas. Mobilising inter-professional resources may be an effective way of organising crucial services and reaching the hard to reach with skilled help and support that is satisfying to both practitioners and clients. Unfortunately, many of the most promising programmatic experiments have been short lived and few have been taken to scale.

The aim of this paper is to provide a review of a unique full scale children's services integration initiative that has been implemented and comprehensively evaluated. Located in Ontario's northern regions, it is one of the world's few large scale children's service integration initiatives. The story that contains the yield of this undertaking is organised along the story line provided by the CIPP framework that covers context, input, process and product. This framework helps to describe the strategies associated with the initiative by covering the context, background and important surrounding features. The commitment of financial resources and the choice of strategies employed in the delivery of services are captured under the heading Input. "Process" refers to the way implementation is carried out in terms of day to day operations. Finally, "Product" examines the actual practices associated with service delivery (Volpe, 1996). Effective strategies are identified in these four areas in terms of pre-implementation actions; requisite organisational structure; service delivery; and evaluation that, from our experience, were instrumental in the success of ISNC.

Context

The pattern of the development of social and health services for the children of the Province of Ontario has been one of separately acting ministries who have functioned in relative isolation from one. A further division has been experienced between the direct provision of institutional care by government employees and the provision of "softer" services such as counselling by agencies and staff from the voluntary and transfer payment agency sectors.

Although some attempts have been made to rationalise the system (*i.e.* such as the transfer of the responsibility for children's mental health services to the Ministry of Community and Social Services from the Ministry of Health), the traditional divisions of responsibility among ministries persisted until as late as 1988 in most of Northern Ontario and is only now being addressed in the rest of Ontario. With a number of notable exceptions, the current state of affairs is as follows: the Ministry of Community and Social Services (MCSS) is responsible for the provision of all child protection services, most children's mental health services to the developmentally handicapped and most services to young offenders; the Ministry of Health (MOH) is responsible for the provision of institutionally-based health services for children (and adults), community-based physical rehabilitation services and public health services; and, the Ministry of Education and Training (MET) is responsible for the provision of all basic education and most special education services for children.

MCSS has a history of creating and funding distinct streams of childrens' services (*i.e.* Childrens' Aid Societies, Children Mental Health Centres, associations and programs for developmentally disabled persons and programs and services for young offenders). Similarly, MOH has created and funded separate institutional and community-based sectors of health care. MET, for its part, has directly delivered some special education services itself but has funded the majority of services in this area through relatively autonomous and separately acting school boards. In short, the system of childrens' services in the Province has been quite distant from the concept of "service integration".

The roots of the current Integrated Services for Northern Children (ISNC) program are imbedded in the policy known as "Northern Initiatives for Children with Special Needs". The policy created the new funding for the current ISNC program and was a direct descendent of earlier work in a number of areas including most directly, the work of the inter-ministerial Northern Assessment Task Force (NATF) between 1980 and 1987.

Historically, Northern Ontario has suffered from a lack of services for children with this situation being particularly acute in the rural/remote areas of the region. Many services which the children of large urban settings such as Toronto or Ottawa take for granted are simply unavailable or available only by travelling hundreds of kilometres. The children suffering the most from this unfortunate situation are those who experience a combination of difficulties which cut across the traditional divisions of responsibility among the various government agencies and their transfer payment agencies (*i.e.* a child who needs both special education and physical rehabilitation services).

With the goal being to consolidate children's services as well as to improve the co-ordination across program streams, MCSS underwent a reorganisation in 1978. Also around this time, the Ministry of Education (MED) presented a proposal for the provision of assessment and psychological services in Northern Ontario. This proposal apparently was a major factor in causing the (Ontario) Deputy Ministers' Ad Hoc Committee on Childrens' Services to direct MCSS and MED to prepare a long term strategic plan for the provision of assessment services for the children of Northern Ontario. A committee was formed, comprised of senior ministry managers from the regional level in Northern Ontario, and was charged with the responsibility of developing long range strategies. This new committee quickly appointed a number of ministry staff to the "Northern Assessment Task Force".

The basic premises upon which the NATF was based included a desire to maximise inter-ministerial co-ordination and inter-agency and inter-professional co-operation at the level of the individual case.

Although the NATF was initially comprised of only MCSS and MED staff, it was quickly recognised that involvement from the Ministry of Health was required and MOH staff members were added to the group. The first concrete result of the inter-ministerial efforts of the NATF was the creation of an inter-ministerial protocol which clearly specified each ministry's responsibilities with regard to assessment services for children and which set the stage for later developments.

The Northern Assessment Task Force operated from 1980 to 1987, accomplishing a number of important tasks including a survey of Northern Ontario-based childrens' services providers and a pilot test of a co-ordinated assessment program in the Temiskaming District. The work of NATF formed much of the basis of the Cabinet Submissions and MB20 (the formal request for funding from the Management Board of Ontario) which eventually lead to the creation and approval of the Northern Initiatives (policy) Project in early 1988. A major component of the new policy called for the creation of a system of integrated services (*i.e.* assessments, interventions and consultations in the areas of childrens' mental health, physical rehabilitation and special education) for children who resided in the rural/remote areas of Northern Ontario. This new program was called the Integrated Services for Northern Children (ISNC) program.

The geographic expanse for which the ISNC program was responsible includes over one million square kilometres, representing almost 90 per cent of Ontario's land mass. Geography and population distribution made the delivery of professional services a formidable task. Only 10 per cent (approx. 850 000) of Ontario's population resides in Northern Ontario, and 400 000 of these were sparsely distributed among four hundred rural/remote communities which range in size from a few hundred to a few thousand residents. Adding to the challenge for service delivery is the climate of Northern Ontario which is often extremely harsh in winter, creating frequent travel disruptions due to snowfalls, blizzards and (- 40° C) temperatures.

Input

Efforts required to support the implementation of the inter-ministerially sponsored ISNC program commenced in mid 1988 and the first children from rural/remote Northern Ontario were referred to the program in late 1989. The scale of the ISNC initiative called for innovative approaches in terms of organisational structures, service delivery elements and quality control. From the outset, ISNC was more than a program of services targeted to a particular client group. It was instead similar to the launching of a national or state policy. And its scope called for the implementers to step away from traditional thinking and practice regarding the delivery of services to children and their families.

Implementation issues

A number of issues impacted on the implementation of the new Integrated Services for Northern Children (ISNC) program which included: creation and empowerment of new inter-ministerial management structures; specification of the requirement that program implementation and operation be formally evaluated; allocation of new financial resources to the program; a decision to fund each of the six sites equally despite major differences in rural/remote population sizes; an initial decision as to which groups of organisations would be invited to participate in the new program; the specification that the new program would serve rural/remote areas only; and, the advancement of a policy which mandated inter-ministerial co-ordination and integration in a context where intra-ministerial integration lagged significantly behind.

In preparing the "field" to implement the new ISNC program, it was recognised by senior government managers that the service delivery and management processes and structures required by the ISNC program represented "a new way of doing business" for the majority of program participants. Members of Ontario's Management Board, aware of past difficulties in implementing new human service policy directions as intended, specifically tied a program requiring monitoring and evaluation, of funding made available through the new Northern Initiatives policy. To facilitate this, the Northern Initiatives policy specified, in considerable detail, the inter-ministerial management structures which were to be created and/or empowered to oversee the implementation and evaluation of the new policy.

Two of the required management structures have played critical roles in ensuring that the ISNC policy/program was implemented as intended: a senior management group and a team of co-ordinators. The policy called for the empowerment of a Northern Ontario, regional-level inter-ministerial management committee that was comprised of senior government managers from the four ministries formally involved with the project. The management committee was responsible for developing the policies that would foster inter-ministry co-operation and co-ordination in program implementation and also provided direction to the evaluation of the policy/program.

The second management structure consisted of a team of ministry-based co-ordinators, including three area co-ordinators assigned to one of the three geographic areas (North-East; North-Central, North-West) and a regional co-ordinator that managed the group. The co-ordinators were the formal mechanism for implementing the policies that were generated by the senior management group, and emerged as one of the most vital mechanisms in the success of the program.

The original ISNC policy also called for the equal resourcing of six separate sites (two sites per geographic area noted above) despite the differences in the rural/remote populations of the sites. For example, the 1991 Canadian census indicates that the rural/remote populations of the six ISNC program sites ranged from a low of 37 000 people in one site to a high of 120 000 in another (with a mean of 67 700 per site). As a result of site-based evaluation results, this policy is now under review by the ISNC management system.

The fact that substantial new resources were made available to implement the ISNC program provided the "carrot" to accompany the potential "stick" function played by the evaluation requirements. The ISNC program carried with it approximately nine million Canadian dollars in new, annualised funding. It was therefore, quite attractive to the MCSS and MOH transfer payment agencies who were invited to participate. This move however, proved to be a two-edged sword, as some participating agencies merely wanted the new resources and made repeated attempts to divert these new resources to unintended uses. Fortunately, most of the participating agencies did utilised the resources as intended, to create the new service delivery model specified by the ISNC policy.

Initially, the sponsoring ministries chose to invite groups of their transfer payment agencies to participate in the new program. For example, MCSS chose to invite all 12 of its Northern-Ontario based, childrens mental health centres to participate in the program. Similarly, MOH chose to invite all four of its Northern-Ontario based, childrens' treatment centres to participate in the program. These decisions failed to recognise that substantial intra-group variability existed within both groups with regard to organisational maturity, quality of leadership and commitment to implement the program as intended. Subsequent difficulties in implementation have caused both ministries to seriously rethink these initial decisions, to drop a sponsoring agency from within each group and to replace the original sponsoring agencies with new agencies from outside of these groups. In retrospect, program implementers have observed that a more appropriate strategy for the selection of sponsoring agencies might have been to "tender" the new program within each site and to select agencies for participation based upon factors other than membership in a particular group of agencies.

An additional pre-implementation policy decision has had significant impact on the multi-site implementation of the new ISNC program: restricting the new program's target population to children from rural/remote areas, thereby excluding the five major population centres of the region of Northern Ontario. The developers of the new policy/program judged the urban centres of Northern Ontario to be substantially better resourced in terms of childrens' services than the rural/remote parts of the region. As a result, they created the requirement that all ISNC program resources be targeted to rural/remote children only. This decision was lauded by many and criticised by some. According to program implementers it assisted in creating a situation in which the most needy clients were assured of receiving services and successfully guarded against a historical trend for the urban centres of Northern Ontario to absorb available service capacity. On the other hand, the decision lead to a number of conflicts within organisations which serviced both urban and rural areas, causing some amount of uneven organisational behaviour in which an organisation integrated its efforts with others for some of its clients but not for others.

One final issue which has significantly affected the implementation of the ISNC program is the fact that while the new policy and program has lead to significant advances in inter-ministerial co-ordination and integration of service delivery with respect to multiple problem children and their families and the management of service integration, two of the major sponsoring ministries (MCSS and MOH) have been challenged in their abilities to achieve wider intra-ministerial integration. For example, MCSS funds and manages a number of quite separate service streams including children's mental health, child protection, young offender services and services for individuals with developmental delays. Each stream is characterised by separately mandated and administered agencies with separate boards of directors, administrations, client intake procedures, target groups and widely varying program evaluation abilities. MCSS is now in the early stages of implementing a comprehensive integration policy "Making Services Work for People" that is focused on achieving wider integration within its ministry (MCSS, 1997). Other joint initiatives are underway, including the Development of a Speech and Language Services System for Pre-school Children (MOH, MCSS, MET) and Healthy Babies Healthy Children Program (MOH, MCSS). Perhaps most important, the Province has established a separate portfolio with an Assistant Deputy Minister, Office of Integrated Services for Children. The intent of this office is to integrate childrens' services of the three ministries (MOH, MCSS, MET) which, coincidentally represent the participating ministries in the ISNC policy experiment.

Pre-implementation strategies

Over the years there has been a growing recognition that programs are not always implemented as originally intended by policy makers (Palumbo and Calista, 1990; Pressman and Wildavsky, 1986; Weatherly, 1979). In fact, there is often significant misalignment across various levels of an organisation which results in program objectives being interpreted differently with consequent variations in action. In the present context, considerable attention had been given to understanding organisational development and change as a lead in to implementation. Both the extant literature and our own experiences with the dynamics of systems and people underscored the need to spend time at the front end of the project in deciphering the policy and mobilising the various stakeholders in the system who would have to 'own' the program for it to be successful. Ignoring the pre-implementation phase increases the likelihood that unwanted features which limit effectiveness will be built in to the program. Five pre-implementation practices from the ISNC project are particularly noteworthy for advancing service integration: establishing a dedicated implementation team; dissecting and translating the policy; developing a communication strategy for moving the policy into the field; assessing the readiness to integrate; establishing a procedure for formal sign-off of key program elements.

The base policy which drives an integration project should provide sufficient resources to establish a dedicated implementation team that is responsible for transforming the policy into action and engaging the key stakeholders in a strategic planning process that leads to field commitment and ownership of the project. In the ISNC project, an Implementation Planning Process was developed by a small team of personnel who were assigned exclusively to the integration initiative. This team was given the requisite authority from senior levels to engage various sub-groups in discussions regarding the scope of the policy as well as the specifics of program parameters, proposed organisational structure and management mechanisms and the role of monitoring/evaluation. The team was charged with 'making the policy come alive' by developing the policy in operational terms.

The Implementation Team functioned as a critical bridge between the two upper levels of management and the six field sites. The ISNC experience is that the task of moving stakeholders toward the goal of services integration is a delicate balance between leadership and management.

The team played a critical role in informing senior management of the way in which the policy was being interpreted and received. Team meetings were deliberately structured to make decisions regarding specific implementation activities that could be used with groups across sites, to identify emerging points of resistance and to monitor the communication strategy for its consistency. The team also served as a critical base of support for those moments when a team member was experiencing significant resistance to change.

It is important that implementers be identified early in the process and that their role and responsibilities be clearly defined so that they are dedicated to the project. Implementation cannot be done part-time because this creates conflicts in commitment similar to the conflicts that the integrating organisations will experience when asked to do something different.

Selection of individuals to be part of an implementation team can be guided by the following skills and attributes: ability to analyse systems both operationally and politically; ability to deal with conflict; good communication and mediation skills; team building and team playing; highly organised; high energy; ability to dissociate self from parent organisation because they are the "inter-ministerial" or "interdisciplinary" mind sets.

Policies that are large in scope typically provide a general framework for action which is then further interpreted or translated at various levels of the system. Given the complexities inherent in a multi-ministry, multi-agency, multi-site initiative, it was critical that interpretations of the policy be in line with its intent. The implementation team was given the authority to interpret and specify operational details of the policy in terms of the program parameters (*i.e.* location of case managers; choice of participating agencies; creating staff job descriptions), clarify the proposed management structure including Terms of Reference for the Inter-Ministerial Management Committee, create regional and site-level structures (*i.e.* arranging for transfer of authority between organisations), and make operational the interdisciplinary service delivery model. A Program Analyst took the lead in dissecting the policy and identifying areas that were then addressed by the Implementation Team.

Through this process, non-negotiable parameters and mechanisms (*i.e.* facets of the policy that could not be altered) were clarified and detailed and then put forward to the senior management levels for approval as policy prior to implementation. Upon approval, these non-negotiables became a key component of the discussions as the team members interacted with agencies and individuals.

If you want people to embrace a different way of doing things, it is critical that they understand very clearly what is being asked of them. The stakeholders who were expected to work together had only their current service delivery experiences to draw upon. Consequently, their mind set would have to be expanded to include the vision of integrated services that was embedded in the policy. In order to frame a vision statement, it was necessary to develop a communications strategy that included an initial detailed, clear and simple description of the integration model and how it was intended to work. This description captured the underlying principles of the innovative approach that did not exist at the time in the various sites. Therefore, the output of the policy analysis identified areas that needed to be introduced and explained to stakeholders at the various organisational levels. It also assisted in the identification of entry points to the field.

Contacts were deliberately planned and communication content and strategies worked out in advance to ensure that the same sets of messages were being communicated regularly and repeatedly across all sites and stakeholders. Repeated contacts were used to establish informal relationships and communication patterns. During these contacts, careful attention was paid to exploring the impact of prior contacts and clarifying or re-aligning as necessary. The target was to build sets of relationships within and between the various organisational levels and to establish a common vision and language through which the program could be described and discussed as implementation proceeded.

As the communication strategy unfolded across the six ISNC sites, it became evident that readiness to integrate varied both within and between communities. Three types of communities can be identified: those willing to try and ready to go; those needing assistance to become ready; those that are inflexible and cannot adapt to required changes. Implementers must determine the "readiness" of the community-based organisations, and professionals and individuals must experiment with new service delivery relations and be prepared to work in different ways with those at different levels of readiness. Some indicators of readiness are:

— the extent to which co-operative service relations already exist (*i.e.* the level of development of these relations and their effectiveness);

— the level of organisational maturity of the potential sponsoring organisations and their executive or management staff;

— the extent that a history of positive relations exists among the potential program sponsors;

— the level of development of community boards or ministry management structures;

— the capacity for the organisations and staff to handle change in terms of resources, time, energy, maturity and commitment.

One effective tool for exploring the readiness of a community or catchment area is to engage key stakeholders in a mapping exercise that generates a picture of the service flow as currently experienced by a consumer/customer. This pictorial representation can then be used to ask key questions that could impact on implementation. How is the service flow currently operating? What are the 'lines of responsibility' for service delivery? What is the nature of the formal and informal power structures? What is the history of inter-organisational and interpersonal relations among key players? How will the non-negotiables of the policy affect the site? How must the service flow in the site be altered to accommodate the non-negotiable parameters? It is important to address readiness and be prepared to delay implementation in some communities since they will absorb progressively more resources, particularly in the form of time of the implementation team and the management committees.

The authority to implement must be clear in the eyes of the participants. Written documentation as an instance of formal signing-off on the key program parameters and organisational structures will communicate clearly to the various stakeholders that the initiative is actively supported at the highest senior levels. In the case of ISNC, the Deputy Ministers of the four participating ministries gave formal, visible authority to the implementation team that could be used when unwanted variation in implementation had to be addressed. For example, at the agency level it was critical that the disbursement of ISNC funds be monitored, particularly during the early phase, to ensure that existing programs did not begin to consume the targeted operating dollars. Sign-off provided the co-ordinators with the tools to undertake this monitoring and ensure that ISNC funds were directed solely to ISNC activities.

In dealing with government ministries and bureaucracies, it was necessary to contain the desire to change the model at the local level. Formal authority enabled ISNC management to ensure that the intended model was the one acted upon. For example, dedicated staff and single point of entry were attractive targets for local modification. In some sites, these efforts had to be addressed repeatedly.

Process

Comprehensive program evaluations of health, social service and special education programs in Ontario have been few and far between. There is no clear policy within the Ontario government which requires the evaluation of the human service programs which it funds. For example, in the 1993 report by the Auditor General of Ontario, it was reported that the Ontario Ministry of Community and Social Services' (MCSS) Child and Family Intervention program provided funds to approximately 200 not-for-profit agencies, including 85 children's mental health centres which provided a wide variety of services to children and their families. The auditor observed, that as of 1991/92, the ministry lacked procedures to measure the effectiveness of agency-based treatment programs for children and that the ministry could not be fully assured that its transfer payment agencies were providing adequate or cost-effective services.

Until recently, few human service programs in Ontario had developed systems for the ongoing monitoring of program performance. Reasons for this included no requirement to do so; untested beliefs that programs are performing well; and, the lack of internal program evaluation expertise. In the instances when the funding ministries have required evaluations of individual programs or when agencies have voluntarily evaluated their programs, the evaluations have generally been of the "one shot", time-limited variety and have occurred after the program being evaluated had been in operation for a number of years. In general, evaluation is not viewed as an essential aspect of program managers' ability to perform ongoing monitoring of program performance for the purposes of continuous quality improvement.

Learning from ISNC

In late 1987, when the Northern Initiatives Policy which eventually led to the creation of the Integrated Services for Northern Children (ISNC) program was in draft form, it was made clear by senior members of the Ontario government that the new program was to be viewed as an "experiment" in inter-ministerial co-ordination and co-operation with regard to service delivery and program management. Explicitly recognising the lack of service integration in the current system in Ontario, the new program was meant to create an innovative new system of children' services. The ISNC policy initiative had anticipated not only the current trend toward integration, but also the recent emphasis on organisational learning.

Given the significant amount of resources made available for the program and the desire on the part of the government to learn from their experiment in integrated service delivery, the new MB20 which authorised the funding for the policy/program included a clause which called for careful monitoring and evaluation to be overseen by a committee of ADMs (Assistant Deputy Ministers).

In order to ensure that the program was actually implemented as intended in the multiple sites in Northern Ontario, the ADMs Steering Committee took two important actions:

- they empowered a group of senior, Northern Ontario-based managers from the Ministries of Community and Social Services, Education, Health and Northern Development and Mines to form the "Northern Project Management Committee" to address developments on the front line of each of the three areas of the North and empowered other middle level ministry managers in each of the three areas of Northern Ontario to form area inter-ministerial management committees;

- hired, as civil servants through the Ministry of Community and Social Services (MCSS), one regional and three area co-ordinators to take on a project management function and provide staff support to the regional and three, area-level inter-ministerial management committees.

In May of 1988, the first ISNC regional co-ordinator was recruited through the Ministry of Community and Social Services (MCSS) and in late 1988 and early 1989, the three ISNC Area Co-ordinator positions were filled by MCSS. At approximately the same time, the selection of the MCSS and Ministry of Health transfer payment agencies who would serve as sponsors of the ISNC program was begun. Recruitment of line staff members commenced later in 1989 and by early 1990, the ISNC was accepting referrals in all six sites.

The ISNC regional co-ordinator took a number of initial steps which were designed to ensure that the ISNC policy would be translated accurately and that the program activities could be monitored and evaluated centrally as mandated by ISNC policy. The regional co-ordinator formed a project management team consisting of the three area co-ordinators and himself, to develop the necessary operational policy required for the ISNC program to function consistently across multiple sites and to monitor and correct any unwanted variations in site-level implementation. To assist the project management team with these tasks, the ISNC Regional Co-ordinator also arranged, through an 18 month secondment from an MCSS transfer payment agency, to add a second member to the ISNC Regional office and for this program analyst to provide support to the Co-ordinators team.

During this time period the ISNC Co-ordinators and Program Analyst performed a number of pre-evaluation activities which helped to set the stage for later developments in this area including: the development of a statement of the non-negotiable parameters (service delivery and organisation) of the ISNC program that was formally approved and signed-off by the Deputy Ministers of the four ISNC-sponsoring ministries; an identification of key program stakeholders at the provincial, regional, area and site levels (for management and service delivery); a survey of stakeholders to determine their information needs with regard to ISNC program implementation and ongoing operation; a survey of key stakeholders to identify the core sets of evaluation questions at the whole program and site levels; and performance of the initial steps required to implement a computerised management information system (MIS) to track both client and staff activity. These activities resulted in the development and deployment of the organisational structure and service delivery model from which a number of practices contributed significantly to the success of ISNC.

Launching the evaluation

As 1989 drew to a close and the first referrals began to be made to the ISNC program, the Northern Project Management Committee and the ISNC Co-ordinators jointly came to the realisation that external assistance would be required in order to formally evaluate ISNC program implementation, processes and outcomes. The rationale for the involvement of external evaluators included: the multi-ministry sponsorship of the program required that the evaluators not be located within a single sponsoring ministry so that bias could be eliminated; the recognition that the Ontario government did not possess the required evaluation expertise in Northern Ontario; the desire to play an active role in shaping the evaluation process; and, the need to have reliable and valid information on the success in implementing as intended, the program at both the whole program (regional) and site levels.

In early 1990, the ISNC Regional Co-ordinator at the direction of the NPMC negotiated a legal agreement with the Centre for Research in Human Development (CRHD), an interdisciplinary research institute of Northern Ontario's Laurentian University, to work with the NPMC in performing an evaluation of ISNC program implementation at the whole program and site levels. The formal evaluation of ISNC program implementation commenced in August of 1990 and formally ended in late 1993 with the distribution of the "Final Report on ISNC Program Implementation" (Shea and Lewko, 1993*a*).

The overall approach to the evaluation of ISNC program implementation can be classified as a hybrid "internal/external" model (Love, 1991), in which the evaluators work closely with internal program staff who have formal evaluation responsibility to ensure that they jointly produce the desired evaluation processes. Program staff participated fully in the vast majority of decisions with regard to evaluation activities and actively played roles in instrument design, data collection, reporting and utilisation. In addition, the evaluators consciously and deliberately employed a number of aspects of the "Utilisation-focused" approach to program evaluation described by Patton (1986) including the facilitation of stakeholder involvement in planning, data collection, reporting and utilisation of the evaluation.

One of the first steps taken by the evaluators was to create an ISNC Program Evaluation Advisory Committee (PEAC) whose membership included the ISNC regional co-ordinator and one elected representative from each of the six ISNC site-level management committees. Formal terms of reference for the PEAC were developed in co-operation with committee members. PEAC members were given the following responsibilities: reviewing drafts of all evaluation instruments prior to their use; providing assistance with data collection efforts in their respective sites; reviewing drafts of evaluation reports prior to their finalisation and distribution; and serving as a communication channel between the evaluators and their respective management committees. Over the course of the evaluation, based upon the leadership of two PEAC members and the ISNC regional co-ordinator, a format for tracking the utilisation of evaluation findings at the site level was developed and implemented across the program's six sites. Overall, the PEAC played an important role in ensuring that the evaluation process was understood by site level stakeholders and functioning smoothly.

One other initial step taken by the evaluators was the creation of a Technical Advisory Group (TAG) of experienced and well known program evaluators from other universities. The TAG members were chosen based upon recognised expertise in the three domains of service delivery addressed by the ISNC program (children's mental health, physical rehabilitation and special education) as well as experience with large scale, multi-site evaluations. TAG members served as consultants to the CRHD-based evaluators with regard to the technical aspects of the evaluation design, the creation and selection of data collection instruments and the analysis and interpretation of results. Through their involvement in the ISNC project, the TAG members also assumed an active role in the production of written products with regard to the ISNC program evaluation.

The research design chosen by the evaluators was the multi-site, embedded case study approach which has been described by Yin (1989). As Yin noted, case study research designs are effective when many of the evaluation questions are of the "how" or "why" type, when the focus is on contemporary events and when the evaluator has little or no control over the events being studied. In addition, case study methodology is particularly appropriate to the evaluation of program implementation due to its ability to capture complex processes and its ability to utilise both quantitative and qualitative data.

The policy requirement that identifiable elements of the ISNC program be implemented consistently across multiple sites, created a situation in which implementation efforts in a single site had to be compared to both overall program standards as well as to implementation in other sites. In evaluating the extent of implementation of success in a single site or "case", the evaluators were required to continually relate the findings with regard to the single case to the overall context in which it was embedded.

Within the context of this research design, the CRHD-based evaluators employed a multi-phase data collection process which produced six interim reports and one summative report, each of which provided both whole program and site-level findings. Findings with regard to a single case were continually related back to the overall context of the ISNC program/policy. In addition, each report presented data at two levels to ensure that both major sets of ISNC program stakeholders received useful information. Data was first presented in a form which "rolled-up" the results from across all program sites to produce regional (whole program) summaries of implementation success. In addition, the evaluators reported data at the level of the individual site and also assisted site-level stakeholders with additional analyses of site-level data to increase the amount of information available to inform decision making and policy development in each of the six, separate ISNC sites. By producing a series of shorter reports, as opposed to one or two large reports, the evaluators provided information on a periodic basis in "digestible chunks" which did not overwhelm the capacity of stakeholders to utilised the evaluation data.

Beginning with the first evaluation report, the findings were divided conceptually on the basis of whether the information pertained to either the management or the service delivery subsystems of the

ISNC program. This conceptual tool assisted managers and policy makers in determining where to intervene in correcting unwanted variations in implementation. In relating the data on the two subsystems of the ISNC program, stakeholders were reminded that the management subsystem existed to support the delivery of services.

A final critical feature of the ISNC evaluation process that warrants mention here is the amount, type and quality of contact between the evaluators and the regional-level, inter-ministerial ISNC Northern Project Management Committee (NPMC). From the commencement of the ISNC Program Evaluation Project in mid-1990, evaluation issues became standing agenda items for this senior management group. The two senior evaluators from CRHD (Shea and Lewko, 1993*b*) have attended approximately 80 per cent of the meetings of the NPMC held since early 1991. The close and continuous relationship between evaluators and policy makers/senior managers ensured that the evaluation was maximally useful to the ISNC program in terms of policy development and program implementation. When senior managers needed assistance in interpreting evaluation data or considering implications, the evaluators were there to provide it. The result of this interactive process was the development of a strong feeling of ownership of the evaluation process and the evaluation results by ISNC managers and policy makers.

Evaluation strategies

Monitoring/evaluation was included as a non-negotiable in the MB20. Had this not been the case, it is highly unlikely that the ISNC project would have attained full scale integration. Four points are worth addressing that would have a general impact on the success of evaluating other service integration initiatives: applying logic model techniques to policy analysis; instituting a management information system; monitoring during the implementation phase; integration of efforts by the stakeholders and evaluators.

Service integration is a complex, multifaceted process. Evaluators must approach any such initiative armed with their logic modelling skills. Logic modelling is a powerful analytic tool that enables the user to generate an organising framework that includes the key conditions and relationships of the initiative under consideration. As such, it can also be used very effectively in the realm of policy development, analysis and review. The core policy and its embedded program must be disaggregated through a process of generating multiple logic models. Through this exercise, an evaluator should identify the key elements of the policy and then confirm their interpretation and intent with the most senior levels of management who have the greatest vested interest in the fate of the policy. Only after doing so can an evaluator proceed to lay out an evaluation design, including measurement tools, units of analysis, data collection strategies, etc. At this point in the process, the evaluator would also be well advised to establish a Project Evaluation Advisory Committee (see Shea and Lewko, 1995 for details) to advance the stakeholder-based approach that we found to be so valuable in conducting the evaluation.

A computerised "Management Information System" was implemented at the same time as the service delivery and organisational elements of the program. The MIS was designed as an internal management tool that would provide detailed information on sets of activities across the six sites. Relational data was available in the following areas: client characteristics, client transactions (*i.e.* all service assignments by type of professional and type of service); specific amounts of time spent by each staff member on a specific case. The design of the data base also allowed for use of data at multiple levels of the program including whole program summaries, site-level data and case-specific data. Internal ownership of the MIS was fostered through data collection, entry and storage, and analysis being performed at the site-level by ISNC staff. Monitoring would have been virtually impossible had there been no MIS. Furthermore, the embedded multi-site case design that was adopted would have been greatly limited by the absence of MIS data. In our experience, some form of MIS is critical to successful service integration, at both the implementation and maintenance stages.

In the early stages of policy implementation, continuous monitoring and on-line feedback is essential in order to detect and correct unwanted variations. Old organisational behaviours are most likely to appear early in the initiative and must be spotted or behaviours will quickly regress to what was a comfort level. Such monitoring and on-line feedback will enable senior managers to exercise their authority. It also provides them with an early warning system to address issues or areas that had not been anticipated to that point. Evaluators should talk often and regularly with senior managers. We also highly recommend that you not rely on the first evaluation report to provide the necessary feedback. It may be too late. Monitoring allows determining when attention can be shifted from program implementation to impact/outcome evaluation.

In order for the program to derive the greatest benefit from an evaluation component, monitoring/evaluation must be integrated into the program, especially with the implementers and managers. An understanding must be reached with senior management so that all stakeholders can be informed about the evaluation at the earliest possible moment and also have a mechanism for direct input to the activities (such as PEAC). In our case, we negotiated the stakeholder-based approach with the Inter-ministerial Management Committee before agreeing to undertake the evaluation. Part of that understanding was the inclusion of a communication strategy that would have evaluation reports distributed to all 270 individuals involved in the initiative. A more important feature was our having direct and ongoing access to key decision making activities such as having evaluation as a standing item on the agenda of the IMC meeting, attendance at meetings of the Area Co-ordinators and access to service delivery personnel in a timely fashion.

Organisational strategies

At the onset of the program, the policy laid out a clear expectation for the establishment of an accountability structure to oversee the development, implementation and ongoing management of the program. What evolved was an inter-ministerial, inter-agency organisational structure that encompassed the four Assistant Deputy Ministers at the most senior level, to the 39 individual case managers who provide direct services to children and their families. The structure consisted of four levels: Six Site-level Inter-agency Management Committees; three Area-level Inter-ministerial Management Committees; one Regional-level Inter-ministerial Committee (IMC); one Provincial-level Inter-ministerial Assistant Deputy Ministers (ADM's) Committee. Also included was an operational team of Area Co-ordinators that served as a key link between the two senior management groups (ADM's and IMC) and the field (Area and Site Levels).

Success of the ISNC program rested on the adequacy of the organisational structure and its functioning. Since service integration is evolutionary in nature and relies very heavily on interpersonal skills of the players, resistance to change and conflict was inevitable in ISNC. It also became evident during pre-implementation that each of the participating organisations had their own deep structures which could interfere with service integration. Off-setting this was the general understanding from within the human services that collaboration between services or agencies is most easily sustained at the front-line level. What emerged was a matrix form of management where areas of decision-making were clearly delegated to various levels, while the decision process rested with the senior leadership (see Hoge and Howenstine, 1997 on participatory management and integration). Therefore, it was critical that the organisational practices took this into account. A number of key points emerged that could assist others intending to embark on an integration venture.

- *Detailed Policy Specification*: The integration policy must specify in detail the composition of the various structures, their roles and responsibilities. These specifications must be formalised in written documentation and signed off on prior to the formal launch of the program. The ISNC policy was specified in some detail through the activities of the Implementation Team and the management structures were able to compel compliance with program policies and to enable appropriate actions or decisions to be taken when non-compliance was identified.

- *Centralised Controls:* A formalised structure is essential and lines of authority must be clear. While simple structures are favoured, they must be vested with strong central control, especially in a multi-site situation.

- *Integrated Management Committees:* Joint management committees which include representatives of the key integrating organisations are critical to maintaining service integration. These committees must have clear terms of reference clear authority and open lines of communication to the central decision making authority within their organisations, stable membership with strong leadership from both within and above, members of equal power and status, and clear task assignments with specified time frames. The ISNC policy specifications reflected these points for committees at each of the four levels. Joint membership reinforced the sense of ownership of the program and provided the key ingredient for sustaining the initiative.

- *Co-ordinator's Role*: A co-ordinator role is essential for achieving and maintaining full scale integration. Within ISNC, the Area Co-ordinator role was only second in importance to the case management role in determining success. The Area Co-ordinators provided inter-ministerial co-ordination and facilitated the accountability mechanisms between the program, the sponsoring transfer payment agencies and the senior inter-ministerial management committees (ADM's & IMC). As employees who were fully dedicated to the program, they were able to perform inter-ministerial functions that could not have been performed by employees of a single ministry/organisation. Based on our experience, key Area Co-ordinator functions should include: serving as the champion of managements' vision of the program at the operational level; negotiating and signing legal agreements with sponsoring agencies; developing the main policies and procedures material; facilitating the flow of communication throughout the levels; ensuring that the joint committees develop and maintain their essential characteristics; providing staff support to the joint committees; conflict management, particularly at the operational level; providing orientation/training to new members of the management system.

Product

The service delivery model in the ISNC program is innovative insofar as it crosses the traditional service responsibilities of many agencies, ministries and professional disciplines. Multi-disciplinary teams of professionals work together on a collaborative basis to serve the "whole child". Parents experience a "one stop shopping/single point of access" for children's services. The inter-agency and inter-ministerial co-operation and co-ordination resulted in the pooling of agencies' resources without requiring the full scale integration of many community agencies into a single mega-agency. ISNC can be viewed as a consortium or 'umbrella organisation' along the lines of that described by Hoge and Howenstine (1997).

The groupings of staff that work in the program include program managers, case managers, paraprofessionals and resource group members (psychiatrists, psychologists, psychometrists, speech pathologists, physiotherapists, occupational therapists, teacher diagnosticians). These team members collaborate to provide case co-ordination/case management, assessments, treatment planning, consultation to other agencies and parents and intervention services for children with multiple needs.

The key elements of the ISNC service delivery model include: a single entry-point for clients through rural/remote based case managers; case management with all cases to facilitate the delivery of integrated packages of care; inter-disciplinary resource teams who provide assessment, intervention, consultation, in-service training and supervision of paraprofessionals; travel to rural/remote communities by resource teams and paraprofessionals to provide services; provision of intervention services by paraprofessionals, collateral agencies and families. Over the course of implementation, a number of service delivery practices were identified as crucial for the success that ISNC has realised. These practices include case management, interdisciplinary resource teams and paraprofessional intervention.

Case management has emerged as the core element for integrated services delivery in ISNC. Given the rural focus of the program and its targeting of multi-problem children and their families, it was critical to establish and maintain effective relationships between the professionals of the Resource Group and the more local, community-based resources. ISNC case managers were based in these rural communities and had their offices in or very near to their home community. They served as integrators of service by being the central figure at the interface between the client (and their primary caregivers) and the service delivery system (resource group; collateral agencies; informal care sector). Case managers performed six core functions: intake (they are the single point of access to service); assessment; planning; intervention (client and community based); monitoring; and discharge. A number of steps were taken to ensure that case managers were able to function as intended.

- The case managers were totally dedicated to their ISNC roles and responsibilities. Some sponsoring agencies and government civil servants wanted to use the case managers primarily to do the work of the agency and not the ISNC program. Pressure was often exerted towards diverting and changing the role to be more in line with normal agency business.

- The ISNC Program Managers were delegated the authority and responsibility for managing the case managers by the Site-Level Management Committee. This ensured that the individual agencies did not control the time and functions of the Case Manager.

- The job descriptions of the case managers were included in the legal agreements signed by the sponsoring agency and the ministry.

- The activities of the case managers were closely monitored by the respective Area Co-ordinators, the other non-sponsoring agencies on the Site-Level Management Committee and through detailed activity logs entered into the Management Information System.

- The agency sponsoring a Case Manager was held directly responsible if the activities of the Case Manager were not fully dedicated to ISNC.

- As the single source for the integrated service in the target communities, the case managers were very important to the children's parents and other community professionals, police, physicians, nurses, teachers, social workers and religious leaders. These groups also ensured that their Case Manager was able to fulfil the role which he or she was contracted to play in the ISNC service delivery process.

Based on our experience, full scale integration would have been difficult to achieve had the community-based case managers not been part of the model. As O'Connor (1988) and others have observed, the interactions that revolve around the case management process represent the "fuel" which powers high quality service.

Properly structured and managed interdisciplinary teams were essential to ISNC service integration. The challenge of multi-problem children and remoteness from central services required that the most comprehensive spectrum of services be assembled as quickly as possible. A team-based approach where key relevant sources of expertise could be obtained simultaneously added to the development and delivery of comprehensive packages of care. However, such team work was not without its problems, not the least of which were the differences of opinion and conflicts that are frequently observed between human services professionals.

The integration of professionals from different organisations into interdisciplinary teams was meant to begin reducing the undesirable effects of professional boundaries while maintaining the strengths of professional specialisation. Some professionals were very excited by the prospect of sharing the burdens of professional work with other colleagues. In other cases, professionals took issue with each other about professional jurisdiction, professional competence, comparative salaries, team leadership.

Shared experiences and mutual respect are two cornerstones of relationship building. Team members came into the program with strong uni-disciplinary experiences and little if any interdisciplinary contacts of a professional nature. To encourage team building, a number of strategies were adopted, perhaps the most powerful of which emerged as a non-negotiable parameter of the model co-location. Wherever possible, professionals from the different agencies were located in one place thereby ensuring greater interaction. A second strategy was to assign the role of team leader to the Program Manager, thereby eliminating (at least at a formal level) the inevitable conflict that arises between the various human services professionals. The third strategy focused on actual skill-based areas such as assessments, consultations and interventions. Interdisciplinary team members were expected to collaborate and integrate their knowledge and expertise in these areas. This was further reinforced through case conferencing that resulted in the development of an Integrated Treatment Plan. Through repeated encounters, team members came to appreciate that co-ordination and collaboration was in the best interests of the child and family.

Given the itinerant nature of the team of professionals and the level of available resources, it quickly became obvious to ISNC professionals that the opportunities for extensive intervention services were limited. While assessment and treatment planning could be provided to large numbers of children, the Resource Teams were too small in size and the geography to large in scale for interventions to be delivered as needed. In order to provide consistent and accessible treatment services to children located in rural and remote areas of the North, a method was devised to extend the intervention capacity of the Resource Team through paraprofessionals.

The ISNC Paraprofessional Model provides intensive direct services to multi-problem children through paraprofessionals who are trained and supervised by the ISNC Speech and Language Pathologists, Occupational Therapists and Physiotherapists. The Resource Team members provide the assessment and consultation services and outline a treatment plan which is implemented by the paraprofessional. The paraprofessionals are hired on the basis of their qualifications (diploma in a related field), experience working with children with special needs, and personal suitability. They are then trained and supervised regularly by the appropriate members of the Resource Team. The use of paraprofessionals has significantly increased the number of clients that have received intensive treatment.

Conclusion

In every organisational initiative, such as ISNC, the opportunity is presented to learn from the multitude of choices and actions that are experienced as 'the program'. Learning from dynamic environments such as ISNC is determined in large part by the capacity to observe, record and distil what appeared to work the best.

The intent of the evaluation was to examine the service integration model on which the ISNC program is based and to determine the extent to which the model had been implemented across the entire region. Therefore, of necessity, the focus of the evaluation was on the two subsystems of the ISNC program and on the way in which they evolved. In order for service integration to be successful, the program subsystems of service delivery and management/program monitoring have to function in a harmonious manner.

The significance of this project can not be understated. Successfully implementing and effectively evaluating a delivery effort in a context that reaches a large enough population with a comprehensive variety of services, overcoming and encountering a full array of jurisdictional and legal issues, and constructing a durable financial, governance, and information system that provides likely program viability is truly one of the world's few examples of going to scale with services integration. Moreover, ISNC remains a manifest model of 'true service integration" that has the potential to inform service improvement initiatives in urban or rural areas and in developed and developing countries.

REFERENCES

Boschen, K.A., Shea, M.P., Flynn, R., Lewko, J.H. and Volpe, R. (1994), "Family Satisfaction with a Rural/Remote Service Provision Program for Multi-Need Children In Ontario", Paper presented at the Canadian Evaluation Society 14th Annual Conference, May, Quebec City, Quebec.

Flynn, R.J., Volpe, R., Boschen, K.A., Lewko, J.H., Salhani, D.P. and Shea, M.P. (1993), "Issues and Choices in Evaluating Out-Reach Rehabilitation Programs", *Canadian Journal of Rehabilitation*, Vol. 6(4), pp. 266-280.

Flynn, R., Shea, M.P., Boschen, K.A., Lewko, J.H. and Volpe, R. (1994), "Experiences and Findings from an Implementation Evaluation of a Multi-Ministry, Multi-Agency and Multi-Disciplinary Children Services Program", Paper presented at the Canadian Evaluation Society 14th Annual Conference, May, Quebec City, Quebec.

Hoge, M.A. and Howenstine, R.A. (1997), "Administrative update: Organisational development strategies for integrating mental health services", *Community Mental Health Journal*, Vol. 33(3), pp. 175-187.

Integrated Services for Northern Children, North Regional Office (1989), Deputy Ministers' Policy Introduction, Appendix in the ISNC North Regional Policy and Procedures Manual, North Bay, ON.

Lewko, J.H., Shea, M.P. and Salhani, D. (1991), "Can You Ensure What Must Be Said, Is Said in a Multi-Stakeholder Evaluation?", Paper presented at the Canadian Evaluation Society 11th Annual Conference, May, Vancouver, British Columbia.

Love, A. (1991), *Internal Evaluation: Building Organisations and Program from Within,* Sage Publications, Newbury Park, CA.

Ministry of Community and Social Services (1997), *Making Services Work for People,* Queen's Printers of Ontario, Toronto.

O'Connor, G. (1988), "Case Management: System and Practice. Social Casework", *The Journal of Contemporary Social Work*, Vol. 69(2), pp. 97-106.

Ontario Management Board (1988), Northern Initiatives Project: Description and Application for Funding, Toronto, ON.

Palumbo, D.J. and Calista, D.J. (1990), *Implementation and the Policy Process: Opening Up the Black Box,* Greenwood Press, New York.

Patton, M.Q. (1986), *Utilisation-Focused Evaluation* (2nd Edition), Sage Publications, Newbury Park, CA.

Pressman, J.L. and Wildavsky, A. (1986), *Implementation,* University of California Press, Berkeley.

Salhani, D., Shea, M.P. and Lewko, J. (1994), "Issues in the Measurement of Integrated Service Delivery in Human Services", *Canadian Journal of Program Evaluation*, Vol. 9(1), pp. 1-14.

Shea, M.P. (1992), "To Boldly Go Where No One Has Gone Before: Seeking Out New Life from Program Evaluation", Paper presented at the 2nd Annual ISNC North Central Area Conference, October, Foleyet, Ontario.

Shea, M.P. and Lewko, J.H. (1993*a*), "Final Report on ISNC Program Implementation", Laurentian University, Centre for Research in Human Development, Sudbury, ON.

Shea, M.P. and Lewko, J.H. (1993*b*), "Transferring Knowledge in Order to Influence 'Small p' Policy Development: Examples from Case Studies in the Implementation of Integrated Service Delivery Systems", Paper presented at the International Evaluation, Social Science and Public their Policy Conference, June, Ottawa, Ontario.

Shea, M.P. and Lewko, J.H. (1995), "Use of a Stakeholder Advisory Group to Facilitate the Utilisation of Evaluation Results", *Canadian Journal of Program Evaluation,* Vol. 10(1), pp. 159-162.

Shea, M.P. and Salhani, D. (1992), "Using a Stakeholder-Oriented Approach to Design and Implement Management Information Systems in Human Services Organisations."

Shea, M.P., Hewitt, M. and Lees, C. (1993), "Engaging Program Stakeholders in the Utilisation of Evaluation Findings for the Purpose of Program Development: A Case Example", Paper presented at the 55th Annual Canadian Psychological Association Conference, May, Montreal, Quebec.

Shea, M.P., Boschen, K., Flynn, R., Lewko, J. H. and Volpe, R. (1994), "Facilitating Program Evaluation Utilisation in the Context of a Human Service Program Which is Sponsored by Multiple Government Ministries and Multiple Transfer Payment Agencies", Paper presented at the Canadian Evaluation Society 14th Annual Conference, May, Quebec City, Quebec.

Shea, M. P., Boschen, K., Flynn, R., Lewko, J. and Volpe, R. (1996), "Design and Measurement Considerations in Evaluating Systems of Integrated Human Service Delivery", *Evaluation Practice,* Vol. 16 (3), pp. 247-257.

Shea, M. P., Salhani, D.P., Boschen, K.A., Flynn, R. J., Lewko, J. H. and Volpe, R. (1993), "Integrated Services for Northern Children: A Network System Out-Reach Program for Children", *Canadian Journal of Rehabilitation,* Vol. 6(4), pp. 230-237.

"Advantages and Disadvantages" (1992), Paper presented at the Canadian Evaluation Society 12th Annual Conference, May, Ottawa, Ontario.

Volpe, R. (1996), "The CIPP model and the case study approach", in Evans, P. (ed.), *Integrated Services for Children and Families at Risk,*. OECD, Paris, pp. 149-152.

Volpe, R. (1998), "Ontario, Canada: Integrating services in Canada's wealthiest province", in Evans, P. (ed.), *Co-ordinating Services for Children and Youth at Risk : A World View,* OECD, Paris.

Volpe, R., Boschen, K.A., Flynn, R.J., Lewko, J.H., Salhani, D.P. and Shea, M.P. (1994), "Best Practices to Provide Integrated Services to Children in Remote Regions", Paper presented at the Tenth International Congress on Child Abuse and Neglect, September, Kuala Lumpur, Malaysia.

Weatherly, R.A. (1979), *Reforming Special Education: Policy implementation from the state level to street level,* MIT Press, Cambridge, MA.

Yin, R. K. (1989), *Case Study Research: Design and Methods* (2nd Edition), Sage Publications, Newbury Park: CA.

PART FOUR

RESEARCH AND EVALUATION OF OUTCOMES

KNOWLEDGE FROM EVALUATION RESEARCH

by

Richard Volpe, Ph.D.
Institute of Child Study, University of Toronto/OISE

Introduction

The specific challenge of the OECD Children and Youth at Risk Study was to describe, some of "the world's best efforts to integrate services" (Volpe, 1996). The more general task, however, was to provide an evaluation framework that would enable the interdisciplinary research team, diverse stakeholders, and an international dissemination audience to make sense out of the enterprise. A complication associated with this endeavour is the paradigm shift that has occurred in evaluation research (Lincoln and Gupa, 1994). This shift reflects a profound change that has taken place throughout the social sciences constituting what is valid knowledge and who are the legitimate creators of such knowledge (Polkinghorne, 1983). An increased appreciation of context in human development has contributed to the need for more holistic and naturalistic ways of studying human existence that retain the discipline and benefits of science. The aim of this paper is to examine the OECD evaluation model by exploring the question, what does it means to inform policy and practice through naturalistic evaluation research?

Evaluation research efforts without scrutiny of the relationship of research to practice becomes more a political than rational enterprise. The complex relation of interdisciplinary and interprofessional research to practice is easily glossed over, assumed to be self evident, or believed to be part of the decision-making processes (Volpe, 1983, 1990).

The particular challenge of the OECD evaluation of integrated services

Of all helping endeavours, integrated services offer special problematic features. These services are by virtue of their comprehensive and interprofessional collaborative nature, complex and elastic. These features become more problematic when dealing with the variety of cultures and practice histories that were associated with the OECD study. Stakeholders in this study dealt with the needs of citizen-clients in ways that had international implications. The world-wide audience for making sense of these social interventions involved a broad range of stakeholders including practitioners representing a number of disciplines and professional groups and a variety of policy communities.

One consequence of this complexity is that multiple perspectives need to be represented in the design and implementation of the research. For example, the languages and practice traditions of member countries have to be taken into account. An important orienting assumption of the project is that a multinational and multidisciplinary team was needed to carry out the project (Evans, 1993).

Although this orientation helps overcome many difficulties, it is also necessary in holistic evaluation research to structure the evaluation according to the various systems that impact and are impacted upon by programs. Thus, an ecological model that takes into account historical, legal, cultural, ethnic, and personal viewpoints is necessary to pull together questionnaire and interview data from the various levels of participating stakeholders.

The most common problem in evaluating services integration is dealing with the incompleteness of the integration effort. This problem is exacerbated by variable meanings as to what constitutes an integrated service. Policy makers may think of integration as a way making services more effective. Unionised front line workers may find integration a devious means of destroying solidarity and forcing the amalgamation of disparate services for the sake of efficiency. Integrated Services may involve co-location and sharing of resources. Thus, many service arrangements may share the term integration. Although no single dimension characterises integration, most programmes are attempts at system reform. They involve efforts to share power and resources, increase accessibility and effectiveness, and better address the individual needs of clients in a more holistic and seamless way. All of the above leaves the evaluation researcher with the interesting intensified challenge of figuring out just what is being studied and how it is to be characterised.

Although the largely descriptive OECD study was not explicitly designed to deal with outcomes, a focus on outcomes can help clarify the nature of the integration effort and be an important contribution to formative evaluation. More integrated services tend to have more complicated outcomes. Thus, it is important that planners and practitioners learn to reveal their rationales for organising interventions. A vital element in that rationale are the assumptions about the clients for whom integrated services are designed. Their perceived needs and conditions that give rise to these needs, reveal information about stakeholder notions of effectiveness and outcomes. Even if these perceptions are not empirically visible, they are an important means of understanding a programme's origin and the operations associated with its implementation.

Because integration can mean many things it is useful to describe programmes by capturing organisational structures, interplay of providers and clients, sharing and co-ordination efforts of practitioners, and perceived changes and benefits of associated arrangements and practices. In particular it is useful, as was done in the OECD study, to describe programmes that are considered by policy makers to be exemplary instances of their intentions. This approach can help clarify both what integration means and intends by stakeholders.

The changing face of evaluation research

The paradigm shift, noted in the introduction, has made for a changed relationship between researchers and practitioners. Applied areas have become central to the interests of mainstream fields. As a consequence, the pursuits, methods, and conceptualisations of human behaviour have broadened. This expansion of activity has helped blur discipline boundaries and made interprofessional and interdisciplinary teamwork necessary. Practitioners are increasingly becoming full team members. These "practice experts" bring with them questions and problems growing out of their practice. Consequently, increased attention is being paid to context; person environment transaction, and to reciprocal influence in human relationships.

Social scientific research increasingly stresses the transactional character of human relations and the role of social, institutional, and societal supports (Horowitz, 1989). This more complex focus has yielded some important insights that may increase the probability that evaluation research will be more useful. Two such insights into the adequacy of our notions of causality and development are important. Previously we believed in a simple relationship between cause and effect. Faith in a simple linear determinism that allowed cause to be linked to effect, *i.e.* early childhood experience determines later life chances, has been undermined (Volpe, 1988).

This change is reflected in the way the nature-nurture debate has evolved. Simple causal notions gave way to a transitional multivariate probing into the relation of heredity and environment. This variable approach eventually was replaced by current effort to non-deterministically understand the interplay between genetics and behaviour. Similarly, current conceptualisations in the study of mental functioning and neural physiological development characterise environment as the architect of the genotype. Cognitive sciences has moved from employing mechanical metaphors likening the mind to a computer to spatiotemporal conceptions of neural maps or dynamic jungle ecologies (Edelman, 1994). Just as the insertion of self in the stimulus-response paradigm foiled behaviourism, the inclusion of the perspective and appraisal of human actors has necessitated recognition of experiential co-requisites (Novick and Volpe, 1990).

Co-requisites are the multidimensional features of experience that, when translated into concepts (categories and scripts for organising ideas and experiences), complicate their translation into indicators and operations. Illustrative is the way consideration of co-requisites makes it necessary to think differently about the concepts of risk and life chances that are often part of the rationale for integrating services. These concepts are usually thought of and operationalised as individual characteristics. Attention to co-requisites necessitates a more appropriate and methodologically more difficult view of them as social constructs. Consequently, evaluation of integrated services that are designed to reduce risk and improve life chances must deal with the personal, familial, communal, institutional, and structural features of existence. These co-requisites are not hierarchically arranged, linear across the life span, or cumulative in significance. That is, co-requisites are not determining pre-requisite antecedents. Predictive and probabilistic statements about risk are not as important here as descriptions of contexts that can be empowering, develop consciousness and facilitate self determination. The developing person and the practitioner are both embedded in the co-requisite dimensions of their existence. The problem here is not one of better controls, multivariate analysis, or more reliable measures. Rather, it is one of indeterminism, the imputation of causality, and the reality of disorder in the universe. The consideration of co-requisites is not merely a summing up of factors (biological, psychological, and sociological) to make a whole. Rather, it requires identification of patterns that are reflective of the whole. This perspective is supported in the ecological psychology of Bronfenbrenner (1979) that considers a setting in terms of micro, meso, exo, and macro systems and views of life span development in terms of its sociocultural, interpersonal, personal, and physical space dimensions (Volpe, 1993; Fogel, 1993).

Common to these ways of looking at the human condition is the assumption that the context of human existence is problematic. That is, the situations in which people grow and develop contain features that are paradoxically both resources and challenges when viewed in terms of life chances over the course of the life span. Further, they assert that human development involves a constructive problem solving process that is inclusive of all the dimensions of the life space. From these perspectives self and society, the activities of the scientist and the enterprise of science, are complex adaptive systems.

From this standpoint culture is both a collective adaptation and a personal resource. As an extension, public policy may be thought of as both a form of collective practice and a resource to front line or clinical practice. Bakhtin (see Todorov, 1995) describes the fusion of these dimensions and provides a hint as to the role of co-operative evaluation research.

Bakhtin asserts:

> "(...) culture consists in the discourses retained by collective memory (...) discourses in which every uttering subject must situate himself or herself (...) it is the human being itself that is irreducibly heterogeneous; it is human being that exists only in dialogue (...) all discourse is in dialogue with prior discourses on the same subject, as well as discourses yet to come, whose reactions it foresees and anticipates. A single voice can make itself heard only by blending into the complex choir of other voices already in place" (Todorov, 1995).

The concept of adaptation is central here. Adaptation refers to a problem solving process with common elements across biological, psychological, and social systems. Adaptation is the interplay between challenges confronted and the mobilisation of resources to meet them. Human development proceeds as a consequence of disequilibria which stem from an imbalance between challenges and resources. The notion of stress provides a useful metaphor to describe how this discrepancy can be facilitative of growth or paralytic and destructive.

Most challenges are coped with adequately. Problem solving is a daily activity. It involves the almost imperceptible mobilisation of historical and habitual resources. When challenges outstrip resources, old patterns must give way to new ones. Co-requisites present resources and challenges to self and society. Self and society are structured responses to the challenges associated with personal and collective efforts to deal with problems in living. Empowering individuals, groups, and communities with opportunities to produce their own research information needed to solve the problems they collectively face should be one of the chief aims of evaluation research.

The scientific method as a method of problem solving

The scientific method has proven itself one of the best methods for problem solving, and gaining knowledge. Moreover, it provides an effective tool for dealing with the physical and social environment and promoting empowerment and adaptive change. Traditionally, however, the social sciences and their erroneous technical preoccupation's have been disempowering (Sarason, 1981). Mistakenly, social sciences have in the past mimicked an outdated image of the natural sciences as value free and more concerned with facts than ideas.

Because science is a value laden method of progress it is an apparatus for bringing larger and greater ideals within the vision of humanity. The changing scientific paradigm allows adaptive social change to be hastened by critical and reflective analysis. Basically, science is an open, communicable, and systematic attempt to solve problems and answer questions. Moreover, it provides a historical community, a basis for consensual validation, and a means by which time consuming and wasteful trial and error can be avoided. The truths associated with both scientific means and ends are not absolute or static. Rather, they are provisional and dynamic. Provisional truths are more accurate and better suited to producing adaptive social change and serving as a basis for social reform. Thus, science is a form of adaptation working as an open problem solving system that operates without expectation of ever reaching a static state.

Technical rationality

Modern science has moved into a radically altered conception of knowledge production and practice. For the physical and life sciences it may be said that they are in a post-positivist phase. The technical contributions of science have been placed in a broadened perspective that includes the reality that they are products of a value laden enterprise.

Social and behavioural sciences are still struggling with the issue of value neutrality and the potential uses, applications, and impacts of their products. Consumers of these products believe that the techniques of science provide, in and of themselves, the means to an end guided by technical rules and the assurance of reliability (truth). The issue of technical rationality is not with its existence, but resides in the belief in its exclusive validity.

According to Schon (1983), technical rationality is the dominant epistemology of practice. Practice is believed to consist of instrumental problem solving made rigorous by the application of scientific theory and technique. Practice is seen as a process of problem solving through the application of scientifically based recipes for action. In this view practitioners are expected to provide researchers with problems to study and opportunities to test research results. Problems are solved by selecting the means most rigorously supported by research. This view ignores the embeddedness of the problem solver in the problem situation and the way the problem and the end sought in its solution have been defined. As Schon (1983) states:

> "Again, it is the work of naming and framing that creates the conditions necessary to the exercise of technical expertise. We can readily understand why uncertainty, uniqueness, instability, and value conflict are so troublesome to the Positivist epistemology of practice, but also why practitioners bound by this epistemology find themselves caught in a dilemma."

The following metaphor of the "cliff and the swamp" is taken from Schon's discussion of the dilemma of "rigor or relevance" in professional practice (Schon, 1983, 1987). Rigor refers to the high hard ground where practitioners make use of rigorous research. In contrast, the swamp is a lowland full of messy and confusing problems. Problems associated with life on the cliff are mostly of interest to researchers and research/practitioners who can function as technical experts.

The problems of greatest social concern and importance, however, exist in the swamp. These are the most challenging and complex.

The study of research utilisation

Difficulty in the application of research findings is increasingly being acknowledged by clinicians and policy makers (Machlup, 1979; Holzner and Marx, 1979; Weiss and Bucuvalas, 1981; Brady, 1986). In psychology this situation has been called a crisis by Westland (1978) and a result of the misdirection of nineteenth century models of science (Sarason, 1981). Fenholt and associates (1986) point out that child psychiatry is struggling with the dilemma of scientific practitioners valuing the precision of epidemiological and quasi-experimental research and finding that the product of these designs fail in helping them diagnose and treat children and families. They assert that the view of science which places experimental methods above clinical inference and decree that mental phenomena must correspond to some measurable behaviour is wrong. They conclude that such a narrow view of science is unproductive and an impediment to progress.

When practitioners seek assistance in their work it is typically not identified as research (Bain and Groseclose, 1979). Rarely are the techniques of the clinician logically entailed or tied to a research based conceptual scheme (Berger, 1985). Although largely educated in programmes espousing some version of the scientific-practitioner model and, consequently, the value of research, practitioners are usually pessimistic about its use in practice (Brown and Wildavsky, 1987). In contrast, researchers are optimistic, they are often the first to claim that an information base is available for such undertakings as primary prevention or effective early intervention (Price *et al.*, 1988).

Because a great deal of private and public funding is directed to research that is socially significant it is important to ask why research results are not making their way into practice. The reasons for this have already been stated. The operations, variables, and relationships found in research often do not correspond with the processes of significance in applied settings. The contrast between the "cliff and the swamp" is a contrast between the "ivory tower and front fine trenches". The motivations, perceptions, and interests of dwellers in these two realms are often at odds. Researchers are usually satisfied with explanation. In contrast, practitioners often want understandings that will help them bring about authentic changes and lasting improvements. Hence, we return to the dilemma of "rigor or relevance". Studies with high application value are generally characterised by less control than studies with low application potential.

These issues have been used to call for the abandonment of science (Feyerabend, 1975), a more open methodological stance (Hoshmand and Lisa, 1989), and the creation of information that can be of use to practitioners through an action science based on ethnography (Argyris *et al.*, 1985). Some of these solutions are extreme and open to a new range of criticism, *i.e.* the hermeneutic circle. Nevertheless, evaluation research professionals need to examine research utilisation and come to grips with the problem of relating research to practice.

Theory-practice

Part of the problem of technical rationality is lack of recognition that the dilemma of "rigor or relevance" includes more than relating research to practice. Perhaps more central is the relationship between theory and practice. The conceptual schemes associated with both the activities of research and practice coexist where these enterprises are joined and opened for epistemological criticism. Habermas (1971) asserts:

> "Science can only be comprehended epistemologically, which means as one category of possible knowledge, as long as knowledge is not equated either effusively with the absolute knowledge of a great philosophy or blindly with scientistic self-understanding of the actual business of research."

Viewing science as one facet of knowledge creation and regarding the products of research as mere information and distinct from knowledge may provide needed insight into the rigor relevance dilemma. Moreover, it may ultimately breathe new life into scientist-practitioner models of professional education. This will be particularly true if theory is viewed as the distillation of the practice of both the front line worker and the researcher (Volpe, 1975, 1981).

The essence of the thesis presented here is embodied in two statements. One advanced long ago by Schelling in 1802:

> "The fear of speculation, the ostensible rush from the theoretical to the practical brings about the same shallowness in action that it does in knowledge (...) only ideas provide action with energy and ethical significance." (quoted in Habermas, 1971).

The other more recently by Freire (1970):

> "But men's activity consists of action and reflection: it is praxis; it is transformation of the world. And as praxis, it requires theory to illuminate it. Men's activity is theory and practice; it is reflection and action."

Knowledge and action

Knowledge is the application of information in practice, "know-how is in the action". The relation of theory and practice present two problems; the problem of the influence of circumstances on thought and the problems of the consequences of thought (McKeon, 1952). Action talks back to thought. If the practitioner is listening, action can itself become informative. Schon (1987) following Dewey (1938) and Mead (1934) discusses the practitioner being reflective, turning experience of the other back onto the self. This accounts for the artistry of practice, the effectiveness of the practitioner in dealing with everyday uniqueness and uncertainty. Every new situation provides the possibility of a new way of responding. Theory and practice blend in action (Connelly and Clandenin, 1988).

Theories embody and enfold the practice of the inquirer. The researcher, client, clinician, and policy maker are joined in action. Theory can help all of these practitioners observe, describe, explain, integrate, and understand experience. Through language communities made possible by theoretical elaboration and exchanges, practitioners can mutually engage in self appraisal and the refinement of their professional knowledge base. Implied here is more than the rationalist's account of theory as words to facilitate thinking or the empiricists belief in the primacy of experience. Rather, this account asserts that understanding the relation of thought and action requires recognition that subject and object interact. The reflective practitioner forms a construction not inherent in either the knower or the known (Volpe, 1981).

Piaget (1971) postulated:

> "(...) knowledge is never a state and always forms a process, this process is essentially the passage of a lesser to a greater validity (...) this concept of knowledge implies adaptations of thought to reality and reveals an inextricable interaction between subject and object."

Several observations summarise the preceding discussion. First, important research questions involve whole human events that take place in a historical and social context. Second, it is important that practitioners see themselves as central to the information generation process we call research. Third, research is essentially, as Dollard (1957) wrote, "human intelligence trying to make sense out of what it observes". Fourth, continuous reflective thought and action give rise to knowledge. Finally, research is a social enterprise that is shared by both researchers and practitioners.

Triangulation

The implications of this view of research, theory, and practice are profound. No single method or methodological strategy can encompass the complexity and levels associated with studies that focus on the personal, interpersonal relations, and human group life. Different methods are appropriate for different types of problems. Arguments over the superiority of one method over another have not been productive. No specific method is always better than another. Methods are part of research designs. Each of these strategies involves decisions that have both strengths and weaknesses. A perspective is needed that will allow problems to be approached in ways that capture all that is important in the life space of individuals and groups. Triangulation or bringing multiple methods and perspectives to bear on research problems is such a perspective (Webb *et al.*, 1981). At least six forms of triangulation can be identified. Methodological triangulation involves either multiple forms of the same method or a variety of different methods. Theoretical triangulation attempts to apply several different conceptual schemes in the analysis of a data set. Investigator triangulation employs more than one observer in a field. Data triangulation utilises multiple sampling strategies in the gathering of information. Denizen (1983) has added an additional form in calling for multiple triangulation or the combination of multiple methods, theories, researchers, and data sources in an effort to provide interpretative interaction. The mix associated with triangulation allows a number of approaches to problems. Most common is the focus of a number of methods on a single problem. This approach facilitates assessing the reliability and validity of observations and revealing the complexity and multilevels of phenomena. Another possibility is that different methods can be applied to different phases or dimensions of a project. One method may be best suited to the process of discovery while another the process of justification. Triangulation also enables flexibility in the design and execution of research. Such a strategy enables adaptation to important and interesting emergent dimensions in ongoing research. Finally, sensitivity to the inclusion of multiple perspectives necessitates recognition and attention to all points of view in research situations.

A descriptive evaluation model that holds onto science

Although described in greater detail elsewhere (see Evans in OECD, 1996), this project essentially involved the implementation of a cross national exemplary practice survey. The following framework proved useful in scientifically mapping programme descriptions in terms of their structure and operation. Moreover, it provided a consistent structure across programmes that facilitated comparative analysis. The framework is based in part on the CIPP Model developed by Stufflebeam (1990). This model was useful in the internal and external evaluations of all participating programmes and in their best practice descriptions (Volpe, 1996). The framework is particularly helpful in generating descriptive information that can be employed in practical decision-making. The components of the model are as follows: C= context, I = input, P = process, P = product.

Context refers here to the description of background and history of programme (climate), antecedent factors -- identified concerns of why is it important for services to be delivered in a particular way that are reflected in relevant policies, legislation, needs analysis, statement of objectives. Input involves the description of the ingredients of the programme (resources), programme planning -- decisions associated with programme design and resource allocation. Process is a detailed depiction of implementation, what people are actually doing in terms of activities and inputs. Product refers to outcomes, the impact of the program, projection of future needs and what clients, designers, workers, managers have learned about the project. This sort of mapping was derived from surveys, questionnaires, programme descriptions, worker and management interviews and testimonials from recipients.

This framework seemed to make sense to both the team and to stakeholders. One reason for the broad intuitive appeal of the framework may be how it addressed the narrative structure inherent in context. Treating context as textual phenomena follows the story line from beginning, middle, and end. Following the CIPP framework the OECD project involved cross cultural intertextual analysis.

The following questions provide a framework for discussing some study design components, questionnaire rationale and data gathering techniques which included group (focus) and individual key informant interviews and questionnaires.

Context:

- What (historical and contemporary) national and international programme antecedents can be discerned?
- Are the public and agency communication materials and strategies appropriate?
- Input and Process:
- Are the programmes being implemented as planned?
- Are the target audiences being reached?
- Who is failing to be reached and why?
- Are those delivering the programmes satisfied with the materials made available?

Product:

- Did the programme have the effect that they were designed to have?
- What plans have been made for the dissemination of lessons learned and the diffusion of exemplary practices?

The identification and description of integrated services as "best practice" programmes required the collaboration of multiple levels of the participating governments. Initial referrals had to be transformed into various information and contact agents, key informants, field practitioners, and participating children and when feasible their caretakers. Close collaboration was needed to generate criteria for the selection of participants and programmes at every level of the survey. The aim of this undertaking will be to describe and analyse programmes in such a way that they can serve as replicable models and contribute to a knowledge base for the development of new programs.

The general aims of this area of research were to:

- describe the range of integrated services and supporting policies in member countries;

- identify examples of best practice and compare and contrast different forms of service arrangements;

- describe, analyse, and evaluate the functioning of these services in terms of their effectiveness for involved clients, service providers, and administrators;

- develop materials for the dissemination of outcomes and the creation of a cross national descriptive inventory of integrated directory.

The OECD project necessitated putting aside methodological disputes and adopting a multi-method approach. Such an approach involved recognition that within limits different methods can provide valid information and insights into a social mobilisation programme that can prove useful in planning and decision-making. Various methods produce different kinds of data and are differentially susceptible to error. The challenge here is to bring the best of what are considered standard scientific methods from a variety of disciplines to bear on the researchable dimensions of the initiative. Each method can contribute to equally valid empirical generalisations and theoretical insights.

Although multi-method research was well suited to the project, it required the team to be ever mindful of measurement burden and to avoid methods that were intrusive and interfere with the lives of programme participants. These requirements indicated the need for insight into the disempowering potential of research and the need for co-operative inquiry. The OECD Project Secretariat provided the locus for project planning and interaction.

Co-operative inquiry

Co-operative inquiry is an approach to social scientific research that maximally involves all stakeholders in the designing, implementation, and analysis of the undertaking. That is, participants help to decide on what questions are to be asked, what methods will be employed, and how outcomes are to be interpreted. Consequently, the participants in the project needed to be engaged in dialogue with all stakeholders, and need to negotiate measures, comparison groups, and procedures with each other. The appropriateness of this approach enabled the alignment of particular methods to meet particular needs. Co-operative inquiry grounds collaborative and open relationships in a shared value of promoting human welfare and a commitment to the importance of systematic inquiry in promoting useful understandings and scientific explanation. Ultimately what is being sought is knowledge through action. Such knowledge serves the immediate aims of partners and should enable them to more effectively act on their own behalf and serve their most pressing interests. Only a multi-method research agenda can serve such ends and retain the integrity and wholeness of human experience. The key to the success use of this approach is assuring that the methods that are employed are consistent with the objectives and purposes of the research.

Methodology

Four different means of data gathering were identified in the evaluation and exemplary practices survey. Documentary evidence was gathered from official documents, census data, programme evaluation reports, historical accounts, year end reports, programme descriptions, and news coverage. Statistical information was collected from the analysis of comparative rates, programme participation records, consumer satisfaction surveys, and previous evaluation studies. Third, both key informant and focus group interviews were conducted. Finally, by the invitation of member countries selective site visits were conducted in Europe, North America, and Australia.

Described below are some specific elements of several of the main data gathering sources that are not usually treated at length. Questionnaires described by Evans *et al.* (1996) covered mandating, strategic, operational, and field levels in each participating member country.

The key informant technique

At the core of the design of both the evaluation and exemplary practices survey is the Key Informant Technique. This approach to doing field work provided a base for both project kick-off and completion. The technique traditionally refers to intensive interviewing of principal members of a community to obtain various forms of information (Tremblay, 1982). Usually this approach conjures images of an ethnographer doing unstructured interviews and collecting almost exclusively qualitative information. This was not be the case in this project. Our interviews were semi-structured and sought both qualitative and quantitative data. Moreover, they had an evolutionary quality that led to the opening up of both the operation and organisation of services and programs. Our informants acted concurrently as expert witnesses, transmitters of lore, knowledge, news, facts, and wisdom. They were both project sponsors and primary sources of information. As theses relationships progressively evolved, deeper understandings emerged that made it possible to obtain cross informant validation and confirmation. All verbal input was translated into English. Translations and reports were always checked by appropriate participants and government staff.

The focus group method

The focus group method involved obtaining data in a one session group interview situation through the facilitation of discussion among participants. The method is designed to collect qualitative material to answer research questions (Krueger, 1988), to hear what participants have to say about their association with programs. Although some group interviews are unstructured conversations, both our key informant and focus group interviews were structured by the use of consistent guidelines or themes. The moderator's role will be to facilitate conversation, keep "focus", and guide discussion along the designated themes.

An important feature of this approach is the intensity and involvement of both the researchers and participants. This is a key source of validity. In and of itself, however, this is also one of its weaknesses. The whole point for doing multi-method research is that each data source needs to be treated with scepticism and that the validity (accuracy and truthfulness) of any particular method arises in its relationship to other sources of information.

Our aim in using focus groups was to find out as much as possible about the range of thoughts and feelings participants have about their programme involvement. These groups also enabled us to get our "feet wet" as we began to operationalise the goals of the project. Moreover, they allowed input from all team members and facilitated team building. An additional benefit of this method is that exchanges among participants help them articulate and clarify for themselves the basis of their opinions and behaviours. This is an often neglected empowering feature of evaluation research.

Narrative analysis

The same procedures were used for analysing the transcriptions produced by both key informant and focus group interviews. Certain characteristics differentiated the groups from one another (*i.e.* parents in contrast to children) and other characteristic were common to all groups (*i.e.* being a worker in a particular program). We have called the former discriminate and the latter uniform characteristics. For example, three discriminate characteristics (child, parent, worker) enable nine points of comparison. Uniform characteristics such as being a parent allowed analysis of these stakeholders as a composite group derived from each program. A discriminate characteristic can thus become a uniform characteristic at another level of analysis. The assumption here is that by holding separate sessions with groups that display different and similar features there will be a greater likelihood of eliciting more information that can be analysed in more depth.

Data analysis was the most difficult aspect of the research. Amassing hours of taped material comes with relative ease. The transcription, sorting, and derivation of meaningful (useful) information creates an enormous challenge. Whenever possible we taped and transcribed all narrative data. The next two phases are the core of our analysis: the physical assembly and subdivision of the transcripts into meaningful segments and the derivation of meaning through the method of "constant comparison"(Stewart and Shamdasani, 1990). The interpretative or meaning making phase involved exhaustively reading and re-reading and marking the less voluminous organised transcripts in search of patterns.

Reading the narrative segments in terms of discriminate characteristics uncovers similarities and differences in the data. Agreement within and between groups is an indication of the reliability of the information obtained. Stakeholders reviews and their indication of whether or not the conclusions "make sense", seem familiar, and appear to an accurate mirror of experience are important manifestations of the validity of how data is being interpreted.

Reliability and validity

The multiple data sources developed in this project elicited verbal accounts, observations, and a variety of policy, historical and demographic reports. With all of this information we expected words-deeds discrepancies and designed the study to reveal and cross check them through the sharing of observational activities in research team meetings within and between partner projects.

The task of the research team was to achieve objectively through opening data gathering methods to public witness and making all findings accessible to others. What emerged was an ability to achieve subjectivity in relating and co-operating with participants and a process of obtaining objectivity through group processes and the "judgements of the larger community. Face, criterion, convergence and construct validity are, thus, achievable. The importance of comparison is also central to the question of reliability. Reliability in the case of this project depended on the explicitness in which observations can be described. Only after events, situations, and processes are characterised can their consistency be assessed. Moreover, the demand characteristics of a study such as this required that we know what comprises the "expected" behaviours and answers. With this understanding we determined the stability of findings through time and similarity of findings within the same time period across situations.

Measurement burden

In a project of this scope, a significant burden was placed on all points where data are generated. Measurement burden can be viewed as consisting of an objective and subjective dimension. The objective reflects the true cost (amount of time that the individual and/or organisation must volunteer, production costs *i.e.* computer time) in order to generate the desired data points. Examples of objective burden at the individual level include participation in interviews and completion of questionnaires. At the community or organisational level examples might be the time required by community personnel to programme materials and descriptions.

The subjective dimension reflects the disposition of the data provider towards the study. The data provider may feel the project is irrelevant or that the data demands are too "personal" and consequently refuse to participate or simply extend the delivery of data beyond the desired time frame. The objective and subjective dimensions tend to be more interactive than independent.

Several strategies were available to the project Secretariat to assist with the management of measurement burden. The first, and in our view most important, is embedded in our collaborative approach to the project. In community research projects of this nature, the relationship between the researchers and the "subjects" must be collaborative rather than authoritarian. Such a relationship shifts the notion of burden from one of imposition to one of consensus. The Secretariat as an organisational structure maximised community input, collaboration and shared decision-making. When data was collected, the data sources in the project agreed to their nature and the process by which they were collected. A second general strategy that complements the development of collaborative relationships is the use of parallel investigators in each partner country. These partners will collaborate in solving various methods issues such as the design of instruments, selection of strategies for accessing particular individuals or data sources, and selecting unobtrusive measures.

A third general strategy involved the identification of natural data collection nodes and integrating project data needs. At the most abstract level, these nodes reflected the key intersects of the various subsystems in the ecological model, such as home and government.

At the more personal level, nodes represented individuals within a community who routinely collected or who have the opportunity to collect information. A variety of individuals, such as front line workers, government programme officials or administrators can be considered. Expansion of these nodes reduced the need for direct contact with subjects. A fourth strategy involved the use of existing surveys or adding items to annual or upcoming investigations. A fifth strategy involved the collection of internal policy descriptions and programme reports that were already in existence.

Discussion

The OECD study well illustrates that as partners in the generation of information, evaluation researchers and practitioners need to confront various notions of knowledge, research methodology, and the relationship of theory and practice. Disagreements in these areas are deeply rooted in epistemological, normative, and attitudinal differences between various interests groups producing and consuming research.

Suggested in this discussion is an orientation toward theory and research in which the acquisition of knowledge is approached through practice, and not as a one way application of recipes for action. Rather, it is an opportunity to create and transform information. This two way process makes it unlikely that practice will provide opportunities for the application and testing of concepts. Similarly, practitioners need not expect that the artistry of their practice will be subsumed by existing theories.

Finally, evaluation research efforts must be responsive to both changing societal needs and perspectives on validity claims associated with the ways programmes are evaluated. A dual commitment exists here. On one hand, we seek to achieve a better understanding of problems in living and, on the other, the application of this knowledge to provide solutions to these problems and to create increasingly refined and informed questions in our ever changing environments both locally and internationally. Responsiveness to this commitment must ensure both accountability and effectiveness. Gaining perspective on the question at hand, the relation of theory and practice should be a major and ongoing aspect of the slow process of promoting our broadening definition of human service.

REFERENCES

Argyris, C., Putnam, R. and McLain Smith, D. (1985), *Action Science,* Jossey-Bass Publishers, San Francisco.

Bain, H. and Groseclose, H.J. (1979), "The Dissemination Dilemma and a Plan for Writing Disseminators and Practitioners", *Phi Delta Kappan*, pp. 101-103.

Berger, L.S. (1985), *Psychoanalytic Theory and Clinical Relevance,* The Analytic Press, Hillsdale, NJ.

Brady, M. (1986), "Why Aren't Research Results in Practice?", Unpublished manuscript.

Bronfenbrenner, U. (1979), *The Ecology of Human Development,* Harvard University Press, Cambridge, Massachusetts.

Connelly, F.M. and Clandinin, D.J. (1988), *Teachers as Curriculum Planners,* Narratives of New York: Teacher's College, Columbia University.

Denizen, N. (1983), "Interpretive Interactionism", in G. Morgan (ed.), *For Social Research,* Sage Publications, Beverly Hills, CA.

Dewey, J. (1938), *Logic: The Theory of Inquiry,* Collier Books, New York.

Dollard, J. (1957), *Caste and Class in a Southern Town*, Doubleday Anchor, Garden City, New York.

Evans, P. (1993), "Personal communication".

Evans, P. in OECD, (1996), *Successful Services for our Children and Families at Risk*, Paris.

Fenholt, J., Holfnunt, R.J., Hunter, P. and Leventhal, J. (1986), "A Debate: Scientific Method and Clinical Research", *Journal of the American Academy of Child and Adolescent Psychiatry,* Vol. 25, 5, pp. 724-726.

Feyerabend, P. (1975), *Against Method: Outline of an Anarchistic Theory of knowledge,* Verso, London.

Fogel, A.(1993), *Developing through Relationships,* University of Chicago, Chicago.

Freire, P. (1970), *Pedagogy of the Oppressed,* Continuum, New York.

Habermas, J. (1971), *Theory and practice,* Beacon Press, Boston.

Holzner, B. and Marx, J.H. (1979), *Knowledge Application: The Knowledge System in Society*, Allyn and Bacon, Inc., Boston.

Horowitz, F.D. (ed.) (1989), "Special Issue: Children and Their Development Knowledge Base, Research Agenda, and Social Policy Application", *American Psychologist*, Vol. 44, No 2.

Hoshmand, T. and Lisa L.S. (January, 1989), "Alternate Research Paradigms: A Review and Teaching Proposal", *The Counselling Psychologist*, Vol. 17, No. 1, 3-79, Fullerton, CA.

Krueger, R. (1988), *Focus Groups*, Sage, Newbury Park.

Lincoln, Y. and Gupa, P. (1994), *Fourth Generation Evaluation Research*, Sage, Newbury Park.

Machlup, F. (1979), "Uses, Value and Benefits of Knowledge", *Knowledge Creation, Diffusion and Utilisation*, Vol. 1, No. 1, pp. 62-81.

McKeon, R. (1952), "Philosophy and Action", *Ethics*, Vol. LXII, No.2, pp. 79-101.

Mead, G. (1934), *Mind Self and Society*, University of Chicago Press, Chicago.

Novick, M. and Volpe, R., *Social Practice*, Vol. 1, Laidlaw Foundation, Toronto.

Piaget, J. (1983), "Piaget's theory", in P. Mussen (ed.), *Handbook of child psychology*, Vol. 1, Wiley, New York.

Polkinghorne, D. (1983), *Methodology for the Human Sciences: Systems of Inquiry*, State University of New York Press, Albany.

Price R., Cowen, E., Lorien, R. and McKay, J. (eds) (1988), *Fourteen Ounces of Prevention: A Case Book for Practitioners*, American Psychological Association, Washington, DC.

Rychlak, J.F. (Fall, 1969), "Lockean vs. Kantian Theoretical Models and the 'Cause' of Therapeutic Change", *Psychotherapy/ Theory, Research and Practice*, No. 6.

Sarason, S.B. (1981), *Psychology Misdirected*, The Free Press, New York.

Schon D. (1987), *Education the Reflective Practitioner. Toward a New Design for Teaching and Learning in the Professions*, Josey-Bass, San Francisco.

Schon, D. (1983), *The Reflective Practitioner*, Basic Books, New York.

Stewart, D. and Shamdasani, P. (1990), *Focus groups: Theory and Practice*, Sage, Newbury Park.

Todorov, T. (1995), *Mikhail Bakhtin: The Dialogic Principle*, University of Minnesota Press, Minneapolis.

Tremblay, M. (1982), "The key informant technique", in R. Burgess (ed.), *Field Research: A Sourcebook and Manual*, George, Allen, and Unwin, London.

Volpe, R. and Posener, J. (1997), "Hunting for Etiology: conceptual Problems in Primary Prevention", Unpublished paper, University of Toronto.

Volpe, R. (1996), "The CIPP Framework", in P. Evans *et al.* (ed.), *Successful Programmes for Children and Families at Risk,* OECD, Paris.

Volpe, R. (1993), *Human Development in Context*, Innocenti, UNICEF, Florence, pp. 1-20 (Italian and English).

Volpe, R. (1990), "Risk, empowerment and research", in M. Novick and R. Volpe (eds.), *Perspectives On Social Practice*, The Laidlaw Foundation, Toronto.

Volpe, R. (1988), "Complexities in the Cycle of Abuse", in P. Sebald (ed.), *Ontario Papers for the Prevention of Child Abuse,* COMSOC, Toronto.

Volpe, R. (1983 October), "Conceptualising professional judgements", *Journal of Teacher Education*, Vol. 23, pp. 37-48.

Volpe, R. (1981), "Knowledge from theory and practice", *Oxford Review*, Vol. 7 (1), pp. 4151.

Volpe, R. (1975), "Behavioural science theory in medical education", *Social Science and Medicine,* Vol. 9, pp. 493-499.

Webb, E.T., Campbell, D. and Schwartz, R. (1981), *Nonreactive Measures in the Social Sciences,* Houghton Mifflin Company, New York, Boston.

Weiss, C.H. and Bocuvalas, M.J. (1981), *Social Science Research and Decision Making*, Columbia University Press, New York.

EVALUATING POLICY INITIATIVES

by

Alejandro Tiana Ferrer
UNED, Madrid, Spain

In the last years, the development of evaluation initiatives in public services has been a world-wide trend, which has deeply influenced the field of education. Not only developed, but also developing countries have set in place a number of programmes, created some outstanding institutions and started public debates aimed at implementing new educational evaluation policies. It can be said that evaluation is becoming a new instrument for monitoring public policies which is being widely used in different fields and places.

Also Spain has participated in this trend, by creating a new National Institute for Quality and Evaluation (INCE) at the beginning of the 1990s. Its Governing Board approved in 1994 a programme of activities which included different studies, both national and international, and the publication of a set of education indicators. During the last few years it has developed a number of activities, thus contributing to spreading a new *culture of evaluation* among teachers and schools in the country. As the first director of such an Institute, I had a wonderful opportunity to participate in the definition and implementation of a new evaluation policy.

Having been invited to participate in a panel presentation about "Research and Evaluation of Outcomes", but not being an specialist in the field of children and youth at risk, I will try to draw some reflections from my experience in evaluation which might be relevant for the subject of the meeting. I will particularly try to establish some connections between evaluation in education and in the field of integrated services for children and youth at risk.

In order to make a presentation which could complement the others in the panel, I have organised it in four main issues, centred around four central questions: why, what for, what and how to evaluate. In other words, I will address the issues of the main reasons, aims, areas and approaches of evaluation as it is conceived and applied today.

Why to evaluate? Reasons for evaluation

There is currently a growing demand of evaluation in a number of very different fields. Even if this can be considered as a new trend, it is not to be forgotten that evaluation and assessment have been an outstanding element always present in school practice. The novelty is that not only students are now subject to assessment, but also educational programmes (a field with a long tradition in the United States), schools as institutions and education systems as a whole. Assessment in education has been so developed from students to system evaluation by colonising close, broader fields.

Not only education has experienced this demand and expansion of evaluation in the last years. A new and strong movement of evaluation can be identified in other areas of public services and policies. Of course, it has also affected the field of social services. So, what is being said here about evaluation in education can be easily transferred to social (and integrated) services for specific populations.

There are both internal and external factors explaining why evaluation is now a subject of public interest for broad audiences. Among the external factors, the impact of economy on social and educational services is probably the outstanding one. The pressure for reducing public deficit has resulted in significant budgetary cuts which have affected important areas of social activities and forced authorities to set new priorities. This trend has obliged a reconsideration of the situation and limits of welfare systems, thus opening a vivid debate about the role of the state in contemporary economies. In this new context, education and social services are subject to public scrutiny asking them to improve their efficiency and effectiveness without investing more resources -- and hopefully reducing them. In some cases, specific programmes have been downsized or just closed, to reduce costs. And evaluation has been seen as a credible, reliable instrument for making such decisions, even if it is not always the case.

This new regard on the efficiency of social and educational programmes has resulted in a growing concern about their accountability. Schools and programmes are expected to account for their outcomes, opening the traditional "black box" to interested audiences. The way in which this accountability movement is translated into practice has significant differences from one country to another, but it can be clearly identified in very different contexts.

Besides these external factors explaining current interest in evaluation, there are some internal reasons pushing in the same direction. The first one is a growing concern about the quality of services offered, which obliges educational and social agents to reflect about how best to use the available resources to get the best possible results. Evaluation is an extremely useful tool for providing such agents with relevant data, feed-back and interpretations. The second one is the need to offer new possibilities for programme and professional development. Evaluation is not the only tool which can be used to meet this objective, but it can make a significant contribution to it by giving programmes and agents an external image of them, thus allowing them to design development plans.

Of course, some other reasons could be underlined trying to explain the growing demands and interest in evaluation. But I think this combination of the above-mentioned external and internal factors explains public attention towards evaluation to a large extent.

What to evaluate for? Aims of evaluation

There are three interrelated aims which evaluation has traditionally pursued. The first one is to assess the work done in some specific field, institution or programme. This purpose is and has been the most common one when thinking about evaluation. The heading of this panel also makes reference to that approach. In fact, resources put in place and hopes and expectations generated by education and social services deserve a clear answer about questions on their quality, efficiency and effectiveness. And evaluation can provide the public and authorities with such an answer, based on systematic data collection and analysis.

This first aim has supported what is usually called "summative evaluation". Its purpose is to offer some conclusive information and judgements to make decisions about a specific initiative. After such an assessment exercise, those who have the responsibility for doing so may decide to introduce some changes or even close the intervention activity. But making such kind of decisions is only one of the possibilities that evaluation offers in education.

In fact, a second aim is to improve the services and activities subject to evaluation. This is a crucial function, because the most usual objective for assessing something is improvement. Evaluation may show some strong and weak points of the activity or programme and suggest how to take advantage of the former and to reinforce the latter. Improvement also means giving some room to professional development of participants by sharing with them data, interpretations and conclusions. This view implies giving a central place to the "formative" role of evaluation. When thinking about how to use evaluation in the field of public services, one has to bear in mind that it is simply not a research exercise nor a management tool, but an instrument for improving the services we render.

Evaluation has as its third aim to improve our knowledge about the factors associated with success in our activity. This reflection about the reasons explaining why our actions are successful or not is a prominent one, because it allows us to set the objectives and to steer change and improvement. This third aim is a shared objective by evaluation and research, the last one making a contribution to investigate the points raised by the former.

So, when designing an evaluation project in the field of education and public services, attention must be given to those three aims. Even if in some occasions one of them may prevail over the others, usually the three of them are more or less interrelated. And special attention should be given to the "back-wash" effects over the other aims when trying to get one of them.

What to evaluate? Areas of evaluation

When talking about evaluation of outcomes in the field of integrated services for children and youth at risk, several areas should be considered. As a result of this CERI project, five main domains for evaluation have been identified:

- *Client outcomes:* The first and most prominent area to be assessed is that of client outcomes. As it has been frequently stated, integrating services is not an aim in itself, but a mean to support personal development of children and youth living under difficult conditions. So, assessing what are the respective levels of development of these persons, in several dimensions (education, health, well-being, social integration) is a fundamental task for making judgements about the quality of such services.

- *Outcomes for agencies and professionals*: Outcomes of integrated services cannot only be assessed among clients or users. Agencies and professionals working in that field also are affected by their own activities and need to receive feedback about those effects. So, institutional and professional outcomes should also be taken into account when designing evaluation in that field.

- *Financial costs*: Current budgetary and financial difficulties have made it obligatory to assess financial costs, a main component in evaluation projects of integrated services.

- *Cost-effectiveness*: Similar arguments can be used to support the inclusion of cost-effectiveness analysis into a general evaluation framework in the field we are considering.

– *Process of service integration*: As it is the case in evaluation in education -- and in general terms -- assessment of outcomes cannot be fully separated from the study of processes. The evaluation of this crucial component of every activity is a very useful tool for improvement. So, as it was argued before, the analysis of service integration processes is an unavoidable task if we want more effective and helpful programmes.

Even if these five fields are currently receiving closer attention than before, not all of them have been similarly developed until now. In fact, a number of projects aimed at assessing client outcomes have been set in practice in the last years, even with some gaps in coverage. The other four areas have been less explored and deserve some more attention.

How to evaluate? Approaches to evaluation

The last question to be addressed in this short presentation deals with the issue of approaches to evaluation. An important rule to bear in mind is that evaluation projects should respect the characteristics of programmes and activities subject to assessment, so adapting methods and techniques applied. But every programme or activity has different components with their own features and not all approaches fit to all of them. For assessing aspects such as the client outcomes of a programme, its social impact, its professional implications, its cost-benefit balance or its efficiency, different approaches and methods should be used. And when trying to assess the whole complexity of a programme, a set of such approaches and methods has to be applied. Consequently, there is a need for adopting integrated approaches and complementary methods in evaluation.

One interesting approach to be considered in this context is self-evaluation. In essence, self-evaluation is a process of reflection and development, conducted by service agents themselves. This approach plays a crucial role in the process of improving institutions or programmes, as it implies an active attitude of social agents and a knowledge-based reflection on processes and outcomes. Evaluation lays the groundwork for a rationale process of decision-making.

While self-evaluation is an extremely important tool for institutional or programme development and improvement, it must still be complemented by external evaluation. Persons and organisations need to contrast their own images with some perspective from outside. External evaluation plays such a role. Some concepts try to combine the benefits from external and self-evaluation, integrating both approaches in the same project.

External evaluation is a central instrument for public accountability. It can adopt different shapes by using different techniques. On the one hand, it can turn to quantitative methods, such as indicators. Indicators have been widely used in the field of education, due to some national and international projects -- *i.e.* the OECD/CERI project called INES (Indicators of Educational Systems). They are currently being used in some countries to offer visible, reliable data on education systems and institutions. On the other hand, external evaluation can be based in qualitative, interactive methods. This last approach can lay the foundation for defining and starting development and improvement plans.

Defenders and opponents of quantitative or qualitative methods have argued against each other, trying to impose their respective viewpoints. But evaluation has evolved, in the sense of what some specialists call integration and others eclecticism. Evaluators tend today to be more pragmatic and use all the existing set of techniques and methods, trying to select among them in accordance with the objectives and the subject of evaluation.

Some concluding remarks

In conclusion, I would like to underline a few ideas about the use of evaluation in the field of integrated services for children and youth at risk. The first one is that evaluation is a task to be developed if integrated services want to gain credibility and receive greater support than they have now. All innovative experiences have to demonstrate their capacity to generate better results than the traditional ones. Evaluation is an important tool in this process, even if it implies some risks.

A second idea is that the possible uses and misuses of evaluation make it a controversial activity, subject to debate and discussion. Nevertheless, it has to be developed in this as in many other fields. When necessary, decisions have to be made to reduce their risks and enhance their possibilities.

A third idea is that evaluation has to be considered an integral part of an activity and not only something to be performed at the end of the activity. It does imply the need to include it in the design of the full operation. Evaluation is a process to be followed from the starting point to the end of an activity. This view will allow it to become a powerful instrument for programme development, so improving our action.

THE BUILDING BLOCKS OF A COST EFFECTIVENESS ANALYSIS OF INTEGRATED SERVICES FOR AT RISK CHILDREN AND YOUTH

by

H. M. Levin
Stanford University

Educational success requires not only good schools, but a stable home situation, good health care, and adequate nutrition. Large reductions in class size, outstanding teachers, and good curricula are not adequate to compensate for gaps in health, nutrition, and home support. Children who are preoccupied by insecurity, poor health, hunger, and bad home conditions are unlikely to be able to focus on school-work. By adolescence there are other dangers which serve as obstacles to learning including teen age pregnancy, substance abuse, and involvement in gangs. Unfortunately, students in at risk situations not only encounter schools which do not take account of their educational needs; but often they lack the supportive home, nutritional, and health conditions that promote learning and, as adolescents, they have a higher likelihood than other children of exposure to and involvement in activities which will undermine their educational careers.

In short, learning requires not only appropriate school conditions for at risk students, but appropriate out-of-school conditions and attention to psychological, social, and health needs. Although the OECD countries typically have a variety of government services to provide support to families and children for income maintenance, health, nutrition, and protection from abuse, these services are usually provided by bureaucracies outside of the school. As a result, they are neither informed by the educational needs of the child, nor are they fully co-ordinated with educational services. Educational success requires that children have their educational needs and health, nutrition, and social support requirements addressed in ways that focus them in an integrated manner on addressing the best interests of the child. The provision of these different services by separate agencies with different modes of operation, funding, and geographical locations raises a dilemma. How might such services be combined into an efficient system of delivery to support child welfare and learning? The last decade of educational policy has witnessed a call for integrating such services at the school site and/or in conjunction with school operations. The logic of such integration is that children are required to be in school where their educational progress can be monitored and their other needs can be observed. If those other needs can be met through services provided at the school site, it is possible to co-ordinate both the evaluation of child needs and their provision in an efficient way. That is, gaps and inefficiencies in meeting child needs that would ordinarily arise because of inter-institutional barriers to communication, bureaucratic inertia and rivalries, and inter-jurisdictional service disputes can be overcome by comprehensive school centres that serve the full range of developmental needs of the child, educational, physical, and mental. The dream is to forge a "seamless" approach to meeting the needs of children through integrating a comprehensive range of services in conjunction with education where providers cooperage around a common focus, the promotion of healthy and successfully educated children.

So much for the logic of providing integrated and comprehensive health and social services at the school site. The fact that the services that children need are typically encumbered in independent bureaucracies means that bringing these to school sites in an efficient and co-operative way is difficult to achieve. Indeed, after a decade of developments in the direction of comprehensive and integrated services, there is little success to report. Even when a few successful cases are reported, there has been little replication. The successful cases have typically been attributable to generous outside funding or a strong charismatic leader rather than a shift in institutional priorities (see Knipp in this publication). Yet, the time has come to seek out alternative models of integrated child services that might be recommended for implementation on the basis of their social results relative to costs. Both educational and social services are costly, a particular concern at a time of public economic austerity and relatively high unemployment rates in the OECD countries. Accordingly, a search for efficient models of integrated service provision must be given a high priority, a search that must take account of both costs and effectiveness of alternatives. This note is devoted to consideration of how one might design and pursue a systematic strategy to obtaining cost and effectiveness information on different approaches to integrated school services.

Cost effectiveness as a goal

Cost effectiveness analysis represents a tool for evaluating alternative public investments. It is premised on the assumption that there exist a variety of alternatives for achieving a given set of goals, but that the alternatives differ in terms of their costs and results. It is desirable to identify those alternatives that provide the best educational outcomes for any given cost outlay, and cost effectiveness analysis provides a systematic framework for making such comparisons. A number of conditions must be present to provide useful cost effectiveness results for evaluating integrated services for youth and children at risk.

First, a clear set of alternatives must exist for integrating services either at school sites or in conjunction with schools. Cost effectiveness is not a theoretical exercise, but a form of evaluation that requires real alternatives. This means that the alternatives must exist as tried-and-tested entities rather than those on drawing boards. That is, we are concerned with the actual cost and effectiveness experience of such endeavours. Second, they must be replicable in that under ordinary circumstances they would be likely to be viable. Thus, we need to be wary of programmes that have benefited from special circumstances that cannot be duplicated elsewhere. A typical non-reproducible resource is a unique resource, such as a charismatic leader or one with other special talents, that is not readily or routinely found in other settings. Thus, a programme must be based upon the use of resources that can be readily obtained in the marketplace as one condition of replicability. A different requirement of replicability is that of stability over time and across different settings. Some programmes go through performance cycles where they show strong results early in their histories because of a high level of camaraderie or esprit de corps at the novelty stage, but at later phases they become less productive as the novelty and public acclaim diminish and as staff become less inspired. Other programme have a large variance in results from setting to setting, raising issues of quality control when they are replicated.

Unfortunately, there do not seem to be many comprehensive and integrated service interventions that meet the standards of replicability. While probably every OECD country has at least some examples of integrated service delivery, rarely are these models fully comprehensive and integrated with educational services. Often such programmes have been short-lived because of inadequate attention to implementation. For example, in the United States, government agencies devoted to health, social services, and child protective services have made agreements with schools to provide social services, but such agreements have not worked smoothly or in a "seamless" way. Others have had staying power by benefiting from unique circumstances such as having unusually charismatic and talented leadership which cannot be easily replicated. What is evident is that we do not yet have a range of alternative models which have been implemented under "ordinary" circumstances and which have shown consistent results. Thus, it is probably more appropriate to consider how costs and effectiveness analyses might be linked to a developmental strategy to pursue and evaluate new strategies at service integration. This means that there must be a constant search for new and more effective models and applications of integrated services as well as continuing evaluation of their properties. A major part of this evaluation can include studies of costs and effectiveness with the hope that over time the project builds a catalogue of alternative approaches that have been shown to be viable and replicable as well as useful estimates of the costs and effectiveness of the alternatives using a common methodology and a uniform set of criteria for judging effectiveness. It is to this task that I will turn in the next section.

Measuring effectiveness

Cost effectiveness studies require good measures of effectiveness in order to compare them with costs for each and all of the alternatives. Common measures of effectiveness of integrated services need to be developed before evaluations of effectiveness can be made. There are two levels of effectiveness that can be considered. To the degree that the services are designed to enhance the educational accomplishments of students in at risk situations, one could measure effectiveness in terms of such educational results as student attendance, course completions, grades, examination results, and completion of particular school levels. Surely, this is one of the two major arguments for placing integrated services at the school site, the notion that the common focus of such services will magnify the possibilities of educational success. The other rationale is the view that such services can be provided most efficiently in this integrated setting because it reduces costs of communication, collaboration, and bureaucratic overlap. But, a strong case can be made for a second level of effectiveness measure, that of assessing the degree of effectiveness of each of the services themselves. Beyond their educational consequences, it is important for children to see and hear well, justifying the provision of screening for and remediation of sight and hearing impairments. Children with adequate nutrition are more likely to have vigour and grow to full stature. Those with proper health care are less likely to suffer from debilitating episodes of illness and reduce the likelihood of transmitting infectious diseases to others. Youth who are protected from abusive family situations are likely to develop in more wholesome ways, needless to say, and with less physical and psychological pain. Youth who are guided with positive support are less likely to engage in substance abuse, gang membership, and teen pregnancy.

Thus, at a second level it is desirable to assess the range of services offered and their consequences in terms that are independent of the consequential benefits to education. One could conceive of two sets of outcomes in measuring effectiveness: educational benefits and those tied more directly to each service individually and their overall impact in combination. Presumably, children will be healthier, happier, and more productive in ways that go beyond education and receive valued services that address overall well-being. Accordingly, an effort must be made to identify a common set of categories for assessing effectiveness as well as formulating specific measures for each category. The result will be a range of indicators of success that can be used to compare effectiveness among alternatives.

Of course, the identification and measurement of these dimensions for each alliterative is not an accurate measure of the net contribution of the intervention. In some cases, children will be drawn from social circumstances or settings which would make them better-off in terms of education, health, nutrition, and general welfare than other students, even in the absence of the provision of comprehensive social services. Differences in clientele and in the provision of other supportive institutions in families and communities can create differences in outcomes, independently of any services that are provided at school sites or in conjunction with schools. In theory, one can only get true measures of effectiveness by taking similar students with similar out-of-school situations and placing them in different interventions to ascertain the net effectiveness of the intervention.

The classical design for measuring such effects among differences in intervention is that of the "true" experiment. In such an experiment, a community might sponsor three or four approaches to the provision of integrated services among as many different sites as well as sites that have no such provisions. Students would be randomly assigned to sites to assure that results of the interventions did not coincide or were not caused by selective policies in which some schools enrolled "better" students than other schools. After a reasonable period of time and at specified time intervals, the evaluators would measure the various educational and non-educational outcomes at each site. Over an adequate time period the evaluators would summarise the effectiveness of each of the interventions for purposes of comparison.

The use of a classical experimental design with random assignment of subjects to treatments is considered to be the most acceptable method for measuring effectiveness. However, it is rarely used to do so. Social policy typically precludes the random assignment of students for many reasons. Such assignment would often create disruptive patterns as children are uprooted from their residential neighbourhoods to be sent to schools that are relatively distant and require considerable transport in comparison with neighbourhood assignment. Indeed, such assignment may be at counter-purposes with a policy of trying to integrate social services at the school site within residential communities. Further, in a free society, client families may upset the pristine design of random assignment by assigning themselves to schools outside of the experimental setting. Families who prefer other schools for their children may choose private alternatives or may move their households to other communities, particularly if the experimental study is of long duration. Even if there are financial or other obstacles to residential movement, they may send their children to stay with relatives or friends in other communities. There is also a serious ethical problem to random assignment in that presumably the schools with integrated services will provide more support to families and children than those without such services. Therefore, random assignment discriminates among children in providing greater benefits to some children than others for the purpose of experimentation. For these and other reasons, experimental studies are usually unfeasible.

A second approach is to use a matched-control design. In this case, at least one experimental site is chosen and matched with at least one control site. In the ideal situation, the two schools are identical in their student intakes, curriculum offerings, teacher qualifications, and so on. The only difference is that the integrated services will be provided at the experimental site, but not the control site. Over time, multiple measures are taken of effectiveness indicators in order to compare the apparent effectiveness of the experimental school. Presumably, any differences in outcomes will be due to the experimental treatment. One major drawback of the matched control design is that almost no match is perfect. Although two schools may appear to be closely matched, subtle and unmeasured differences may account for differences in results such as the quality of leadership or a history of community solidarity.

A related design is the quasi-experimental approach. In this case there is an attempt to match as closely as possible the school settings that will be the subject of study for the alternative delivery systems. However, the statistical design takes account of, or "controls" for, a wide variety of student and school characteristics that may vary among schools and influence results independently of the interventions. That is, by controlling statistically for differences in students, families, and other school characteristics, there is an attempt to isolate differences due to the interventions themselves rather than differences among schools due to other causes. This design is widely used in social evaluations, although there is a history of controversy on its efficacy in deriving net effectiveness measures. That is, it may over- or under-compensate in adjusting for confounding influences.

Each of the designs set out above has relatively high validity in comparison with assessments where no controls are used. That is, by using random assignment, a matched design, or a quasi-experimental design with statistical controls, there is an attempt to isolate the unique effects of the particular integrated service interventions that are under scrutiny. A less valid approach and one whose results are likely to be contaminated by other factors is the use of change scores with no adjustments for other influences causing change. Unfortunately, the cost of designs using controls is high and the expertise required for evaluation is great. In contrast, the cost of simply measuring changes over time at an intervention site is relatively low, and expertise is not needed in evaluation design. The result is that the most common form of evaluation is that of measuring changes over time in the various criteria and attributing any change to the intervention. The problem with this approach is that other factors may be changing over time which may account for changes in apparent effectiveness. For example, if unemployment and poverty fall (rise) in a neighbourhood, the educational performance and social and health status of students may rise (fall) because of factors that are independent of the intervention. Controlled comparisons will enable one to ascertain the unique impact of the intervention, independent of these external factors. Therefore, designs with controls (either experimental, matched, or statistical) are to be preferred vastly to those without such controls, and one must be sceptical of designs that simply attribute any change over time to an intervention. The only possible exception is when the change is very substantial (not just statistically significant) and the predicted effects and timing coincide precisely with the implementation of those parts of the intervention that are expected to have these impacts. Where effects are large it is possible to use a design called an interrupted time series to infer if the long-run trend in the criterion measures are substantially "interrupted" by the advent of the intervention.

In summary, there are two phases to the evaluation of effectiveness of different approaches to providing integrated services for at risk children and youth. First, one must establish categories and uniform measures of effectiveness that can be used to assess the outcomes of the various alternatives. Secon, one must construct and implement valid evaluation designs for using these measures to ascertain effectiveness. For both cases there is a large literature that might provide guidance.

Cost estimation

The estimation of costs of interventions is rather straightforward. Although it may require the assistance of someone with expertise in cost estimation, much of the general procedure follows a logical progression of steps which can be readily understood even among persons who are not cost specialists. The goal of the cost estimation is to estimate the value to society of the resources that must be given up or sacrificed to provide each intervention. Some interventions will require more resources than others such as more personnel. These differences will translate into differences in costs which must be taken account in cost effectiveness analysis.

There exist standard sources on cost-estimation for cost effectiveness studies (*e.g.* Levin, 1983), so the purpose of this section is only to provide a brief overview. The most acceptable method of cost-estimation is to use a resource or ingredients approach. The first step in the ingredients approach is to specify in detail the ingredients or resources that are required for the intervention. Not only are quantities of resources identified, but their qualities as well. Thus, we are concerned with the qualifications of personnel and the characteristics of facilities and equipment as much as we are with their quantities. The details on what resources or ingredients are required are derived from studies of the details of the intervention, field surveys of the actual resources that are used, and interviews with those who are involved in and knowledgeable about the intervention. Once a detailed list of ingredients is compiled, it is necessary to "cost-out" or determine the value of these resources. Not all resources are purchased in the marketplace, so a variety of procedures have been established to provide a consistent methodology for obtaining costs. For example, "donated" space or volunteer labour is still costed out in terms of its value if such services were purchased in competitive markets in order to find the total cost of the resources that were required regardless of who bears the cost in the particular examples being studied. The concern is to determine the value of all of the resources needed to provide the impact that will be ascertained in the effectiveness studies, regardless of who "pays" the cost. Even volunteer time and donated space have a cost to someone when used for an intervention as long as they have value in alternative use.

Finally, the total cost of the ingredients is calculated, and further analysis is done by determining the distribution of cost burdens for the intervention as well as using common units of costs (*e.g.* costs per student) to make comparisons among interventions. Depending upon the intervention, it may be possible to get different levers and agencies of government, charitable agencies, volunteers, and families to participate in providing resources, both financial and in-kind. The analysis of the distribution of costs is a secondary analysis in terms of determining how an intervention has been supported. But, the primary analysis is to determine the overall cost and the unit cost of each intervention for comparative purposes. Obviously a uniform system of cost accounting must be employed across interventions in order to derive comparable cost information.

Combining cost and effectiveness

Ideally, the measurement of costs and effectiveness among interventions for integrating services for children and youth at risk will result in ratios of costs to effectiveness for each of the alternatives. Presumably we wish to choose that alliterative or combination of alternatives which has the lowest cost for any given outcome. This is known as the most cost-effective alliterative and enables the largest impact to be achieved for any given resource constraint. Of course, the cost effectiveness analyst is not responsible for decisions, but only for informing decisions by providing a competent and lucid analysis of the cost effectiveness consequences of the alternatives. The decision maker may also have to take account of other considerations which are not in the analysis. For example, the most cost-effective alternative may require major institutional changes which might be difficult to achieve politically. In that case, there might exist an alternative that is almost as cost effective in service delivery that builds more fully on existing institutional mechanisms and traditions. The point is that cost effectiveness results must be considered in a larger framework of information and criteria rather than being used mechanically to make decisions.

Cost effectiveness calculations and comparisons are most nearly straightforward when there is only a single measure of effectiveness and when all of the effects are captured by the single measure of outcome. Thus, if the effects of integrated services can be summarised in a single educational measure such as school completions, the analysis and comparisons of cost effectiveness will be uncomplicated. However, by the very nature of this type of intervention, the outcomes would seem to be multi-dimensional. Earlier we identified two levels of effectiveness, one based upon educational results and one based on other measures of well-being. Even within these two levels there are multiple dimensions that must be considered. Cost effectiveness analysis becomes complicated for multiple outcomes in the following way. What if one alternative is superior by cost effectiveness comparisons according to one effectiveness criterion, but inferior according to a second criterion? How does one choose between two alternatives that produce conflicting conclusions, depending upon which criterion of effectiveness is used?

The solution is to create a "numeraire" which will summarise the value for all of the outcomes of each alternative so that the summary measure can combined with costs to be used as a basis for comparison. The most common approach is to shift from cost effectiveness to cost benefit analysis where the entire range of outcomes is converted into monetary values. For example, school completions translate directly into better labour market opportunities and higher earnings. Better health status has been shown to have similar effects in labour markets. To as great a degree as possible, ostensible effects of the intervention can be converted into the monetary payoffs for those outcomes using a separate statistical analysis on other data sets that enables the linking of education and health status to employment and earnings. The variety of effectiveness measures are now converted to an overall measure of estimated monetary benefits for each alternative. These benefit-cost ratios can be compared directly among alternatives in order to recommend those with the highest benefits relative to costs. Benefit-cost ratios also permit a preliminary screening of alternatives in which only projects whose benefits exceed costs will be considered for adoption. That is, projects whose costs exceed benefits should not be considered further because they represent a net sacrifice for society rather than a net gain and, thus, a poor use of resources.

Unfortunately, it is not always possible to convert all of the valued outcomes of an intervention into monetary benefits. For example, what is the value of reduced suffering or discomfort due to the provision of nutritional meals or availability of counselling, reduction of child abuse, or diagnosis and provision of appropriate medicinal, optical, or auditory interventions? Even if some of this translates into superior labour market outcomes for both individuals and society, the accounting for benefits is incomplete by not including the improvement of well-being. An alternative approach that takes account of a wider variety of dimensions of effectiveness is that of cost-utility analysis which considers the value of each and every outcome and aggregates these individual values into an overall utility index. While this approach offers advantages in comprehensiveness, it, too, is characterised by a number of methodological challenges, not the least of which is the subjectivity of value associated with each outcome. A discussion of cost effectiveness, cost benefit, and cost-utility analyses can be found elsewhere and should be referred to for further details.

The fact that cost effectiveness analysis is not a simple recipe should not disqualify its use for purposes of comparing the efficacy of investments in integrated services for at risk youth and children. Even highly imperfect cost effectiveness evaluations may provide more useful information and better guidance to policy than ignoring this information. Indeed, a number of historical examples have shown that in the absence of any cost effectiveness analysis, major policy decisions have resulted in extremely wasteful decisions. An informed cost effectiveness analysis can provide an overall framework for discussion and debate that is superior to one that is not informed by these dimensions.

Some building blocks

In the absence of a concerted effort to do a cost effectiveness comparison of alternatives, it is possible to take steps that will lead in that direction. For example, it might be possible to begin the design of evaluations that can ultimately be applied to alternatives that would appear to meet the initial criteria of ostensible success and replicability. As countries get experience with initial efforts at integrated services and work to improve their interventions, they should also begin to consider how they will evaluate the different models for effectiveness. At the same time, they should begin to set out cost-analyses of interventions. One of the claims of integrated services is that through their integration one can reduce the cost of service delivery. Even in the absence of effectiveness results, one can compare the costs of different approaches to service integration by using the cost-side of the cost effectiveness methodology. This preliminary analysis of costs will also build capacity to use the tool in full cost effectiveness studies at some later date. Such analysis could also consider the potential sources of more efficient service delivery. Will the models of integrated services benefit from reduction of overlap in record-keeping, paperwork, and communication across agencies, and will they provide more harmonious operations by reducing unproductive conflict among service providers by placing their representatives on integrated service teams that focus on the same diagnostic and service teams? Even prior to doing a formal cost analysis, these types of issues with cost implications should be explored.

One other incremental step is to begin to do cost, effectiveness, and cost effectiveness studies on more modest approaches to service integration. It is far easier to find examples where a few child services have been integrated than where the integration is complete and comprehensive. That is, we simply lack experience on the more complex situation of comprehensive service integration and have fewer examples where such integration has been fully institutionalised and would seem to be replicable under ordinary circumstances. But, to the degree that we have more modest examples that have been replicated or seem replicable, it would be useful to "practice" doing cost effectiveness analyses on these alternatives. This would not only allow a comparison of what already exists -- even if far from the integrated ideal -- but it would also build capacity to do cost effectiveness studies as needed when more comprehensive alternatives are established.

REFERENCES

Levin, Henry M. (1983), *Cost Effectiveness: A Primer,* Sage Publications, Beverly Hills, CA and London.

Levin, Henry M. (1988), "Cost Effectiveness and Educational Policy", *Educational Evaluation and Policy Analysis*, Vol. 10(1), pp. 51-69.

MODELS OF COMMUNITY DEVELOPMENT

by

Jennifer Evans
University of London

Summary

An OECD research project looking at the potential of integrating education with other services for children and families, including health and social services, used a four-level decision-making model of services integration as the basis for data collection. The levels were: the mandating level; strategic level; operational management level; and field level. The interface between field level workers and community members was seen as a crucial arena for the evaluation of the impact of integrated services on the welfare of children and families "at risk". The evaluation studies carried out were therefore focused on localised examples, situated in discrete contexts. That is to say, we studied the impact of policies about the delivery of services to children and youth at risk and their families and the ways in which decisions about services integration, at the various levels outlined above, were implemented at the local level. The contexts in which local projects are conceived and carried out are inevitably complex. Localities are permeable; communities are not always easily defined and may have conflicting needs and priorities; community members may have direct influence on decision taken at the mandating and strategic levels through lobbying and other political actions.

This paper will focus on the complexities of evaluating the effectiveness of programmes targeted at particular social groups and communities and attempt to refine the four level-model described at the outset to include the crucial element of community participation in decision-making, and the delivery of integrated services.

Introduction

The OECD study of Integrated Services for Children and Families at Risk, was set up to explore the potential of greater collaboration between education, health, social and other welfare services to support children "at risk" of school failure (OECD, 1996). The rationale for promoting an integrated approach to the provision of services for children and youth "at risk" rests firmly in the notion that the problems confronting these young people should be viewed holistically: that children's problems cannot be tackled in isolation from their context within their families and local communities (Evans, 1995). Therefore, the concept of "community" and of "community participation" in tackling the problems is crucial to the formulation and implementation of policies and practices in this area.

However, the terms "community" and "participation" are ill-defined and can have multiple meanings depending on who is using them. As Vincent (1993) points out they are *"condensation symbols"* (Edelman 1964). They evoke positive emotions by appearing to promote such ideas as "belonging", "equality, respect", "involvement" and so on, but the meanings of the words and the ways in which they are used are rarely subjected to close scrutiny or analysis. They are "motherhood and apple pie" words and as Vincent points out "their usage can obscure more than it can illuminate" (Vincent, 1993, p. 231).

What do we mean by "community"?

A definition of "community" is provided by Carr and Reigeluth (1993) in a paper discussing the role of community members in re-structuring school systems. They quote a "classic social science definition" offered by Warren (1978):

> "(A community is) a social unit which consists of persons who share a common geographic area interacting in terms of a common culture and which incorporates a range of social structures which function to meet a relatively broad range of needs of all persons who make up the social unit" (p. 36).

This rather broad definition glosses over the fragmentation and isolation which is experienced by many members of poor communities with transient populations -- those whom the integrated services are attempting to reach. The definition of "community" quoted above presents a picture of cohesion and stability, rather than of fragmentation and change.

Chaskin and Richman (1993) discuss concerns about school-linked services and suggest that community-based models may be more effective in reaching disenfranchised communities. Their definition of a community is similar to that of Warren quoted above:

Broadly conceived, community here relates to the local context in which people live. It is referred to by its geographic identity, but its place on the map is only one of its attributes. It's a place of reference and belonging. The community includes dimensions of space, place and sentiment as well as action. It is defined by a dynamic network of associations that binds (albeit loosely) individuals, families, institutions and or organisations into a web of interconnections and interaction.

However, these authors acknowledge that in low-income urban communities, individuals often identify and concentrate their activities within a much smaller area than the city as a whole. The boundaries of their neighbourhoods are constructed from their own "mental maps" of their community and may not coincide with those of the planners and politicians.

Chang (1993) notes that service providers need to be aware of the cultural and linguistic diversity of the communities being served. She adds that "current methods of analysing the needs of children and families seldom differentiate between the conditions of different ethnic populations." One step which often takes place prior to establishing a plan to integrate services is to conduct a community-wide needs assessment. But, she argues, the results of such assessments are seldom disaggregated to take into account the diverse populations found within quite small geographic areas.

Jones (1991) criticises the tendency of policy analysts and programme evaluators to conflate the interests of community leaders with those of the broader membership of communities. She suggests that those in powerful positions in local communities will often use their involvement in government or state initiatives as a way of consolidating their power, and that they might not necessarily be representing the best interests of ordinary community members.

The dilemma therefore, for those wishing to serve adequately and to empower local community members, is how to identify and involve them and support their participation in planning and policy-making.

What do we mean by "participation"?

The development of Western democracies in the twentieth century has placed more or less emphasis on some form of community participation in political decision-making. The forms this has taken have varied, depending on the sophistication of the understanding of the location of power and the complexity of the society. In the United States the concept of a pluralist society, with wide representation of varying interest groups in political life, has sometimes obscured the relative lack of power, and therefore of the opportunity of some groups and communities to participate effectively (Lukes, 1974; Bachrach and Baratz, 1962). In other, more homogenous countries such as the Scandinavian group, it was assumed that elected representatives at local level would provide community representation and that there was a consensus between professionals and community members about the aims and organisation of welfare services. Contestation and conflict were not seen as part of policy-making about the Welfare state (Mishra, 1984).

More recent analyses have cast doubt on the effectiveness of both the pluralist and the consensus perspectives to be inclusive of all sections of the community, especially those whose powerlessness positions them as passive recipients of services which they have had little say in designing. The power has lain either with the professionals (Scandinavian model) or with politicians, both local and national (US model).

Vincent (1993), quoting Pennock (1979) suggests four main reasons for introducing community participation in decision-making:

1) it will serve to legitimise to the work of any institution;

2) it will make institutions more responsive to their clients;

3) it will aid the personal development of those involved;

4) it will overcome the alienation of groups served by the institution.

Vincent points out that aims 1 and 2 can be fulfilled without any transfer of power, but that aims 3 and 4 may be more threatening to the status quo, since they involve the potential empowerment of disenfranchised groups.

Recent moves in many of the developed Western states to decentralise their education and social welfare systems could be seen as a response to criticisms that the institutions of the Welfare state (education, social services, health services, housing etc.) have become self-serving bureaucracies, out of touch with the needs of their clients and lacking in accountability. Thus there have been changes in many countries towards site based management" of schools and the introduction of "choice" to make schools and other services more responsive to the needs of their users. It has been argued (Tooley, 1995; Chubb and Moe, 1992) that so called representative democracy does not work and leads to excessive bureaucracy and that "market forces" ensure much greater participation of individuals in decisions about which services should be offered and how they should be organised.

However, the involvement which the market offers is limited, in the sense that individuals do not have a "voice" in what is offered; their influence is felt by their acceptance or rejection of services. So they would not be involved in planning or policy-making, only in consuming (or not consuming) what is on offer. "This is a very limited form of participation and one which denies the existence of "communities". As Margaret Thatcher once famously said: "There is no such thing as society -- there are only individuals and their families". So far from empowering, market solutions may fragment and prevent the formation of interest groups within communities.

Paradoxically, at the same time, there has been a growing interest in the notions of "communitarianism" (Etzioni, 1993) and of "stakeholding" (Hutton, 1995). Both these concepts revolve around the idea that individuals are part of communities and must take responsibility for the well-being of community members. For its part, the state should ensure that all members of society have a "stake" in that society and that businesses should take a wider responsibility for the prosperity of their workers and members of the communities in which they are located and not just respond to the wishes of their share-holders. Hutton emphasises that stake-holding is not a return to the monolithic state planning, characteristic of post-war social democracy, but that it is an attempt to recreate a sense of mutual responsibility and to counteract the individualism of the Thatcher/Reagan era.

Models of community development

It was against this background of contrasting values and ideologies that the OECD project on Integrated Services for Children and Youth At Risk was carried out. The project team visited examples of integrated services in three countries in Europe, as well as in the United States, Canada and Australia. In each country we visited a number of different sites based in different states and giving examples of different communities. Not surprisingly, therefore, we encountered a range of different models of community development.

The model used by the project to provide a framework for data-gathering suggested four levels of decision-making about services integration: the mandating, or political level; the strategic or executive level; the operational or managerial level; and the field or professional level (OECD, 1996). However, in operationalising the model as a framework for data collection, questions were asked to respondents at each level about the involvement of community members and clients in the decision-making at that level. "This has offered an opportunity to refine the model to capture the complexity of policy-making across different services and at different levels of governance.

Four models of community development have emerged from our case studies. These are:

1) community development as part of an overall strategy mandated and promoted at the political level through legislation and funding arrangements;

2) localised autonomy where funding and decision-making is devolved to the community level and services are developed by local professionals;

3) community autonomy, where decisions about the needs of the community are made by local community members and funding is delegated to community support specific community projects;

4) a mixed economy, where there are elements of top-down and bottom up decision-making, but where legislation is permissive to allow the development of localised services to meet local needs.

Model 1 was evident in Finland, where recent legislation has devolved all responsibility for the provision of health and social services from the central government to the local level. The State Subsidy Reform, implemented in 1993, has given the Municipalities greater freedom to use central government funding according to local priorities. The funding is given by central government on the basis of a profile of the population of the Municipalities and they are free to allocate between health and social services as they see fit. An Integrated Customer Services Act, passed in 1993 removed obstacles to the provision of integrated services at the "field" level.

At a more local level still, a policy of "Local Population Responsibility" has given a multi-professional team of social welfare and health professionals the responsibility to serve the needs of a small geographically defined area of 2 000 to 4 000 people. Thus a system has been set up which has the potential to meet more effectively the needs of small communities.

The main objective of this type of services integration appears to be to make services more efficient and effective. Finland has a very low infant mortality rate and high rates of participation in education. However, the involvement of local community members and clients of services in planning and policy-making does not appear to be a key feature of these initiatives -- they are driven more by the concerns of politicians and professionals. One example studied by the OECD team, an elementary school and day care centre on the same site, was unusual in that efforts were made to involve the local community in the planning and operation of the centre. Those in the community were encouraged to use the centre for community meetings and to work in the centre on a voluntary basis.

Model 2 -- localised autonomy -- has been a feature of welfare provision in Germany since 1945. Each Land is autonomous and has developed welfare and education policies according to its own political and cultural traditions.

In Bremen, the Office for Health, Youth and Social Welfare is divided into four regional departments for North, South, East and West Bremen. These are further divided into districts and then into neighbourhoods of between 5 000 and 10 000 people. In Huchting, one of the most disadvantaged areas of Bremen, a committee made up of professionals from the education, health and social services as well as representatives of youth organisations, a city farm, churches and leisure clubs and other non-profit organisations, researches the needs of the community and plans new provisions to meet those needs. This committee has become influential at the strategic level in advising policy-makers and politicians about the needs of the community, and this has led to a decision to devolve control over funding for social and health services to the local level.

One of the key provisions of the organisation in Huchting is the "House of the Family", where health, psychological, social and welfare services for the local community are housed in one building, along with adult education to provide a "one-stop shop" for disadvantaged members of the community.

Classes organised for women and girls, in particular, are an important aspect of the community development role of the provision.

Model 3 -- community autonomy (or "bottom-up" development) -- was exemplified in two areas of Saskatchewan, Canada. Both of these involved local community members in setting up initiatives to tackle social problems in their areas. In Saskatoon, the concerns of a group of residents about petty crime and the general deterioration of their neighbourhood has led to the setting up of a Citizens" Group. This group carried out a survey of community members to gather information about local population needs and the encourage community involvement. The group obtained the support of local welfare professionals and funding was made available for the provision of integrated and community based services through Saskatchewan's Action Plan for Children. Four types of programme were initiated by the group: educational, recreational, housing and community policing. Each of these addresses the expressed needs of community members. Community members are involved in the organisation and delivery of each of these programs. Therefore the sense of ownership by the community is very marked. However, it must be pointed out that support for community efforts was provided by local professionals (a local community school principal was a key figure) and by the ability of the community to access funding through a Provincial policy to provide locally-based integrated services.

Model 4 -- a mixed economy -- was a feature of many of the sites we visited, as all the countries involved in the project were attempting to provide integrated services which were responsive to local community needs. The differences between them could be described as differences of emphasis, rather than of policy goals. In California, for example, legislation authorised counties to establish inter-agency Children and Youth Services Councils to co-ordinate local services for children. This legislation provided for counties to obtain waivers against state regulations which inhibited services integration.

At the same time, the state established the Healthy Start programme which was designed to bring together public and private sector social welfare, health and educational support services at the school site. Funding decisions about projects were to be made at the state level. Another initiative by private foundations, set up at around the same time, was the Foundation Consortium for School-linked Services. This consortium entered into agreements with the state to provide support for school-linked services, to develop stable funding mechanisms so that projects would continue once the foundations grants were ended and to try to initiate state-wide changes in the ways in which services are organised and delivered.

The example of the involvement of private foundations in influencing policy decisions about welfare services at the state and national levels appears to be quite common in the United States. Very often, foundations have strict requirements about the involvement of community members in the design and delivery of services -- thus providing models for state bureaucracies to emulate. For example, in New York City, we visited several community schools which had been used as the sites to provide a range of educational, social and health services to local communities. These services were funded by private foundations and a key feature of each of them was the close involvement of community members in the schools, as users of services, volunteer helpers and as paid employees.

Discussion

A number of questions are raised by these different approaches and models of community development:

- What counts as "a community?" Many localities contain several communities who have children and youth at risk and who see themselves as in conflict?

- Who decides what the community's needs are? Professionals and community members may have differing views about the services they need.

- Where should the responsibility for services integration lie? Is it up to local professionals or community members, or should strategic and political actors take the lead?

- What are the lines of accountability for the delivery of well organised, flexible integrated services? Should professionals be accountable first of all to the communities they serve, or to their managers and politicians?

- Will integrated services targeted at communities lead to greater empowerment of community members or are they a device to ensure better control of troublesome populations and to "keep the lid on" potentially explosive social situations?

Firstly, what counts as "a community?" As argued above, communities in urban areas are complex and diverse. These communities will have different needs and different attitudes towards the provision of services. For example, one of the problems perceived by the West Flat Citizen's Group was the anti-social behaviour (as they perceived it) of some First Nations people who moved into the area from the Reserves. From the "professionals and politicians" perspective, the community as a whole was needy, but the means of achieving an orderly community was to put one group (the older-established population) somehow in control of the other.

In California, it is estimated that children attending the state's schools speak more than 100 languages and that one in every five children is an immigrant (Chang, 1993). Chang argues that services set up to serve such diverse communities must be sensitive to the different cultural traditions within them if they are to be effective. Consequently, the Healthy Start Programme does not impose a single model of service delivery. Rather, "each community must tailor programme design to respond to its citizens' needs and expectations and build upon local strengths" (Lewis, 1994).

This leads to a consideration of the second of my questions: who decides what the community's needs are? Professionals and community members may have differing views about the services they need. Chaskin and Richman (1993, p. 205) argue that a frequently used model of services integration which uses the school as the site for co-location of health and social services may deter many disenfranchised families from using the services. They suggest that the most needy and alienated groups may see schools as unfriendly institutions and may associate them with failure and trouble. They argue for "multiple access points" to services and that, most importantly in the context of my current argument about participation:

"This access must include not only physical or eligibility access to existing services but also the opportunity for citizens to participate in the process of defining community needs and the strategies for meeting them (p. 204)."

To go back to "Healthy Start", the model adopted by this programme allows for flexibility in programme delivery including: school site provision, community based provision, provision by teams not based around a physical location and youth service programs. Evaluations indicated that each of these models has strengths and that no one model could be seen as "the best". The Healthy Start programme must include involvement of parents, teachers and community groups in programme planning, design and operation. But it is not clear whether the potential recipients of the services were included in this.

My next question concerns the location of responsibility for services integration. Is it up to local professionals or community members, or should strategic and political actors take the lead? This is the well known dichotomy of "top-down" and "bottom-up" origins of policy-making. It is clear, from our research, that the organisation and funding arrangements of human services can enable or inhibit services integration significantly. This is why many national and state governments have enacted legislation to introduce flexibility to allow different services to plan and fund joint provision. However, local involvement and commitment is essential to make best use of these new flexibilities. A good example of the coming together of "top-down" and "bottom-up" initiatives is Saskatchewan's "Children First" policy, which has been promoted and supported at the political and strategic levels and which enabled Citizen's Groups in Prince Albert and Saskatoon to bring services together at the local level to meet the needs of the community.

In terms of the need to involve and empower the most needy members of the community, bottom-up strategies are obviously the most effective. This will involve real shifts of power from the centre to local areas, and the realisation by professionals and politicians working locally that they must put power into the hands of citizens. This will involve more than a "market" solution as discussed above. It will require changes in our views about how local democracy can work (Ranson, 1992).

These lead to a discussion of my fourth question: What are the lines of accountability for the delivery of well-organised, flexible integrated services? Should professionals be accountable first of all to the communities they serve, or to their managers and politicians? This is a dilemma which faces all professionals working within communities. They are the "gate-keepers", or "street-level bureaucrats" as Lipsky (1980) has termed them. Those at the "field" and "operational" levels according to our model, have a responsibility both to the local communities which they serve and to the more senior managers and politicians. As I suggested in my introduction, community members may also have direct access to politicians and senior executives, so that a hierarchical model is not necessarily appropriate as an accountability structure. Sometimes, because of local professional issues about the limits of responsibility of different services (so-called turf issues), local professionals do not best serve the needs of community members. Therefore, there need to be lines of accountability which will ensure that the local community will have access to powerful decision-makers.

My last question: "Will integrated services targeted at communities lead to greater empowerment of community members or are they a device to ensure better control of troublesome populations and to keep the lid on potentially explosive social situations?" relates back to the four purposes for introducing community participation in decision-making discussed above: legitimation, responsiveness, personal development and over-coming alienation.

Scheurich (1994) is extremely cynical about the role of integrated services in improving the lives of those in disenfranchised communities. He suggests that the projects designed to help those communities serve, in fact, as a demonstration to society as a whole what is a normal and acceptable life-style. He argues that, given the size of the problem (*i.e.* "20 per cent, of all US children live in poverty; 32 per cent of African-American children live in poverty; 34 per cent of Hispanic children live in poverty": 1994, p. 309) the solution offered by services integration is "small". He suggests that the label "at risk" tends to focus on the children and families and does not question the underlying social and political order which results in such large sections of the population becoming "at risk".

From our studies, it appears that the more severe the problem of alienation of a particular community, the more concern there is to empower that community and to encourage community development through participation in decision-making. For example, it is at the core of many of the programmes in the United States and in Canada. However, where there is less alienation and, perhaps a more effective existing infrastructure to involve local people in local decision-making, such as in Germany or Finland, the emphasis on community empowerment is not so great.

It seems that there may be an optimum amount of participation, for too much would threaten the stability of existing power structures and too little creates an alienated and disaffected populace. Evaluations of programmes to serve poor and disenfranchised communities currently concentrate on outcomes concerned with improved health, reductions in school drop-out, improved take-up of benefits, improved mental health, and so on. They do not typically address wider issues of feelings of empowerment and increased participation. The OECD project explored some aspects of the involvement of local community members in decision-making but no clear pattern has emerged which could be related to outcomes in terms of the success of programs. Partly, this is due to the difficulties, described above, of having a clear idea of what is meant by community and participation, and partly due to the remit of the project which was to address how services integration had been achieved in a range of countries and not to look at what Scheurich has called "the deep structures of inequality" which underlie many of the problems of children and youth "at risk".

REFERENCES

Bachrach, P. and Baratz, M. (1962), "The Two Faces of Power", *American Political Science Review*, Vol. 56, pp. 947-952.

Carr, A. and Reigeluth, C. (1993), "Community Participation in Systemic Restructuring: Member Selection Procedures", *Educational Technology*, Vol. 33, No. 7, pp. 36-46.

Chang, H. (1993), "Serving Ethnically Diverse Communities", *Education and Urban Society*, Vol. 25, No. 2, pp. 212-221.

Chaskin, R. and Richman, H. (1993), "Concerns about School-Linked Services: Institution-Based versus Community-Based Models", *Education and Urban Society*, Vol. 25, No. 2, pp. 201-211.

Chubb, J. and Moe, T. (1992), *Politics, Markets and America's Schools,* The Brookings Institution, Washington DC.

Edelman, M. (1964), *The Symbolic Usage of Politics*, University of Illinois Press, Chicago.

Etzioni, A. (1993), *The Parenting Deficit,* Demos, London.

Evans, P. (1995),"Children and Youth at Risk", Chapter I in OECD/CERI, *Our Children at Risk*, OECD, Paris.

Hutton, W. (1995), *The State We're In*, Jonathan Cape, London.

Jones, A. (1991), "Community Participation in Frontier Education Planning", *Educational Management and Administration*, Vol. 19, No. 3, pp. 160-165.

Lewis, M. (1994), "California Case Study of Service Integration for Educationally Disadvantaged Children and Youth", unpublished report for OECD.

Lipsky, M. (1980), *Street Level Bureaucracy*, Sage, New York.

Lukes, S. (1974), *Power: A Radical View*, Macmillan, London.

Mishra, R. (1984), *The Welfare State in Crisis*, Hemel Hempstead, Harvester-Wheatsheaf.

OECD (1996), *Successful Services for our Children and Families at Risk*, Paris.

Pennock, J. (1979), *Democratic Political Theory*, Princeton University Press, Princeton, NJ.

Ranson, S. (1992), "Towards the Learning Society", *Educational Management and Administration*, Vol. 20, No. 2, pp. 68-79.

Scheurich, J. (1994), "Policy Archeology: a new policy studies methodology", *Journal of Education Policy*, Vol. 9, No. 4, pp. 297-316.

Tooley, J (1995), "Markets or Democracy for Education, A Reply to Stewart Ranson", *British journal of Educational Studies*, Vol. 43, No. 1.

Vincent, C. (1993), "Community Participation: The Establishment of "City's" Parents' Centre", *British Educational Research Journal*, Vol. 19, No. 3, pp. 227-241

Warren, R.L. (1978), *The Community in America,* Rand McNally, Chicago.

ISSUES IN THE EVALUATION OF INTERSECTORAL INITIATIVES: A BACKGROUND PAPER

by

Craig Shields, M.A.
Human Services Consultant

Introduction

When I was approached to participate on the panel exploring issues related to the evaluation of intersectional initiatives, I thought it might be useful to know something about the extent of such activity on a national basis. With Health Canada support, I asked a colleague, Coletta McGrath, to do a telephone survey of relevant activity across Canada. The findings from this survey are included in Attachment 1, and constitute a major part of this background document.

The paper itself is intended to provide background for the panel presentation on "Intersectional Initiatives: Research And Evaluation of Outcomes" at the OECD/Canada conference on Integrated Services For Children And Youth At Risk And Their Families. Since the amount of time allotted for the panel presentation is quite brief, it was felt that a background paper would be a helpful way to provide more information than can be provided through the presentation alone.

The paper, in keeping with its collaborative nature, is organised into two sections. The body of the paper focuses upon some of the general patterns and specific issues related to the evaluation of intersectional collaborations, based upon the survey findings and upon personal experience. The attachment contains a summary and analysis of the findings from the survey on current activity across Canada.

The authors wish to acknowledge and thank the Children's Mental Health Unit and the Work and Education Health Promotion Unit of Health Canada for their financial support for conducting the survey and the preparation of this paper.

General patterns

What is the state of the art of the evaluation of outcomes from intersectional collaborations where the education sector plays a prominent role? That is essentially the question we set out to answer when we designed the survey of current activity across Canada. The responses, while only a sampling in the end, nevertheless revealed some interesting patterns. The most obvious is that each of the four elements -- intersectional collaboration, prominence of education, formal evaluation, and a focus on outcomes -- were found to occur at differing rates of frequency.

Let me explain what I mean by this. In searching for initiatives to include in the survey, we began by identifying intersectoral collaborations where the education sector played a prominent role. Having identified these through our provincial/territorial contacts, we then contacted individuals associated with each of the initiatives and asked them to what extent their initiative included a formal evaluation component. Where it did, we then asked to what extent the evaluation focused upon process, impacts, and child-centred outcomes.

What we discovered was that there are lots and lots of intersectoral collaborations underway across Canada focused upon young people and their families. Only a percentage of these, however, include education as a prominent partner. Of the twelve initiatives that were identified to us where this was the case, only nine included a research or evaluation component. And of these nine initiatives, only three are using objective measures of child-centred outcomes (though five more are using subjective measures).

In other words, the results of the survey suggest a pattern that looks a bit like the pyramid in Figure 1. Across the base we have a large number of intersectoral collaborations. However, when we add the element of education being a major partner, the number drops. Similarly, when we add the element of a formal research component, the number of examples decreases again. And finally, when we add the element of the research including a focus on child-centred outcomes, the number decreases even more.

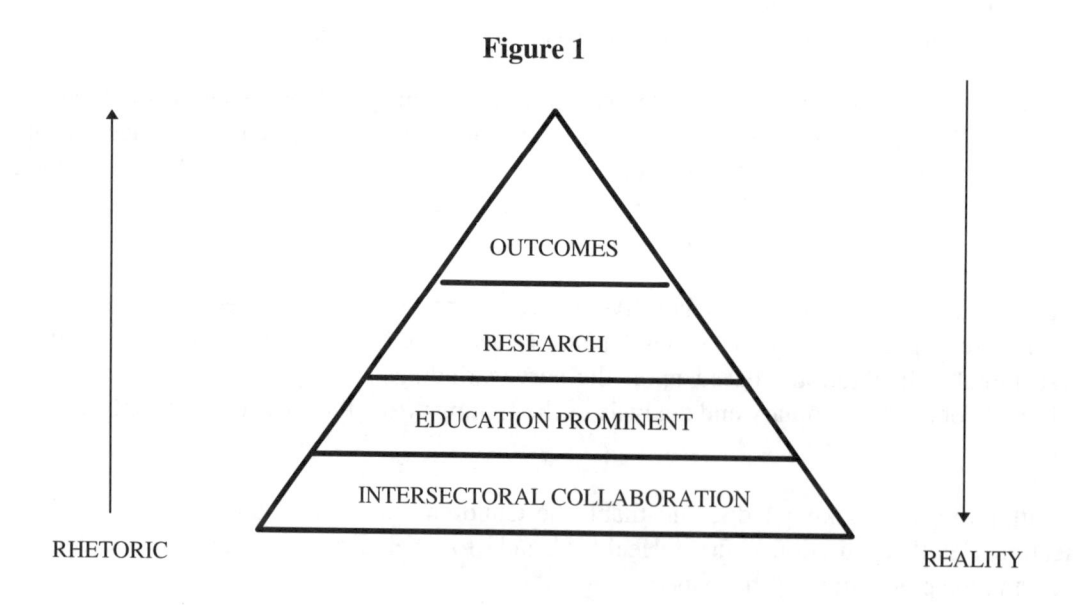

Figure 1

```
                    /\
                   /  \
                  /OUTCOMES\
                 /----------\
                /  RESEARCH  \
               /--------------\
              / EDUCATION PROMINENT \
             /----------------------\
            / INTERSECTORAL COLLABORATION \
           /------------------------------\
```

RHETORIC   REALITY

The interesting thing about this pattern is that it goes against the grain of our current rhetoric. Virtually everyone recognises the necessity of the education sector being involved in intersectoral collaborations that focus upon school-aged children and youth. And there is lots of talk about the need to shift to more evidence-based decision-making, including evidence that services and supports actually make a difference in the lives of young people and their families.

So the question becomes, if we value all four elements as part of a package for successful intersectoral collaborations, why aren't all four elements present more often? There are no doubt lots of reasons for this gap between rhetoric and reality, some of which are captured in the comments and analyses included in the survey findings. However, I would like to add my own thoughts on some of the issues and challenges to establishing initiatives that include all four elements.

Specific issues

My comments are based upon experience with a major intersectoral collaboration currently underway in four localities across Ontario. In my role as co-ordinator of the Laidlaw Foundation Children At Risk program, we have been working with broad community networks, local neighbourhoods, levels of government, and non-governmental organisations to build "community systems" of support for young people and their families. While this 4 1/2 year process has offered a good number of insights into the challenges of designing and carrying out intersectoral collaborations and outcomes oriented research, I will restrict myself to discussing just four: one for each of the elements of the pyramid.

Re: Intersectoral collaborations -- The challenge of emerging design

Most intersectoral collaborations are by their very nature "fluid." Often they have different starting points for different sectors, as partners join the initiative at various stages in its evolution. And they almost certainly have multiple visions or agendas, at least at the outset. The result is that sectors often come together over some broad common interest, such as getting children off to a good start in life, or making sure that they are ready to enter the formal education system. These broad shared objectives provide the glue for the initiative that keeps the sectors, despite their different world views and mandates, working together towards a common end.

In other words, often these intersectoral collaborations begin with participants coming together with a commitment to do something together, but without the details of that "something" clearly worked out. The details are developed over time, as are the specific contributions of the various partners which may change over the course of the initiative, influenced by all kinds of factors. The design of the initiative, in effect, becomes a function of process, and emerges as the process evolves.

This fluid quality of intersectoral collaborations presents obvious challenges for researchers who are used to the more disciplined world of programme evaluation, with its design phases, pre- and post-tests, comparison groups, and so on. My experience with the Community Systems initiative is that there are few researchers with the skills and competence to study these more systemic and fluid initiatives. When we tendered for the design of our study, what we found was that most of the respondents were programme evaluators who were intending to adapt programme evaluation techniques to the study of our intersectoral collaborations.

Re: Prominence of education -- The challenge of a new framework of understanding

Why isn't education more prominent in intersectoral collaborations? Indeed, given that as a sector it serves all children, and therefore has a very real interest in the well-being of all children, why isn't it leading the charge? There are no doubt many responses to this question, and I won't presume to answer it with any finality. I do think, however, that part of the answer is related to what might be called the new "framework of understanding."

It used to be that there were normal kids and other kids, and the "others" fit into some relatively simple categories such as "mad," "bad," or "sad." By and large, education looked after the normal kids, and the special service sectors, such as mental health and corrections, were called upon to look after the others. The categories were simple, the causes of deviation seemed clear, and the roles of the various sectors were well-defined. But all that has changed.

The new framework of understanding suggests that a child's development is the result of a complex interaction between personal attributes, contextual factors, and previous life experience. Not only that, but school performance can be seen as a measure of the extent to which the child has successfully adapted to the school environment; a process which has interaction variables as well, in the sense that parents, child, and teacher share responsibility for the results.

In the old framework of understanding, for example, reading ability was viewed as primarily a function of a child's skills and motivation. If either of these were deemed lacking, the child might be slotted for remedial instruction. In the new framework, reading ability is seen as the result of a complex interaction of a child's innate abilities and motivation, the teacher's expectations and instructional style, the family's values, literacy levels and degree of involvement, and community attitudes.

One implication of this new framework of understanding, with its emphasis on multiple influences and ecological adaptation, is that there are few if any simple causal relationships, and therefore few if any simple solutions. Another is that formal services have only a limited influence on a child's overall development and well-being, and many of the factors that do influence these lie outside the reach of those services.

This new framework presents challenges for all service sectors, but particularly for the education sector which, given its resource base of administrators and classroom teachers, may just view it as too complex or too removed to be relevant. And until education sees not only its place but also its possible contributions in the context of this new framework of understanding, it is not likely to take a stronger lead in intersectoral collaborations which operate from such a perspective.

Re: Research -- The challenge of differing traditions

It is a given that service sectors, like professions, have their own research traditions, and that these traditions differ not only in terms of what constitutes acceptable methodology, but also in terms of what constitutes valid proof. When it comes to intersectoral collaborations, however, these traditions can extend to fundamental differences about the desirability and value of research.

Let me give you a recent example to try to illustrate this point. The foundation I work for has been funding a number of community networks to test the possibility of improving child outcomes through finding ways of using existing community and service system resources to better effect. Each of the networks has been exploring whether this is possible through following a series of steps such as routinely reporting on the well-being of young people, mobilising communities around positive outcomes for all children, planning in a more strategic and unified manner, and so on. The steps were spelled out in an original agreement between the foundation and the networks, and are incorporated in their local workplans.

We are now nearing the end of a multi-year grant to assist the networks in implementing this approach in their localities. In discussions regarding future funding to carry on with the initiative we have heard from some groups that they find the expectation that they implement the approach as designed to be both rigid and intrusive. Furthermore, they say that some aspects of the design don't "resonate" with community members.

This will be a familiar experience to many, because it represents a very strong tradition in some sectors, particularly social services with its long history of community development. But let's compare this experience with another tradition. Suppose the foundation had wanted to test the possibility of improving heart health by controlling for diet and exercise. And suppose it had funded a number of community health centres to be partners in the initiative. In this tradition you would not expect to hear somewhere down the road that adherence to the original project design was a sign of inflexibility or intrusiveness. On the contrary, in this tradition, adherence to the original design would not only be a virtue, but a necessity. Similarly, you would not expect the community health centres to say, "Well, we didn't follow through on the exercise part because it didn't resonate with participants."

The point here is not that one tradition is necessarily right or the other wrong. The point is that there are significantly different traditions with regard to the value of research, and the role of different partners in collaborative efforts in the design and implementation of it. This is particularly true when these collaborations have a strong community dimension to them, and may help to explain why more intersectoral collaborations do not have a strong research component.

Re: Outcomes -- The challenge of shifting the focus

It is not surprising that of the four elements we have focused upon, the one that is least often present in intersectoral collaborations is a focus on outcomes. This is because the desire to focus on outcomes appears to be ahead of the development of the tools and methods enabling us to do so.

But the challenge is greater than simply one of technology. It has two dimensions, both requiring a fundamental shift in focus. The first is making the now well understood shift from the traditional focus on "outputs" to the new focus on "outcomes." Of course, we have always had a focus upon some types of outcomes. However, in the overwhelming majority of cases these have been from the negative side of the ledger. They have been outcomes that we want to avoid like low birth-weight, accidental injury and death, school non-completion, substance abuse, suicide rates, and so on. What we haven't had in ready supply are positive outcomes that we want to promote, other than the inverse of the negatives, such as school completion. This, then, is the second shift in focus that needs to be made.

My own experience to-date suggests that this second shift is going to be more challenging than the first. This is partly because the existing literature, particularly in the area of child status indicators and their measurement, reflects the earlier tradition of focusing upon the negative. But it is also because focusing upon the negative is how we've learned to play the game in terms of mobilising support, acquiring funds, and proving the necessity of our programmes and services.

Concluding comments

This is obviously a short list of issues related to the evaluation of intersectoral collaborations. But it includes, I believe, some of the most significant challenges to strengthening the state of the art in Canada.

What needs to be done in order to achieve this? To begin with, we have to de-mystify research and humanise it. One way of doing this would be to promote the view that knowledge development and experience are different sides of the same coin, and they need to continually interact to inform the other. Another way would be to anchor research capacity in local process so that it can be used not just as an evaluative tool but as a learning tool to strengthen that process. And finally, it would be very helpful if we had more researchers who had the ability to find the best balance between studying process, impacts, and outcomes, and the skills to carry out all three.

ISSUES IN THE EVALUATION OF INTERSECTORAL INITIATIVES: SURVEY FINDINGS

by

Coletta McGrath, M.S.W.
Human Services Consultant

Introduction

This report summarises the findings of a brief cross Canada survey of current, intersectoral initiatives where education is a prominent partner, and where there is a formal evaluation component.

The information contained in this document was gathered by first contacting a key informant employed in a provincial education or social services ministry or department. The names of local initiatives that incorporate the features described above (*i.e.* intersectoral, education as a prominent partner, formal evaluation component) were obtained, together with the names of appropriate contact persons. A telephone survey was subsequently conducted with staff representing 11 of these initiatives. Programme materials regarding collaboration, research and evaluation, and findings were collected, reviewed and documented for these initiatives as well as a twelfth initiative for which no survey information was collected. The project survey asked a series of questions designed to collect information regarding whether or not a project evaluation was being implemented, the nature of the evaluation or research activity being undertaken, and findings to date. Informants were also asked to describe the challenges they faced in designing and implementing the evaluation as well as any lessons that had emerged in the course of the evaluation.

In addition to the information about research and evaluation, programme related information was collected, creating a relatively broad picture of the intersectoral work being done across Canada. It should be noted that the initiatives included in this survey represent a wide range of approaches and use different personnel and service strategies. A significant amount of time and space would be required to provide a comprehensive overview of each. Instead, each initiative is briefly summarised according to its goals and objectives, the various sectors participating in service delivery, the nature of the evaluation being undertaken and findings to date, and the duration and current status of each initiative.

The results of the survey and the information collected during the review of relevant programme materials are described on the following pages. The information is organised according the questions that were asked in the survey.

Survey findings

Is there a formal research and evaluation component and what does it include?

Informants were asked if the initiative includes a research or evaluation component. If so, they were also asked if the research or evaluation includes a process evaluation, an evaluation of the project's impact on influences and determinants, an evaluation of child centred outcomes or a cost benefit analysis.

The survey, as well as the review of programme materials provide useful and encouraging information. Of the twelve projects included in this report, nine are implementing an evaluation or undertaking research. The three that have not yet undertaken an evaluation have acknowledged the need to do so. Two of these indicate that they will be designing and/or implementing an evaluation should they receive continued funding for their projects.

The number of projects implementing child centred outcome evaluations or research is equally positive. Eight of the nine projects indicated that their evaluation is intended to measure child centred outcomes focusing on such outcome measures as physical health, self esteem, communication, interpersonal relationships and academic performance. However, of these eight projects, five are measuring these outcomes using primarily subjective or secondary data sources (*i.e.* information collected from parents, teachers, other relevant staff or community/school statistics).

Four of the projects undertaking evaluations appear to be measuring indicators or determinants of children's well being, examining parental attitudes, parental competencies and parental self-efficacy for example.

Cost benefit analysis appears to be the least common type of evaluation. Only two of the twelve projects have undertaken a formal cost benefit analysis with respect to their work, although others indicate that their projects have resulted in cost savings as experienced and reported by various agencies and sectors. The absence of a "context" or "frame of reference" within which to implement a cost benefit evaluation was noted by several informants.

While three projects reported that they were undertaking research, six projects indicated that they were involved in programme evaluation. The distinction between research and evaluation was somewhat unclear. It appears that the term research is being used where projects are attempting to determine the effectiveness of various service interventions over an extended period of time and where randomised control groups or comparison groups are in place. The research challenges and requirements noted by two informants, specifically the perceived need for research questions/ hypotheses/premises to take priority over the programme and needs of the community, may provide some insight into the apparent lack of research activity. The cost of longitudinal research was also cited as being fairly prohibitive, particularly where only local dollars are available.

What are some of the more important research or evaluation challenges and lessons that have emerged?

The informants contacted for this survey were asked to identify challenges in designing and implementing research and programme evaluations as well as lessons they have learned as a result of their efforts. The responses are summarised and discussed below.

Research challenges

A wide variety of research challenges were identified in the course of the survey and in reviewing the project materials. The challenges are organised according to four categories. They include challenges related to programme characteristics, community characteristics, research and evaluation design, and research and evaluation support.

- Programme characteristics

Many of the services described in this report tend to be customised to individual clients. In order to maximise effectiveness, services will vary to reflect the characteristics and needs of the programme participant. This degree of variation has significant implications for evaluation including making the selection of measurable programme outcomes very difficult.

Another significant challenge is created as a result of multi-disciplinary service approaches. Different disciplines have different expectations regarding evaluation. There exists a great deal of variation regarding what exactly should be measured. While there is a tendency to look for different kinds of things through the evaluation, there tends to be agreement that evaluation designs need to be kept reasonably straightforward and as simple as possible. Yet the more demands being put on the evaluation by different service providers and disciplines, the more complex, and often expensive, the evaluation becomes.

Agency restructuring, which is currently being experienced by many organisations, can also significantly confound the research/evaluation process. Depending on the nature of the restructuring, original evaluation measures may no longer be appropriate. In addition, service may be disrupted or members of the original sample may no longer be considered part of the agency's target population.

Finally, voluntary programme participation was cited as problematic with respect to implementing evaluations or research. Participant attrition is sometimes quite high. The use of control groups and treatment groups in measuring outcomes can be significantly jeopardised as a result of this attrition problem. The use of consumer survey instruments to determine issues such as parent satisfaction becomes particularly questionable as a result of voluntary participation as well. Given the voluntary nature of the programs, most parents who are dissatisfied tend to withdraw their participation.

- Community/Participant characteristics

Obtaining data in a timely way and obtaining hard data is difficult at times. It seems that various community or participant characteristics contribute to this situation. For example, sometimes it is difficult to contact families to arrange appointments or, once a family is contacted and an appointment set up, families may not show up. In addition, some parents simply cannot be interviewed. For example, the residential mobility of poor families creates a definite barrier to obtaining data. In many cases parents of children who no longer participate in programmes have left the area. Parents often say they are too busy or some parents are simply not interested. As a result it becomes difficult to ensure that data is collected from a random sample of parents.

The inability of many families to regularly participate in programme activities seems to be a fairly common problem which impacts negatively on programme evaluations. It was pointed out that programme attendance has an impact on programme effectiveness, while at the same time being difficult for service providers to control.

- Research and evaluation design

Combining the strengths of traditional research design and procedures for controlled experiments with more qualitative and participate evaluation and research approaches has resulted in a number of challenges specific to the programmes described in this report. For example, often the background of the evaluation committee members tends to divide them between "hard data or quantitative people" and "soft data or qualitative people." It seems that the processes involved in setting up and implementing evaluation designs for integrated programmes often frustrates the "hard data people," sometimes to the point where they are no longer interested in participating. As a result, the evaluation design tends to be influenced by more participation and input from " soft data people." Similarly, recruitment and ongoing participation of researchers/evaluators capable of accepting a participatory approach or the lengthy and sometimes thorny interactions with parents and local organisers is at times difficult and even impossible.

Given the challenges that it presents, to date not many researchers appear to have undertaken an evaluation process that requires shared and equal decision-making power between programme participants, community residents and researchers with respect to all facets of the research/evaluation process (*i.e.* design, pilot testing, review, revisions, implementation, analysis and reporting). Establishing these kinds of relationships can be time consuming and stressful. The involvement of multiple disciplines seems to make the process that much more challenging.

At least three informants identified lack of control, invasion of privacy and the lack of positive outcomes for children and their families as characterising earlier research and evaluation designs, implementation and results. There also appears to be a tendency for neighbourhoods to associate research and evaluation with having a stigmatising effect on children and the community as a whole. As a result community members are described as having become cynical, suspicious and resistant to yet another research project being carried out in their neighbourhood. This general attitude has resulted in the perception that government, researchers and other stakeholders need to explore new ways of gathering information from the community that are more sensitive and attentive to the needs of community residents and programme participants.

While programmes today tend to focus on promoting positive behaviours and outcomes, it was pointed out that many of the measures being used still tend to reflect a more deficit oriented approach. Furthermore, there is some concern that child and family impact measures are not sufficiently sensitive to detect small behaviour changes. Yet these minor shifts in behaviour are considered to be quite significant by many of the programme participants and service providers. It was also noted that, so far, our evaluation measures continue to be somewhat limited in their capacity to document noticeable changes in the social and psychological status of children.

- Support for research

Many of these intersectoral initiatives have been in place for a relatively short time. They also tend to have time limited funding. As a result of their short lifespan to date, they have not yet passed through their evolutionary and developmental stage and become truly grounded. Furthermore, this developmental stage seems to take much longer when integrated programme approaches are being implemented. At the same time however, outcome evaluations, which inform decision-makers as to whether or not programme goals are being achieved, should not be undertaken until the programme is solidly established. The initial and sometimes the only funding for the project is often close to ending when the programme is finally at a stage where it makes sense to implement an outcome evaluation. This has proven to have significant implications for the feasibility of undertaking the evaluation at all.

The short term or time limited nature of the funding for many integrated projects has created a great deal of uncertainly regarding whether or not the programmes will continue. Unfortunately, under these circumstances, evaluation seems to become a secondary consideration to obtaining secure funds. It was further noted that programme evaluations tend to give programme participants the impression that if the results are positive, the programme will continue. This appears to raise some ethical issues for service providers, particularly in light of their perception that positive results are often unrelated to ongoing programme funding. Under these circumstances there is a reluctance to undertake evaluations too quickly.

A third challenge with respect to designing and implementing programme evaluations relates back to the deadlines established for proposal submissions. These deadlines tend to be quite tight. When staff preparing the proposals are delivering programmes at the same time, proposals are often developed on the run. There may be minimal if any time to consider incorporating an evaluation component. Instead, energy is focused on accessing dollars within a very short period.

Research lessons

The evaluations and research activity undertaken by the programmes included in this report, have given rise to a number of lessons and insights. A number of these focus specifically on research or evaluation design. Others simply reflect general insights that have emerged over the course of implementation. They are outlined below.

Most projects noted that shared decision-making power between residents, participants and researchers, while time consuming, results in greater participation in research/ evaluation activity and a sense of community ownership of the results. This increases the credibility of the evaluation process and the likelihood that the results will be used in the future.

Unfortunately there seems to be a tendency for evaluations to intimidate programme participants. They are not particularly trusting of evaluators. Not only is there a risk of losing programme participants as a result of this attitude, but it decreases the likelihood of participants contributing to the evaluation's design and implementation. Strategies to ensure sensitivity to the needs of "at risk" populations should be in place at the outset.

It was suggested that evaluations should be undertaken within the context of what has been termed a "quality improvement cycle." Within this context the idea is to evaluate on a short term cycle first, for example week by week, revise the programme as appropriate and then move toward evaluating larger programme goals. Furthermore, since process evaluations tend to provide ongoing and continuous feedback it was pointed out that they can be particularly useful as programmes are developing in order to improve operations, revise or alter services or problem solve, for example.

Putting the evaluation or research design in place prior to starting the programme can be particularly helpful. The need for Funders to be aware of this in terms of the dollars they make available and the time frames they establish was noted. While the design may be subject to revision once the programme has stabilised, at least it reduces the likelihood that there will be missing data.

The management and organisational structure of the programme is rarely if ever evaluated. In the case of integrated programmes these features would seem to deserve particular attention since new, never before tested organisational designs and management structures are often put in place to accommodate the "integration factor."

Finally, the distinction between research and evaluation was pointed out. Specifically, it is important to keep in mind that implementing a programme evaluation is different from implementing a research project. In the case of evaluation, making the programme work and providing service is the primary consideration, implementing the evaluation tends to be considered secondary. As a result, service providers feel that if it is not absolutely essential to ask a question or if asking questions will reduce the likelihood that a family will participate, the questions are not likely to be asked.

Programme descriptions: what are the program's goals, objectives and findings?

Each informant was asked to describe their project's goals and objectives and the various participating sectors. In addition to the nature of the evaluation being undertaken, information concerning the findings to date, the duration, and the current status of each initiative was also collected. This information is presented on a project by project basis below.

Child Development Centre Infant and Early Intervention Project. This Yukon-wide resource specialises in early intervention services for children from birth to school age. The project is a combined effort of the Child Development Centre, Kwanlin Dun First Nation, the Dawson City Interagency Committee and the Community Health Centre. It was developed to provide three programs: Dawson City Infant and Early Intervention; Kwanlin Dun Infant and Early Intervention and Kwanlin Dun First Nation Pre-school.

Evaluations of the Child Development Centre (CDC) as well as the individual programmes have been completed. Over 70 children and 28 adults have received services through the Centre. The majority of these participants are members of the target group and all those interviewed for the evaluation spoke highly of the services received. The CDC has successfully enhanced and expanded community supported and culturally relevant child development programmes in Dawson City and the Kwanlin Dun community. Individual programme evaluations indicated that the staff of the Dawson City Infant and Early Intervention programme have most successfully enhanced and expanded services by providing early assessment, therapy and support for pre-school children identified as being at risk. Staff of the Kwanlin Dun Infant and Early Intervention Programme and the Kwanlin Dun Pre-school programme have enhanced existing services to the community but there need to be continued efforts to provide comprehensive services to more members of the target group in the former case and to establish and implement a culturally and developmentally appropriate curriculum in the case of the pre-school program.

These programmes have been operating since March, 1995. A two year time-limited grant was provided through the Community Action Programme for Children. Substantial and growing support for the project among stakeholders in the community is reported.

The Early Intervention Co-ordinator Project. This was originally a joint initiative of the North West Territories Counsellors Chapter of the Canadian Guidance and Counselling Association and the

Student Support Division, Department of Education, Culture and Employment, Government of the Northwest Territories. Recently the partnership has expanded to include partners at the regional and community levels. A Memorandum of Agreement has been signed by the Ministers of Health and Social Services, Justice, Education, Culture and Employment and the Northwest Territories Housing Corporation whereby the four departments agree to work collaboratively to provide service to their clients. Through this initiative an Early Intervention Co-ordinator works with the Northwest Territories School Boards and other interested government or non-government agencies to advance Early Intervention initiatives. Overall project objectives include providing support to Early Intervention programmes in design, implementation, evaluation and accessing funding; ensuring the availability of staff development opportunities; promoting culturally appropriate early childhood education programs, supporting the Aboriginal Headstart Committees in developing and implementing the Aboriginal Headstart in the Northwest Territories and documenting the long term impact of the early intervention programs.

While a formal evaluation of the project has not been undertaken, a review of the project prepared by the co-ordinator indicates that the project has successfully achieved a number of its objectives. Two communities have received support in preparing funding proposals for early intervention programs. A large amount of time was spent sharing information regarding services that are provided by the Co-ordinator and assisting communities interested in early intervention programs. The Co-ordinator has been included in developing Terms of Reference for the Aboriginal Headstart Programme and developing the two Advisory Committees to that program. Finally, the Co-ordinator has served as a resource to the Federal Government's Nobody's Perfect parenting program.

The Community Action Programme for Children made funding available to this initiative for approximately 18 months. In the meantime however, it appears that many of the project activities have been picked up by the Student Support Division of the government of the North West Territories.

The Small Steps Program. Sponsored by the Shared Care Day Care Society, Small Steps provides support to children and families enrolled in child intervention, parent child programmes and family support programmes in the town of Arviat, Northwest Territories. Operating out of the local school, the programme is intended to assist children between the ages of 0-6 years who are deemed by the referring agency to be "at risk" of experiencing oral language deficits, hearing/speech/visual impairments, gross/fine motor delays, physical/emotional/psycho-social developmental delays, family problems which interfere with adequate parenting or any other factor which is deemed to limit the child's ability to cope successfully in the community. The Small Step Project Worker, in conjunction with staff from other partnering agencies, develops and monitors a programme plan for the child and family. When the child enters the school system, the student Support Team from the school follows up on the plan.

At present no formal programme evaluation is in place. Individual children are monitored on a client by client basis however. Individual case files show improvements among participating children. Referring agencies also report that the programme has had a positive impact on child development.

The programme received Brighter Futures funding from Health Canada for a three year period beginning in September 1994 and ending in March, 1997. Since its inception, Small Steps popularity has grown significantly, with over 50 clients currently on the referral list. The original survey, prior to receiving funding, had identified 11 children requiring support. In addition, the need for access to expertise in speech pathology, physiotherapy and developmental assessment work has been identified by Small Steps.

Partners for Kids and Youth. Working with at risk families in Edmonton, Alberta, Partners for Kids and Youth helps ensure safe and healthy kids by providing programmes intended to prevent children abuse and neglect, connecting families with community resources as required and promoting the development of needed resources if they are not available. Programme partners including Public Health, the Children's Health Centre, Public and Separate Schools, Police, Edmonton Social Services, Child Welfare, Income Support, Justice, Children's Mental Health agencies, the YMCA and Catholic Social Services work together to develop and monitor individualised programme plans for children and their families.

A formal programme evaluation has produced encouraging results. The project has been well received by the community, despite some initial concern regarding the involvement of child welfare and the police. While past referrals came primarily from the school system, over 50 per cent of the clients are now self-referrals. Parents have reported that accessing services is much easier and less stressful given that they are often interviewed only once, rather than two or three times by different agencies or organisations. Joint interviews conducted by the police and child welfare are a case in point. Family participation has increased. Having staff out in the community getting to know people on a positive social basis rather than only under negative circumstances is one of the key explanations for this increase. School support has also contributed to the programmes success. Specifically it was noted that teacher appreciation of the importance of using a holistic approach and being aware of multiple barriers to kids doing well in school has resulted in particularly effective school linkages and working relationships. The project reports that the frequency of family visits is decreasing, which could mean that families are coping better. Finally, outcomes including improved school attendance and decreases in youth crime are in the process of being measured, although there are no results as of yet.

This three year demonstration project will end in September, 1997. In the meantime it has received a very positive response from all of the key stakeholders involved. It currently appears that the project will be incorporated under the Children's Services Initiatives (CSI), in Alberta. It was reported that this particular project appears to be serving as somewhat of a prototype for service delivery models that are evolving under the CSI.

The La Loche and Prince Albert Pre-school Support Pilot Projects. They operate in the communities of La Loche and the West Flat area of Prince Albert, Saskatchewan, communities that are experiencing significant social, health and economic pressures. These preventative pre-school programmes are intended to improve health, social skills and potential for success in school, particularly among children at risk. The projects develop learning skills to help children make an early and successful adaptation to school, provide assistance in making the transition from a native language to English, ensure ready access to health services and help parents who require additional support to access the necessary services. Modelling a new approach to service integration, the pilots incorporate significant community participation and innovative funding arrangements. The pre-school programmes are a partnership among several government agencies and community organisations including the Provincial Government Departments of Social Services, Education, Training and Employment and Health and the local municipal governments and local businesses.

In each pre-school community, a half-time evaluation co-ordinator collected data to be used in the year-two evaluation report. Among those participating in the evaluation, there is a high level of satisfaction with the way that community resources are integrated into the pre-school programme for the benefit of both children and teachers. Specifically, the integrated nature of the pre-school's funding, administrative and governance structures is perceived as facilitating the integration of the education, social and health services that children and their families need. Major programme components include education, music, cultural activities, nutrition, speech and language, health, family support and transportation. The high level of parent and community involvement in all aspects of programme suggest effective community empowerment. While children were not asked directly if they like the program, parents reported that their children like pre-school. When asked about future changes, 43 out of 58 parents interviewed did not make suggestions for change because they were very satisfied with the pre-school as it is. Staff and Board members also expressed a high degree of satisfaction with the programme and the results being achieved. The role of the Family Support Worker was perceived as highly valuable by both parents and staff, serving as a key link between the parents and the pre-school.

The degree of change experienced by the children and families was also evaluated. With respect to the children, observational checklists were completed by the pre-school staff and the teachers in the pre-schools were interviewed about the progress of the children. The children attending the pre-schools showed growth and development over the course of a year. In La Loche, children made gains, particularly in the areas of social and emotional development. In West Flat, it was clear that the longer the children attended, the more gains they made. The greatest gains were made in the area of social skills and independence/self-help skills. Kindergarten teachers in schools which received children from the two pre-schools indicated that overall, the children stood our from those who had not attended pre-school. Social skills, following routines and fine motor skills were perceived to be higher among the children who attended pre-school than among those who did not. Parents who were interviewed as part of the evaluation indicated that involvement in the pre-school and its programmes had helped them learn parenting and interpersonal skills, brought them together to learn and enjoy activities with their children, raised their self esteem and influenced them in becoming more involved in their community generally.

Both pre-school programmes were initiated as three year pilot projects in 1993. The programmes are currently in their final year of operation. To fund the project, Education, Training and Employment and Social Services re-targeted existing resources to jointly provide $98 000 for the fiscal year operations of each project. The funds were funnelled through the Child Care Division (Social Services) and the pre-schools were developed to meet the requirements for Day Care licensing, thereby receiving 50 per cent federal cost-sharing on the provincial funds. Social Services further allocated $40 000 through the Teen and Young Parent Programme for a half-time parent support worker associated with each pre-school in the two locations. Education, Training and Employment provided $40 000 to cover the cost of the evaluation. Provincial funds leveraged additional community donations for renovations to buildings, equipment, supplies and volunteer assistance. The most important new issue mentioned by most of the people participating in the evaluation was finding some way to keep the pre-schools open after current funding arrangements end. The low income levels among families living in the community, coupled with the transient nature of many of the families make it particularly unlikely that parents can cover the fees themselves. Also, any fund-raising to support the school will likely be limited. The Federal Government and Foundations are being contacted regarding alternative funding options.

The Multi Agency Preventive Programme for High Risk Youth. Operating in Brandon, Manitoba, the Multi Agency Preventive Programme (MAPP), is a systemic, information-based process for ensuring effective planning on behalf of the small population of highest-risk youth in the Brandon community.

The MAPP model emphasises co-ordination and information sharing among the Youth Justice System (*i.e.* Police services, Community and Youth Corrections, Department of Justice) and Youth Social Service agencies (*i.e.* Addictions Foundation of Manitoba, Brandon School Division, Child and Family Services of Western Manitoba, Brandon Mental Health Centre, City of Brandon and the Dakota-Ojibway Child and Family Services) to aid in (a) early identification of the seriously high-risk adolescent, (b) development of an interagency plan for intervention, and (c) timely implementation of appropriate consequences for unacceptable/illegal activity. The MAPP initiative is based on the principle that a more systematic approach to information gathering and dissemination, analysis, planning and integration of agency activity will increase the effectiveness of the network of community resources in dealing with and reducing youth crime in the community.

A formal evaluation was initiated while MAPP was being developed. The evaluation is multi-focused. A risk assessment tool was developed based on a tool being used in Ontario. Its purpose is to identify the highest risk youth in the community. The reliability and the validity of the instrument is currently being tested and data is being collected on comparison groups. The ratings of the youth are being related to incidence reports being completed by workers from different agencies regarding problem behaviour on the part of the youth. Although the number of transgressions increased at the outset, possibly as a result of the youth being monitored, the programme is anticipating improvement in youth behaviour over time. In addition, a school survey indicates that schools have experienced a much greater degree of co-operation in working with high risk youth. Based on a survey of agencies, there has been a significant increase in agency interaction. Finally, parents have expressed very positive feelings about the programme and welcome the support being provided to them by the participating agencies.

The programme was first initiated in 1993. There are monthly meetings that continue to have 90 per cent attendance rates. There is a need for financial support periodically and the problems that tend to arise when funding intersectoral initiatives (*i.e.* who funds?) emerge here as well. To date, Section 25 Staff have been accessed through the Federal Government Unemployment Insurance Programme to carry out the monitoring function. The programme is expected to continue given the positive community response to date.

Better Beginnings, Better Futures. In the province of Ontario, Better Beginnings, Better Futures is a 25 year longitudinal prevention policy research demonstration project. Focusing on children 0-8 years at risk for emotional, behavioural, social, physical and cognitive problems, as well as children and families living in economically disadvantaged neighbourhoods with multiple high risks for poor child development, this integrated service model has been established in eight communities across Ontario. Two types of models have been established: a pre-natal/infant development programme integrates with a pre-school or a pre-school integrates with an elementary school (primary division). Other features of the model may include drop-in centres, recreation programs, breakfast/lunch programs, parent training and single mother support groups. There is significant involvement of families and community leaders. Co-founders have agreed to three main goals: prevent emotional, behavioural, social, cognitive and physical health problems in children, promote healthy child development and enhance the abilities of socio-economically disadvantaged families and communities to provide for their children. Specific objectives are tailored to each of the eight sites for each of these goals.

The research component of the Better Beginnings, Better Futures Project addresses three general questions: is the Better Beginnings Model effective?; what structures and processes are associated with Project results?; and, is the Better Beginnings Model affordable? The first research objective, outcome research, entails the on-going collecting of information on a wide range of child, family and community characteristics so that both short and longer term project effects can be determined. Baseline data has been collected from parents, children, kindergarten teachers and grade two/three teachers. Information was also collected about various characteristics of the Better Beginnings neighbourhoods from existing records of local organisations and agencies such as Public Health Units, hospitals, child welfare agencies, school boards and police files. This was used to create a set of "community indicators" such as child abuse cases reported, children taken into custody, number of individuals/families on social assistance and birth weights, for example. Once the base line data was collected, the research focused on a group of children in each community who are at the bottom of the programme age range. This group of children constitute the longitudinal research group.

The second research objective is being addressed through the collection of extensive field notes from meetings, documents, discussions and interviews, developing reports for discussion with local committees and collecting information on programme participation. The final objective, related to the economic feasibility of the projects, involves undertaking an economic analysis that includes developing and implementing an accounting system and software, collecting direct and indirect programme cost data and eventually relating cost to programme outcomes and benefits.

Current research findings focus primarily on process related issues. With respect to service integration, the research indicates that integration, in the absence of meaningful, significant parent or community involvement, can be more problematic than no service integration at all. Furthermore, integration of services must be realistic when funding remains segmented. As far as community involvement in decision-making is concerned, there must be 50 per cent or more parents or community leaders in every committee and important subcommittee to actually have meaningful, significant involvement of parents and community leaders in decision-making. In addition, there must be a transfer of real decision-making power to the program, or parents and community leaders will not participate in planning and implementation. Preliminary outcomes reported by participants include the development of a sense of community among participants, enhanced self confidence and self esteem, increased number of social contacts, improved skills for finding jobs and improved parental image. Generally speaking however, the impact of the project on influences and determinants of child well being, outcomes for children and cost benefit analyses are still to be determined.

Co-founders for the programme are providing a total of $33.2 million over a five year period. Included among the funders are the Ministry of Community and Social Services (MCSS) ($2.9 million/year for five years), the Ministry of Health ($1.9 million/year for five years), Ministry of Education and Training ($800 000/year for five years), Federal Department of Indian and Northern Affairs ($800 000/year for five years), Secretary of State for Multi-Culturalism ($240 000/year for five years). MCSS research monies are also available to follow children, families and communities until children reach their mid-twenties. Government supports to the Project also consist of a Project Design Co-ordinator, Site Supervisor/Co-ordinators and a Government Committee consisting of 15 members who meeting regularly. Each of the communities has taken three years to become evaluable. All communities are currently in their third year of a four year demonstration of the model.

KIDS COUNT, Partners For Children's Health and Learning. Serving the City of London, Ontario, the overall goal of KIDS COUNT is to co-ordinate the efforts and resources of child serving organisations -- and their ministries -- at the local level, in order to improve health and learning opportunities for children. Eleven neighbourhoods were selected for inclusion in KIDS COUNT based on a scientific assessment of "risk," as defined by the presence of five factors in percentages that were significantly above city averages (low income, single parent families, parental educational attainment, newcomers, rental housing). Final selection was based on the inclusion of other "soft" variables such as community acceptance; school interest; various levels of existing infrastructure; etc. The Social Services, Health and Education (including 25 schools) sectors participate in the project, together with the Chamber of Commerce and the Municipal Transportation System. Other organisations or systems, specific to each neighbourhood are also involved as appropriate. The somewhat open ended nature of KIDS COUNT and the entire notion of "using our existing community resources more effectively" was initially a particularly difficult concept to get across to communities and service sectors. The Public School Board's announcement that some $1.5 million was to be reallocated in support of the initiative has been equally challenging to implement.

The evaluation of the KIDS COUNT project focuses on capturing outcomes at three levels (process, programme and policy). Three areas were analysed as part of the process evaluation: stakeholder participation, the establishment of neighbourhood groups and the development of stronger partnerships. From a process perspective, questionnaires administered to project stakeholders indicate a relatively high level of commitment, involvement and satisfaction among participating organisations. A survey of the local neighbourhood groups, interviews with their facilitators/chairpersons and a review of meetings minutes indicated significant progress on the part of 10 of the 11 groups. Members were relatively satisfied with their involvement and indicated relatively positive group experiences where they were given an equal chance to participate. The three neighbourhood groups that were the quickest to take root and to establish local leadership share three common characteristics. All three exist in areas where there is very little else in the way of community groups, organisations or services. They were all able to draw on a parent population coming from relatively stable, income-secure homes. It seems that parents from less secure situations are often unavailable to volunteer due to their extenuating circumstances. The third common characteristic is school staff who are very supportive and who take a facilitative approach within the group.

Four items were examined with respect to programme outcomes: *i)* the implementation of neighbourhood projects, learning indicators based on information collected using two school-based measures; *ii)* a child questionnaire and a reading ability test; *iii)* health indicators based on information collected using a child questionnaire; *iv)* parental information about their children. Baseline data has been collected in each of these areas and will be used to track changes within each of the 11 neighbourhoods. The use of information from two control schools will be used to account, as much as possible, for outside influences.

The final area of research measures policy outcomes. During a yearly interview with the Resource Steering Committee, four of the seventeen organisations involved indicated that they had made a total of ten policy changes as a result of, or reinforced by, their participation in the KIDS COUNT project. Notable policy changes have been made. For example, the Public Board of Education has changed a policy to accommodate a redistribution of staff and to order the upgrading of computers in the KIDS COUNT schools. Their participation has greatly increased accessibility to the Board by outside organisations and neighbourhood people alike. The city's Social Services Department has offered control of service delivery like public ice skating, to neighbourhood groups and the London Public Library has made a policy to allow for long term off site loans to a Parent Resource Centre, thereby improving accessibility to reading material. Based on annual interviews with agency CEO's and senior staff from other systems, it was reported that approximately $460 000 has been leveraged in the first year as a result of participation in the KIDS COUNT program.

KIDS COUNT is a two year project that began in 1994. Core funding has been provided by the Federal, Provincial and Municipal governments. As the second year draws to a close, training and support continues to be provided to community and neighbourhood facilitators as the project attempts the transition of responsibilities and problem solving to local residents. Given the number of neighbourhood residents participating, the continued operation of the groups is more than promising. The ongoing support of local principals has also been an important contributor to the healthy status of the neighbourhood groups. A more formalised approach to funding and supporting incidental costs related to neighbourhood activities is being explored. In addition, a government relations and communications strategy intended to maximise support for the project, is being developed. The ability of the Resource Steering Committee to function also continues to be enhanced.

1, 2, 3 GO!. As an experimental project operating in five neighbourhoods and one village of the Greater Montreal area, 1, 2, 3 GO! invites community residents, agencies and local organisations to invest their resources in the well being of children aged 0-3 years. The overall goal of the project is to mobilise material, intellectual, social, and political resources in order to develop and sustain a culture devoted to the well being and development of children. In order to achieve this goal, the project is pursuing three specific strategies: enhancement of individual competencies, promotion of institutional and organisational change and mass influence. Participants in the programme include volunteer organisations, government services including health and social services, local schools, local police, recreational services, business organisations, youth protection, child care organisations, workers' unions and local churches. Project strategies include community mobilisation, financial support based on a community's demonstration of the capacity to work together, development of Action Plans that include strategies to reach at risk families, work directly with children and include parents in programme design and implementation and the provision of high quality interventions that involve knowledgeable, well trained service providers.

A research team has recently completed a study aimed at defining the overall research design to be applied over the next five years. The team has borrowed from a participate-research approach. Interviews have been conducted with the initial promoters of the project, members of the programme committee and permanent staff members. Focus groups have been held with members of the local steering committees to identify the main research concerns to be attended to in the research design. Based on this feedback, the team has conceived a research plan that rests both on qualitative-anthropological methods and quantitative methods. Each community will be invited to create an Evaluation Task Group which is going to be in continuous interaction with a co-ordination body. In terms of content, the research will document processes of implementation and project impact at the community development level and the child development level.

The project was initiated in 1993. The community was invited to participated in 1995. Six communities were offered seed money to develop Action Plans. Based on the participation levels to date, the programme has been well received by the community. For example, 230 people participated in local presentations regarding the project. One hundred and thirty of these are actively involved in identifying the best way to establish a local culture concerned with the well being of children. Participation in local steering committees ranges from 12 to 55 people and strong signs of collaboration are showing up in the neighbourhoods. Three hundred parents and others are involved in identifying priorities. Of the six participating communities, two have presented Actions Plans, including detailed and well structured workplans that have received approval.

Support Services to Education. Serving the province of New Brunswick, this prevention oriented project provides students, teachers, administrators and parents with health and social services aimed at improving the functioning of students in the public school system. It was initiated and continues to be supported by the Department of Education as well as the Department of Health and Community Services, Family and Community Social Services Division. The programme is provided under the legislative authority of the Schools Act and the Family Services Act.

Support Services to Education (SSE) objectives were identified as providing better co-ordination of existing health and social services related resources, avoiding service duplication, providing for the development of provincial standards for professional services, insuring more effective use of professional staff, maintaining professional and service linkages with the Health and Community Service network (which may already be servicing the child or the child's family), and reducing unnecessary competition between systems for scarce professionals. The overall target groups include students primarily in grades one, two and three with physical, perceptual, behavioural, communicative or intellectual difficulties where the student, family or school requires support services. In addition, specific target groups and priorities for services will be determined within each region/district. Among its responsibilities, the Department of Education must identify the need for and provide, within available resources, school psychology/psychometry, guidance services, teachers assistants and student attendants, specialised educational materials and equipment and specialised teachers. The Department of Health and Community Services is responsible for the availability and accessibility of health and social service professionals for students (speech language pathologists, nurses, occupational therapists, physiotherapists, clinical psychologists and social workers).

A Two Phase project evaluation has been completed. During Phase I a list of indicators for measuring programme outcomes from the point of view of SSE professionals was developed. The demographics of students receiving service under SSE, the nature of the service, the length of time waiting for service and the major presenting problems were described. A sample population for Phase II of the evaluation was derived using these results, and indicators were selected that would allow the program's success in meeting its goals to be measured. The data collected during Phases I and II of the evaluation indicate that 2 968 student cases received SSE service as of November, 1993. The waiting time for service was just over one month with speech/language pathology clients experiencing the longest waiting time. The highest percentage of SSE service recipients were males in grades one to three receiving service for language and learning difficulties. Of the three models of service delivery available (treatment, monitoring and consultation), treatment was used most frequently for social work and speech language pathology. When individuals associated with the programme were asked to comment on their assessment of improvement in a population receiving service, 81 per cent indicated a positive change in school functioning. Results by presenting problems indicated that a positive change was recorded for 81 per cent, 77 per cent and 87 per cent of students presenting language/learning, psycho/social and health/physical problems respectively. In addition, when presenting problems were in the language/learning domain, perceived positive changes were recorded in academic performance, interpersonal relationships, self-esteem and communications for at least 60 per cent of the student sample. When presenting problems were in the psycho/social domain, attendance was the only aspect of functioning that didn't show improvement. Finally, when presenting problems were in the physical/health domain, self esteem and interpersonal relationships were the two areas where positive changes were most frequently perceived.

This joint initiative was in a planning and development stage from 1988-1993. Although staffing is incomplete due to freezes in hiring, the programme continues to grow and evolve. The Management Committee for the project continues to broaden, recently incorporating representative from Mental

Health and Human Resources. Relationship building has been excellent and services are perceived to be better than they were five years ago, for example. While much is being learned about how to deliver essential services to children in the most effective way possible, questions such as whether or not actually placing community based programmes in schools would result in better outcomes, remain outstanding as does the question of whether or not SSE would be better managed under the Department of Education. These kinds of questions have yet to be explored.

East Prince Youth Development Centre. Operating in Summerside, Prince Edward Island, and offering services to youth and young adults aged 16-29 years living in the East Prince community, the goal of this multi-faceted programme is to improve service co-ordination by providing an easily accessed gateway to information, programming, needs assessment and comprehensive case management and follow-up. The East Prince Youth Development Centre incorporates three major programme components. The Academic Component offers academic upgrading, academic assistance, literacy and numeracy enhancement and vocational skills development. The Employment Support Component focuses on employment enhancement and personal effectiveness addressing areas such as self-esteem and self-confidence, managing anger and other emotions, stress management, time management, setting goals and positive communications skills for example. A second feature of the Employment Support Component focuses on employment assistance and vocational planning, including skills identification, creative job search techniques, volunteerism and career development and work experience programs. A third and final component focuses on youth wellness and health. Services provided include an adolescent addictions programme that incorporates student assistance, outpatient detoxification, a five-week family programme and one on one and group counselling.

Contributing Partners to the East Prince Youth Development Centre include the Summerside Offices of Human Resources Canada, East Prince Health and various of its agencies such as Child and Family Services and Young Offender Custody Programs, the City of Summerside, the Western School Board, and the Three Oaks Senior High School. Additional participants include the Summerside Police Services, the John Howard Society, the RCMP, the Summerside Christian Council and the Greater Summerside Chamber of Commerce.

While the need for an evaluation has been identified for each programme component, a formal evaluation has not yet been implemented. However, programme statistics show that participation levels have been high among youth and the community response is reported to have been positive since the program's inception two years ago. Ongoing funding is presently unavailable. In part, the decision not to implement an evaluation has been linked to the uncertainly of continued funding. At this point several proposals have been circulated to potential funders and the programme is awaiting their responses.

Model for the Co-ordination of Services to Children and Youth and Profiling the Needs of Children and Youth. The Departments of Education, Health, Justice and Social Services of Newfoundland and Labrador committed to the implementation of the Model for the Co-ordination of Services to Children and Youth in June, 1995. The goal of the model is to ensure that a programme planning process is put in place for children/youth with special needs and to ensure service co-ordination when more than one agency is providing service. In support of this goal, the need for a process for capturing information on the needs of children participating in programme planning (Child and Youth Profiles) and the need to ensure the development and co-ordination of policies between the Departments of Education, Health, Justice and Social Services that will support the programme planning and resource co-ordination efforts were identified.

The focused approach being adopted is known as an integrated service management approach. The approach is based on the recognition that many children require supports or interventions for specific periods during or throughout their pre-school and school lives. Those supports often require input from many professions represented within the Department of Education and/or Health and/or Justice and/or Social Services. The model recognises that such professional supports are intended to complement and enhance the role of parents, who along with their child, have a leadership role as team members in the implementation of the programme planning process. All agencies which are providing services to the child/youth form a team. The team is responsible for developing a programme plan and selecting a Support Services Manager who undertakes service co-ordination and programme planning team facilitation.

In addition to including parents and the child/youth as partners in the process, and developing the concept of an individual Support Services Manager, the key components which are believed to ensure success when implementing the programme planning process include using an integrated management team approach at the local, regional and provincial levels and the profiling of children/youth and their needs. The role of the regional and provincial level teams in this model is one of ensuring that service needs are identified, service barriers are minimised and resource issues are addressed. The region/provincial role also includes the development, monitoring and evaluation of programme standards. The Profile is designed to capture information on the needs of children identified in the Programme Planning Process, for the purpose of service and resource planning at the local, regional and provincial levels. The Individual Support Services Manager is responsible for ensuring that the Profile information is completed and updated on each child on a regular basis as required or at least yearly. This information is forwarded to the Regional Community Health Board and, along with summaries submitted by the Regional Offices of Health, Social Services and schools, is used to develop a regional demographic picture of the range of presenting needs and service requirements for the region.

The Regional Integrated Service Management Team has been assigned responsibility for establishing a system for the ongoing evaluation of the effectiveness and efficiency of service delivery, developing, monitoring and evaluating policy and programme standards, and designing a methodology for determining the effectiveness of the Profiling process. In addition to ensuring the development and implementation of Inter-Ministerial Protocols to support co-ordination, the Provincial Integrated Services Management Team will be responsible for reviewing and evaluating their effectiveness.

OECD PUBLICATIONS, 2, rue André-Pascal, 75775 PARIS CEDEX 16
PRINTED IN FRANCE
(96 98 07 1 P) ISBN 92-64-16966-0 – No. 50467 1998